Hugh Despenser the Younger and Edward II

Downfall of a King's Favourite

Hugh Despenser the Younger and Edward II

Downfall of a King's Favourite

Kathryn Warner

PEN & SWORD
HISTORY

AN IMPRINT OF PEN & SWORD BOOKS LTD.
YORKSHIRE - PHILADELPHIA

First published in Great Britain in 2018 by
Pen & Sword History
An imprint of
Pen & Sword Books Ltd
Yorkshire - Philadelphia

Hardback ISBN: 9781526715616
Paperback ISBN: 9781526751751

A CIP catalogue record for this book is available from the British Library.

Typeset in Ehrhardt MT 11/13 By SRJ Info Jnana System Pvt Ltd.

Printed and bound in the UK by TJ International Ltd.

Pen & Sword Books Ltd incorporates the Imprints of Pen & Sword Books
Archaeology, Atlas, Aviation, Battleground, Discovery, Family History,
History, Maritime, Military, Naval, Politics, Railways, Select, Transport, True
Crime, Fiction, Frontline Books, Leo Cooper, Praetorian Press, Seaforth
Publishing, Wharncliffe and White Owl.

For a complete list of Pen & Sword titles please contact

PEN & SWORD BOOKS LIMITED
47 Church Street, Barnsley, South Yorkshire, S70 2AS, England
E-mail: enquiries@pen-and-sword.co.uk
Website: www.pen-and-sword.co.uk

or

PEN AND SWORD BOOKS
1950 Lawrence Rd, Havertown, PA 19083, USA
E-mail: Uspen-and-sword@casematepublishers.com
Website: www.penandswordbooks.com

Contents

(1) Bassets, Beauchamp, Despensers

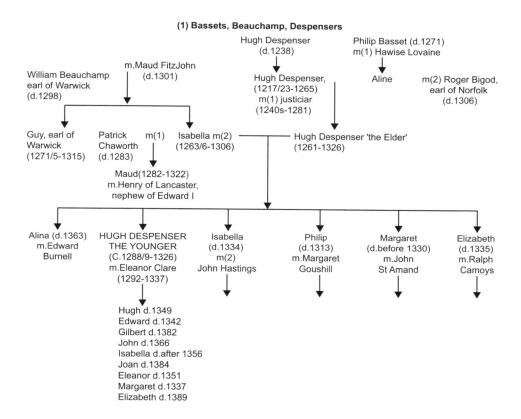

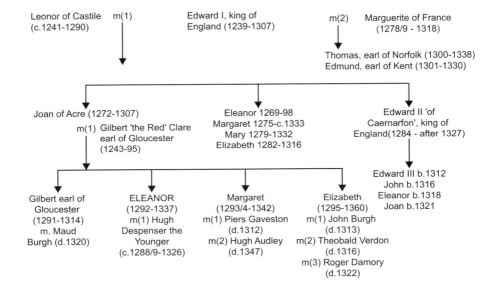

Leonor of Castile (c.1241-1290)   m(1)   Edward I, king of England (1239-1307)   m(2)   Marguerite of France (1278/9 - 1318)

Thomas, earl of Norfolk (1300-1338)
Edmund, earl of Kent (1301-1330)

Joan of Acre (1272-1307)   Eleanor 1269-98   Edward II 'of Caernarfon', king of England(1284 - after 1327)
    m(1) Gilbert 'the Red' Clare earl of Gloucester (1243-95)   Margaret 1275-c.1333
    Mary 1279-1332
    Elizabeth 1282-1316

Edward III b.1312
John b.1316
Eleanor b.1318
Joan b.1321

Gilbert earl of Gloucester (1291-1314) m. Maud Burgh (d.1320)

ELEANOR (1292-1337) m(1) Hugh Despenser the Younger (c.1288/9-1326)

Margaret (1293/4-1342) m(1) Piers Gaveston (d.1312) m(2) Hugh Audley (d.1347)

Elizabeth (1295-1360) m(1) John Burgh (d.1313) m(2) Theobald Verdon (d.1316) m(3) Roger Damory (d.1322)

A Note on Names

Hugh's family name in the fourteenth century was always written 'le Despenser', and female family members were called 'la Despensere'. I have omitted the 'le' and 'la', and the 'de' in noble family names such as de Clare and de Bohun.

A Note on Chapter Headings

All the quotations in italics at the start of chapters are from Hugh's own letters (in French in the original). 'We', 'our', 'us' and 'ourselves' mean Hugh himself; this was a convention of the era.

Introduction

Hereford, Monday the eve of Saint Katherine in the twentieth year of the reign of our lord King Edward, son of King Edward (24 November 1326)

A man tied to a poor, flea-bitten nag was brought into the town of Hereford to the sound of tremendous cheering from the populace. He wore a crown of sharp stinging nettles, and Biblical verses including 'Why do you glory in wrongdoing?' from the book of Psalms were scrawled all over his skin. Men riding alongside him blew bugle horns in his ears, people screamed abuse and pelted him with rubbish, and an ally of his was forced to walk in front of him carrying his coat of arms reversed as a sign of his disgrace. He must have felt weak and faint: he had been refusing food since his capture in South Wales eight days before, and even water as well, with the result that he was 'almost dead for fasting.' [1] The procession which brought him to Hereford took over a week to cover the 65 miles from South Wales, where he had been captured, to show him off to as many people as possible. Numerous people watched and cheered as he went past, delighted that the king's corrupt and loathed favourite had fallen at last.

In Hereford a list of charges was read out against him which ranged from true to dubious to patently absurd, and to the surprise of no-one, the man was sentenced to death by hanging, drawing and quartering without any chance to speak in his own defence. The judge bellowed out 'Go to meet your fate, traitor, evil man, convict!' His feet were attached to four horses which dragged him through the streets. A gallows 50 feet high had already been constructed; the verdict against him had been a foregone conclusion. Watching was the queen-consort of England herself, Isabella of France (*c.* 1295–1358), and her ally Roger Mortimer, lord of Wigmore (1287–1330), the prisoner's deadliest enemy. He was partially strangled on the high gallows, then tied to a ladder and his private parts cut off and thrown into a fire, followed by his internal organs and bowels, as he still lived. He was then lowered onto a table and finally given relief from his terrible agony as his head was cut off. As a sign of his disgrace, and as a punishment in the afterlife as well, his body was dismembered into four pieces and sent to the towns of York, Carlisle, Bristol and Dover for public display, and remained there for four years. His head was placed on a spike on London Bridge to the sound of trumpets and general rejoicing.

He was an English nobleman in his late 30s, born around the late 1280s, and his name was Hugh Despenser, lord of Glamorgan; he is usually known to history as Hugh Despenser the Younger. Hugh was the 'favourite' of King Edward II in the 1320s, perhaps his lover, wielded considerable power over the English government and foreign policy for years, took whatever lands he wished with the king's connivance, and imprisoned, exiled and blackmailed his enemies. Hugh was once voted the 'greatest villain of the fourteenth century' by BBC History Magazine; the twentieth-century winner (or perhaps we should say loser) was Oswald Mosley of the British Fascist Party, while Jack the Ripper took the prize for the nineteenth. [2] From about 1319 until his execution in November 1326, Hugh Despenser was the most powerful man in England and Wales. He has been used in literature for centuries as an archetypal royal favourite. He brought down a king. He was grotesquely executed by a queen. Yet there has never been a biography of him before, nor even an academic thesis dedicated to him (though there is one about his family). Contemporary chroniclers were, without exception, extremely critical and disparaging about him, not of course without very good reason, and not one had a single good word to say about Hugh. Neither has he been depicted favourably in more modern writing. Hugh has appeared in much historical non-fiction and fiction about Edward II (r. 1307–27) and his queen Isabella of France, though for the most part appears oddly one-dimensional, even a caricature, a cackling moustache-twirling villain and psychopath who rapes the queen and murders and tortures people for fun. There has been little attempt in the last 700 years to depict Hugh as an individual, and he is sometimes written merely as a placeholder successor of the much more famous Piers Gaveston (d. 1312), the first great favourite of Edward II, as though the two men were basically interchangeable. As historian J. S. Hamilton has pointed out, '[i]n popular literature and even some historical writing there has been a tendency to conflate the two, and to present them as identical stereotypical caricatures.' [3] The charges of murder and torture were made solely by Hugh's enemies in 1321 and 1326 and have little if any supporting evidence in their favour, and the charge of raping the queen was invented in the early twenty-first century. Hugh Despenser the Younger was emphatically not a nice person, and certainly committed extortion, blackmail, false imprisonment, piracy and other crimes, but it may be that that the most serious accusations against him are fabrications, or at least exaggerations.

Did Hugh have any redeeming features? Edward II loved him for many years and refused to give him up even after an invasion of his kingdom intended to force him to do so. He was highly intelligent, sharp, witty and articulate. He read out letters to Edward so was a fluent reader, by no means a given in the early fourteenth century, and took a keen interest in national affairs and in the affairs of his own lordship. He had a sense of humour and was given to dry sarcasm. He fought at the battle of Bannockburn in June 1314, took part in jousting tournaments and rescued a woman and her servants when they were besieged by a large group of armed men, so was certainly not a physical coward. Although Hugh does not have a reputation as a warrior, perhaps he should: Edward II made him a knight banneret after Bannockburn (at a time when he mostly still ignored and apparently disliked Hugh) which can only mean that Hugh had fought there with notable bravery and honour. He was capable of self-insight and was honest about his ambitions to be as rich and influential as possible, and managed to work his way into a position which enabled him to achieve his aims. If he was arrogant, self-important and grasping, he was not much different in this respect from most of the medieval English nobility. His successor as over-mighty royal favourite, his greatest enemy Roger Mortimer, behaved in much the same way as Hugh had and was executed for usurping royal power, though in modern times Mortimer tends to be viewed and depicted as a considerably more attractive and sympathetic figure.

This book is intended more as a personal biography of Hugh Despenser the Younger using his own letters, Edward II's accounts and other primary sources, than as an account of the politics of Edward's reign which have been extensively discussed elsewhere. Certain aspects of Hugh's life, notably the Despenser War, his possible reforms of the exchequer, the parliament of 1321 which exiled him, and the parliament of 1322 which restored him, have been narrated in detail many times before, and there seemed little point in covering very familiar territory yet again. I have therefore endeavoured to present a fresh and original take on a notorious figure, using his own words wherever possible.

Chapter 1

A Plethora of Hugh Despensers

Take good comfort, and be glad, and bold, and work so well now on the king's affairs that it will be to the honour of yourself and your blood.

The first really important member of the Despenser family was Hugh the Younger's grandfather, who was also called Hugh Despenser and was the son of a man called Hugh Despenser who died in 1238. (No-one would ever accuse the Despensers of being creative with names for their sons.) Born in about 1223 or earlier, though no earlier than May 1217 as he was still underage in May 1238, Hugh Despenser the grandfather was a close ally and associate of Simon Montfort, earl of Leicester (*c*. 1208–65). [1] Montfort was the brother-in-law of King Henry III (r. 1216–72), and his long-term conflict with Henry exploded into open warfare in the Barons' Wars of the 1260s. In 1260 Despenser was appointed justiciar of England, and in the late 1250s or 1260 married Aline Basset, daughter and heir of the royalist baron Philip, Lord Basset, who alternated the office of justiciar with Despenser.

All the way back in February 1238 Hugh Despenser the grandfather had been given permission by Henry III that 'by the counsel of his friends he may marry where it shall seem best for his promotion,' and it seems highly likely that he had been married to another woman before Aline Basset, given that he was at least 37 and perhaps over 40 at the time of his wedding to her *c*. 1260. [2] This would be an unusually advanced age at first marriage for a thirteenth-century nobleman. If this is the case, though, the identity of his first wife has not been established. Aline Basset's date of birth cannot be established more precisely than sometime in the 1240s, and she was considerably younger than her husband. The only son of the Despenser-Basset marriage, the man known to history as Hugh Despenser the Elder and father of Hugh the Younger, was born on 1 March 1261. [3] Despenser 'the Elder' is the only certain child of the marriage between Hugh Despenser the justiciar and Aline Basset; three other Despenser siblings, Hugh the Younger's aunts Anne, Joan and perhaps Eleanor, are likely to have been the children of Hugh Despenser the justiciar with his unknown first wife. The justiciar fought at the battle of Lewes on 14 May 1264 on the side of Simon Montfort, earl of Leicester, against his own father-in-law Philip Basset, King Henry III, Henry's elder son and heir the future King Edward I (r. 1272–1307), and Henry's brother Richard of Cornwall, king of Germany (r. 1257–72). The baronial side won a great victory against the royalists, and the king, his son and brother, and Philip Basset were committed to comfortable custody while Montfort ruled the country for more than a year, with Hugh Despenser as one of his closest allies.

Lord Edward, elder son and heir of the king, escaped from captivity and, with the aid of the young earl of Gloucester who had switched sides, raised an army against his uncle Simon Montfort. The young heir to the throne, then 26, turned the tables on Montfort and defeated him at the battle of Evesham in Worcestershire on 4 August 1265. Evesham was less a battle than a slaughter, and among the many dead on the field lay Montfort himself, his eldest son, and his good friend Hugh Despenser the justiciar. Alongside Edward in victory stood the baron Roger Mortimer of Wigmore, from a great noble family in Herefordshire and the Welsh March, whose grandson of the same name would, decades later, prove to be the deadliest enemy and nemesis of Hugh Despenser's grandson Hugh the Younger. Roger Mortimer may have killed Despenser personally at Evesham, and decades later, Hugh the Younger swore to avenge his grandfather's death on Mortimer's son and grandson. [4] Hugh Despenser the justiciar left his widow Aline née Basset, three or four daughters, and his four-year-old son and heir Hugh 'the Elder'. Fortunately for the little boy, and for the future of his son Hugh the Younger and the Despenser family in general, his maternal grandfather Philip, Lord Basset held considerable influence with the royal family. This saved young Hugh's position and his mother Aline's. On 4 October 1265 two months after the battle of Evesham, Henry III granted to Aline for life the three Leicestershire manors (Loughborough, Freeby and Hugglescote) which had formerly belonged to her husband. [5]

Philip Basset died at his manor of North Weald Bassett in Essex on 29 October 1271, when his daughter and heir Aline Despenser née Basset was said to be anywhere between 22 and more than 30 years old. [6] It is impossible that she could have been as young as 22 in October 1271 which would have made her only 11 or 12 when she gave birth to her son Hugh the Elder. Philip Basset had married again *c*. 1255 after the death of his first wife Hawise Lovaine, mother of Philip's only (surviving) child Aline. His second wife, the step-grandmother of Hugh Despenser the Elder, was Ela Longespée, countess of Warwick by her first marriage and daughter of Henry II's (r. 1154–89) illegitimate son William, earl of Salisbury, and she outlived Philip Basset by more than a quarter of a century. With the three manors she held from her late husband and the 13 she inherited from her father (this figure does not include the third of Basset's estate held by his widow Ela in dower which Aline never held as her stepmother outlived her), Aline became a well-off landowner. [7] In or before 1271 she married for the second time. Her new husband was Roger Bigod, earl of Norfolk and earl marshal of England, nephew of the childless Roger Bigod (d. 1270), the previous earl of Norfolk. The younger Roger Bigod was around the same age as his wife Aline or perhaps a little her junior: he was born *c*. 1245 and was only about 16 years older than his stepson Hugh Despenser the Elder. The marriage produced no children, and Bigod's second marriage to the sister of the count of Hainault also remained childless.

Aline continued to use her first husband's name throughout her marriage to the earl of Norfolk, and Bigod himself referred to her as Aline la Despensere. [8] Medieval noblewomen who were married to more than one man tended to use the name of the highest ranking of their husbands, and, as an earl, Roger Bigod was of higher rank than Hugh Despenser the justiciar had been. Aline's choice to retain Despenser's name throughout her second marriage and until her death may therefore be revealing, and indicate that she had found her first marriage a happy one. Aline Despenser née Basset, countess of Norfolk, died shortly before 11 April 1281. She left a will, though it does not survive, and her son and heir Hugh the Elder was one of her executors. [9] On 28 May and again on 2 June 1281, Edward I's steward was ordered to deliver Aline's lands to Hugh, even though he was still not quite of age; he would turn 21 on 1 March 1282. [10] Also on 28 May 1281, William Beauchamp, earl of Warwick, was granted the rights to Despenser's marriage, a common situation among tenants-in-chief (the important men and women of the realm who held land directly from the king) which generally meant that the earl would expect to arrange Despenser's marriage to a member of his own family, usually a daughter or niece. [11]

From his mother and Basset grandfather, Hugh Despenser the Elder inherited the manors of North Weald Bassett, Wix, Tolleshunt Gaines, Tolleshunt Knights, Layer de la Haye and Lamarsh in Essex; Barnwell in Northamptonshire; High Wycombe, Buckinghamshire; Soham, Cambridgeshire; Vastern, Broadtown, Upavon, Marden, Berwick Bassett, Compton Bassett, Wootton Bassett and Winterbourne Bassett, Wiltshire; Woking and Sutton Green, Surrey; Speen, Berkshire; Loughborough, Freeby and Hugglescote, Leicestershire (originally held by his father Hugh the justiciar); Kirtlington, Elsfield and Cassington, Oxfordshire; Oxcroft, Cambridgeshire; Euston and Kersey, Suffolk; and Mapledurwell, Hampshire. [12] At some point he also acquired Otmoor in Oxfordshire which is now a nature reserve owned by the Royal Society for the Protection of Birds, and in August 1302 complained that five men had 'carried away his swans' from there. [13] Throughout his lifetime Hugh the Elder added considerably to his inheritance, and by 1321 he had 66 manors in 18 counties, though held some of these as wardships. [14] Even without his many later additions, his inheritance from his mother Aline was sizeable enough that her widower Roger Bigod tried to gain control of it after her death. A medieval custom called 'the courtesy of England' allowed a man to keep hold of all his late wife's inheritance until his own death, provided that they had had at least one child together. Bigod claimed in 1281 that Aline had borne him a child at her manor of Woking and that it had lived long enough to take a breath before dying. Despenser vigorously challenged his stepfather, and Bigod was forced to give up his claim; Aline's inheritance passed intact to her son. [15] Sometime before 12 June 1290, the earl of Norfolk married his second wife Alicia, daughter and sister of counts of Hainault, and on that date Hugh the Elder was one of the witnesses to Norfolk's assignment of dower to his new countess. [16]

On 2 March 1282, the day after his twenty-first birthday, Hugh Despenser the Elder acknowledged a debt of 1,600 marks to William Beauchamp, earl of Warwick, to buy the rights to his own marriage from the earl. [17] This association with Warwick would ultimately result some years later in Despenser's marriage to the earl's daughter Isabella Beauchamp, Hugh Despenser the Younger's mother, though in 1282 she was still married to her first husband Patrick Chaworth and bore him a child on 2 February that year. Despenser was allowed on 3 March 1282 to take possession of the Worcestershire manor of Martley which had formerly belonged to his father's cousin John Despenser, whose heir he was, on the grounds that 'it is evident to the king's court that Hugh is of full age.' [18] He later gave Martley to his eldest child Alina, and inherited two more manors in Leicestershire from John. [19]

William Beauchamp, earl of Warwick, Hugh Despenser the Younger's maternal grandfather, was born in the late 1230s or beginning of the 1240s and so was very close to the same age as Henry III's son King Edward I, who was born on 17 June 1239. [20] He was the eldest son of William Beauchamp the Elder, lord of Elmley in Worcestershire, and Isabella Mauduit, whose mother Alice was the daughter of Waleran Beaumont, earl of Warwick. William Beauchamp married Maud FitzJohn, eldest of the four daughters of Isabel Bigod, daughter of the earl of Norfolk and granddaughter of William Marshal, earl of Pembroke. As both their brothers died childless, Maud and her three younger sisters, and their children and grandchildren, were the FitzJohn heirs. Maud had previously been married to Gerard, Lord Furnival, who died before 18 October 1261; they had no children. [21]

William Beauchamp and Maud FitzJohn had one surviving son, Guy Beauchamp, who was born between 1271 and 1275 and succeeded William as earl in June 1298. [22] William and Maud named their son in honour of the literary hero Guy of Warwick. Their daughter Isabella, Hugh Despenser the Younger's mother, was a few years older than her brother; she was born around 1263 to 1266 and may have been the eldest Beauchamp child. As Maud's first husband Gerald Furnival was alive until October 1261, Maud and William cannot have married before 1262, so Isabella cannot have been born before *c*. late 1262 or 1263. She bore her first child in early 1282 so is unlikely to have been born after 1266. Isabella and Guy Beauchamp had several other sisters, Hugh Despenser the Younger's aunts: two who both became nuns at Shouldham Priory in Norfolk, and an uncertain number of others. [23] William Beauchamp, earl of Warwick, was a friend of Edward I, was made High Sheriff of Worcestershire for life in 1268, and played a large part in the king's military campaigns in Wales in the 1270s and early 1280s. [24] He wrote his will on 14 September 1296 21 months before he died, and asked to be buried at the Greyfriars' or Franciscans' church in Worcester. Earl William did not mention his daughter Isabella or any of his grandchildren in the will, though left his son and heir Guy a gold ring with a ruby and the sum of 50 marks to two of his other daughters, the nuns of Shouldham. To his wife Countess Maud, William left several items including 'the cross wherein is contained part of the wood of the very Cross whereon our Saviour died.' [25]

Isabella Beauchamp's first husband Patrick Chaworth died shortly before 7 July 1283 when the writ to take his lands into the king's hands was issued. Patrick's heir was his and Isabella's only child Maud, named after Isabella's mother the countess of Warwick, who was 'age one on the Feast of the Purification last' in July 1283, i.e. she was born on or around 2 February 1282. [26] Maud Chaworth, Hugh the Younger's half-sister, inherited the lordships of Kidwelly and Carmarthen in South Wales, and 16 manors in five English counties, from her father, and was also the heir of her uncle Payn Chaworth. [27] Isabella Chaworth née Beauchamp was granted her dower, the customary one-third of her late husband's estate, on 3 September and 4 October 1283. [28] Only in her teens or at most 20 years old at the time of her husband's death in the summer of 1283, she remained a widow for some years until she married Hugh Despenser the Elder, formerly, albeit briefly, her father's ward.

As the earl of Norfolk's stepson and in possession of a reasonably large inheritance across numerous counties in the Midlands and south of England, Hugh the Elder made a good prospect as a husband for the earl of Warwick's daughter, and probably sometime in 1286, the two married. The date of Hugh and Isabella's wedding cannot be precisely determined, except that it is likely to have taken place after 10 September 1285 when Isabella was still called Chaworth, and definitely before 27 January 1287 when Despenser acknowledged liability for a fine for marrying Isabella without royal permission. [29] Although they wed without a licence from Edward I and were fined, this was a common occurrence. Tenants-in-chief were obliged to obtain the king's permission to marry, but often failed to do so, and a large fine and temporary seizure of lands and goods was the usual punishment. On 8 November 1287, Hugh Despenser the Elder was acquitted of a fine of 2,000 marks or £1,333 'for his trespass in marrying Isabella…without the king's licence.' [30] Their marriage without a royal licence might indicate that it was a love-match, and almost certainly they both freely chose to wed. Isabella as a widow had more freedom than she had before she married Patrick Chaworth; it was the norm for noble families to arrange their children's marriages, but in widowhood women usually (though not always) had more freedom to marry again or not as they pleased, and to choose their own second husbands. Hugh the Elder's brief period as the ward of Isabella's father Earl William presumably gave the two an opportunity to meet. Despenser, despite or perhaps because of his father's rebellion against King Henry III in the 1260s, was himself a loyal royal servant all his life, faithfully serving Henry's son Edward I and grandson Edward II. He was 'going beyond seas' on Edward I's service on 27 May 1286 and again on 10 April 1287; perhaps he married Isabella before the May 1286 visit, or when he returned from it. [31]

The marriage of Hugh Despenser the Elder and Isabella Beauchamp produced six children, two boys and four girls. The eldest Despenser child was Alina, named conventionally after her paternal grandmother the countess of Norfolk. Alina was probably born in 1287 or thereabouts, the year after the likely date of her parents' wedding, and did not die until May 1363 when she must have been in her mid-70s. [32] Sometime after 3 May 1302 at the age of about 14 or 15, Alina Despenser married Edward Burnell, who himself was born on or around 22 July 1287. Hugh the Younger was the elder of the two Despenser sons and the second child. It is likely that Alina Despenser was a year or two Hugh's senior, as she married in 1302 and he in 1306; although it was common for noble girls of the era to marry at a rather younger age than their brothers, the four-year gap between Alina's wedding and Hugh's indicates that she was older than he. Unfortunately, we have no way of knowing exactly when Hugh was born, even to the nearest year, but it was probably about 1288 or 1289. Hugh the Younger married 13-year-old Eleanor Clare on 26 May 1306 a few days after he was knighted, when he was about 17 or 18.

Isabella was the third Despenser child and born perhaps in 1290/92, and named after their mother. She married her first husband Gilbert Clare (b. 1281), lord of Thomond in Ireland, probably in 1306 or soon afterwards. The date is not recorded, but as Gilbert's first cousin was Eleanor Clare who married Hugh the Younger in May 1306, it may be that a double marriage alliance between the Despenser siblings and the Clare cousins was arranged in this year. Gilbert

Clare of Thomond died in November 1307, and in 1308 or 1309 Isabella married her second husband John, Lord Hastings, who, born in 1262, was just a year younger than her father. Next in the list of Despenser children came Philip, the fourth child and second son, named after his great-grandfather Philip Basset. Philip Despenser was born sometime before 24 June 1294, and married the Lincolnshire heiress Margaret Goushill, who was born in 1294, before 29 June 1308. [33] The fifth Despenser child was Margaret, who married John St Amand after 4 December 1313 and was born around the mid to late 1290s and the sixth and youngest was Elizabeth, probably born in the late 1290s or early 1300s. She married the widower Ralph, Lord Camoys, who was born in the 1270s, in or before 1316. All the Despenser siblings except Alina had children of their own; Hugh the Elder and Isabella had at least 20 grandchildren, Hugh the Younger contributing half that total. Isabella Despenser née Beauchamp died in May 1306 when she was in her early or mid-40s and her husband 45. Although Hugh the Elder lived for another two decades, he never married again.

Hugh Despenser the Younger was of almost entirely English origin several generations back on both sides of his family. Going farther back in time, to the mid-twelfth century, one of his five greats-grandmothers on his father's side was German: she was Luitgarde of Sulzbach in north-east Bavaria, duchess of Lower Lorraine, landgravine of Brabant and margravine of Antwerp, and countess of Metz and Dagsburg by her second marriage. Luitgarde's sister Bertha of Sulzbach, renamed Eirene after her wedding, married the Byzantine emperor Manuel I Komnenos (r. 1143–80) in 1146, and another sister, Gertrud, married Konrad von Hohenstaufen, king of Germany and Italy (r. 1138–52). Luitgarde's daughter-in-law, the woman who married her son Duke Godfried III of Lower Lorraine and who was Hugh Despenser's great-great-great-great-grandmother, bore the excellent name Imagina de Looz. Imagina was the daughter of Louis, count of Looz in what is now Belgium and of Rieneck in Bavaria, and also burgrave of Mainz in western Germany. Imagina's younger son Godfrey of Lovaine moved to England in the 1190s and would become the ancestor of the Despensers: his granddaughter Hawise Lovaine married Philip, Lord Basset and was the grandmother of Hugh Despenser the Elder.

Although Hugh never set foot in Ireland, he had connections there: he was the five greats-grandson of Diarmait Mac Murchada or Dermot MacMurrough, king of Leinster (d. 1171), and his great-grandfather John FitzGeoffrey of Shere (d. 1258) was justiciar of Ireland. His grandmother Maud FitzJohn's sister Aveline married Walter Burgh, lord of Connaught, and was the mother of Richard Burgh, earl of Ulster (1259–1326), a first cousin of Isabella Beauchamp. Another of Maud's three younger sisters, Joan, was the mother of the earl of Carrick and grandmother of earls of Kildare and Ormond. Hugh would have been raised to be very aware of his high rank and his noble relatives and ancestors, and to know that one day he would make an arranged marriage to a noblewoman whom his father would choose for him. He was an eligible bachelor, and Edward I himself paid a great deal of money to Hugh the Elder for the privilege of marrying Hugh to his eldest granddaughter.

Chapter 2

Early Life

Work gladly and assiduously on the king's business, and protect his honour and his country, because in doing so he will have such regard for you that you will be rich and will remain always honoured.

Hugh the Younger was of noble origin going back generations and was most probably born in the late 1280s, about halfway through the reign of the man who would become his grandfather-in-law: Edward I, who succeeded his father Henry III as king of England in November 1272. We know nothing about Hugh's childhood or where he grew up; perhaps on one or several of his father's chief manors such as High Wycombe in Buckinghamshire or Soham in Cambridgeshire. Noble boys of the Middle Ages were often sent to the household of a nobleman or noblewoman to serve as a page from the age of about seven, and this is likely to have been the case with Hugh as well. It is possible that he spent time in the households of his maternal grandfather and uncle William and Guy Beauchamp, earls of Warwick, though this is only speculation. Hugh's great-uncle Sir Walter Beauchamp, one of Earl William's many siblings, became steward of Edward I's household in 1289, around the time that Hugh was born, and held the position until his death in 1303. [1] The prominence of his grandfather and great-uncle at court means that Hugh surely spent time there as well as he was growing up. Hugh would have been taught to ride and to wield a sword from a very young age. In England knighthood was not hereditary as such, but a young man of Hugh's high birth could always expect to be knighted and so he would have been trained for this. One day he would come into a large inheritance and would have to learn how to manage it, and would have learnt the courtesy, etiquette and so on which he would need to operate successfully in his society. Hugh's father was often sent by Edward I on important diplomatic missions to the pope and to leaders of other European nations which indicates that he was extremely presentable, well-dressed and well-spoken and must have had excellent courtly manners.

Hugh the Younger's upbringing was as comfortable as anyone's possibly could be at the end of the thirteenth and beginning of the fourteenth centuries:

his father was very well-off, and in 1291 was able to make a loan of £500 to the earl of Arundel, Richard Fitzalan. [2] By 1308 Hugh the Elder owned houses in Paris and elsewhere in France, and at the same time was owed more than £2,500 by Edward II. By March 1318, the king owed Despenser a remarkable £6,770. [3] On top of his sizeable inheritance from his parents, grandfather and father's cousin, Hugh the Elder acquired many other estates in England from the 1290s onwards, sometimes by rather dubious means; he was not overburdened with scruples, and his son was to prove even less so. In 1298 when Hugh the Younger was about nine or 10, one Saer le Barber of London declared that his father was 'unworthy of praise' and claimed that he 'kept more robbers with him than any man in England.' Despenser complained to the mayor of London, and Barber was sent to Newgate prison. [4] Hugh the Elder was accused of brutality and corruption by his contemporaries, especially in his capacity as justice of the forest, and *c.* 1313 a chronicler wrote 'the whole land has turned to hatred of him. Few would mourn his downfall. As an unjust official he did harm to many.' On the other hand, he and his father Hugh the justiciar were talented administrators and estate managers, not to mention diplomats. [5] The three Hugh Despensers of the thirteenth and early fourteenth centuries were acquisitive and often cruel and malicious; they were also intelligent and capable men.

Evidence from the 1320s shows that Hugh the Younger was a fluent reader and was probably able to write. As was the case with all the English nobility of this era, Hugh was French-speaking, and all his surviving correspondence is in that language. Many of his extant letters survive as drafts, kept by Hugh himself, and are fascinating for revealing his thought processes as he ordered his clerks to add or to strike out various phrases as he changed his mind on certain points. The letters also show Hugh's ability to dictate articulate and detailed text, his deep interest in his lordship of Glamorgan in South Wales, and his control over the English government and foreign policy in the 1320s. Whether or to what extent he and his noble peers could speak English can only be guessed at as we have little direct evidence, though presumably as he and the rest of the elite lived in a country where the vast majority of the population spoke only English, he could speak it, and he probably learnt Latin as well.

Hugh would also have received a considerable amount of religious teaching. In 1290 when he was still only a baby or a toddler, Edward I expelled the entire Jewish population from England, with the result that for the whole of Hugh's lifetime everyone who lived in his country was Catholic. Little of his behaviour indicates that he was particularly pious, though he expressed dutiful wishes in many of his letters that God would help him achieve his aims and ended them with conventional salutations such as 'May God keep you' or 'May the Holy

Spirit have you in his keeping.' In the 1320s, his enemies were to call him a 'false Christian' and a 'traitor against God Himself.'

There is, unfortunately, no real way of determining what Hugh looked like, as is the case with almost everyone else of his era (except Edward II, whose tall, fair, bearded and immensely strong appearance was recorded). Whether Hugh was dark or fair or a redhead, tall or short, slim or plump or burly, we cannot know. His uncle the earl of Warwick was nicknamed 'the Black Dog of Arden' presumably because he was dark, while his half-sister Maud's son Henry, duke of Lancaster, was tall, slim and blond. Another nephew, Sir Hugh Hastings, was found to have stood five feet ten inches when his remains were examined in the 1970s. A carved stone corbel of a man's head in Hugh's great hall of Caerphilly Castle in South Wales (which he rebuilt in the 1320s) may depict him with long hair and a goatee-style beard.

Sometime before 24 June 1294 Hugh's younger brother Philip was born, and on that date their father granted Philip two manors and all his goods and chattels in them. [6] Thanks to contemporary English inheritance laws, where primogeniture was in operation – a practice where the eldest son inherited everything – Hugh the Younger was sole heir to the Despenser/Basset estate, and would not have to share it with his brother and sisters. He stood to inherit lands worth at least £1,500 a year and goods worth more than £2,500, in an age when most English people earned one to three pence per day. [7] As Hugh grew up, he must have been accustomed to his father's frequent journeys overseas on Edward I's business: Hugh the Elder went abroad in the summer of 1294, December 1295, August 1297, and so on, and frequently took part in Edward I's military campaigns in Scotland in the 1290s and early 1300s. [8] Hugh the Elder was in England on 30 November 1295, when he witnessed a royal charter with his stepfather the earl of Norfolk and father-in-law the earl of Warwick. [9] In 1294 and again in 1296/7, he received one of his most important commissions from the king when he was sent, with the archbishop of Dublin and the bishop of Durham, as an envoy to the German king Adolf of Nassau (r. 1292–98) and Siegfried von Westerburg, archbishop of Cologne (1275–97). [10]

In December 1295 when he was about six or seven, Hugh the Younger may have been aware of the death of the greatest nobleman in England: Gilbert 'the Red' Clare, earl of Gloucester and Hertford and husband of the king's second daughter Joan of Acre (1272–1307). Hugh would later marry Gloucester's daughter Eleanor. As a very young man in the mid-1260s, Gloucester had switched sides from Simon de Montfort to Henry III and his son, and played a vital role in Montfort's and Hugh Despenser the justiciar's defeat at Evesham in 1265. The earl died at the age of 52 and left one son and five daughters, the youngest of whom, Elizabeth Clare, was only a few weeks old at the time of her father's death. Hugh would later persecute this sister-in-law and deprive her of her lands. Hugh's grandfather the earl of Warwick had played an important role in putting down an uprising in Wales in 1294/5 with the earl of Gloucester, and on 5 March 1295 Warwick was responsible for a major victory at the battle of Maes Moydog when he crippled the forces of the Welsh leader Madog ap Llywelyn. [11] Warwick was also one of the leaders of the force which defeated the king of Scotland John Balliol (r. 1292–96) at the battle of Dunbar on 27 April 1296, when Edward I invaded Scotland and removed Balliol from his throne. [12] These battles and his grandfather's involvement in them, and the death of the immensely influential earl of Gloucester, were perhaps amongst Hugh's earliest memories.

Hugh's future mother-in-law Joan of Acre, the king's daughter and widow of the earl of Gloucester, caused a great scandal in early 1297 when she married a humble squire named Ralph Monthermer without her father's permission. News of this must have reached Hugh's ears. An important event took place in the royal family around this time, on Monday. 7 January 1297. Fourteen-year-old Elizabeth, Joan of Acre's sister and youngest of the five daughters of Edward I and his late Spanish queen Leonor of Castile (c. 1241-90), married the 12-year-old count of Holland, Jan I. Hugh Despenser the Elder was almost certainly present at the Ipswich wedding, and Hugh the Younger perhaps attended too. The elder Hugh's stepfather Roger Bigod, earl of Norfolk, and his second wife Alicia of Hainault were among the guests. [13] Certainly present at his sister Elizabeth's wedding was 12-year-old Edward of Caernarfon, born in April 1284 as the youngest and only surviving of Edward I and Leonor of Castile's four sons, and heir to the English throne. Hugh would of course have known exactly who Edward of Caernarfon was, and Edward would also have been well aware of him as one of his contemporaries, a boy of high rank and part of the elite who surrounded the king and his court. A later chronicler wrote that Hugh was a member of Edward of Caernarfon's household before he became king, and although we have no confirmation of this statement, it is virtually certain that he was, at least on occasion. Two of Hugh's future brothers-in-law, Piers Gaveston and Gilbert Clare of Thomond, were companions of the heir to the throne in the early 1300s. Hugh's half-sister Maud Chaworth and their second cousin Eleanor Burgh, one of the daughters of the earl of Ulster, were also in the company of the future king in 1290 when Edward was six (Maud was two years his senior while Hugh was about four or five years his junior), and perhaps in other years too. [14] As the son and heir of Hugh Despenser the Elder who was a trusted ally of the king, and as the grandson of the earl of Warwick, it would have been an insult to both men if Hugh had not been chosen to spend time with Edward of Caernarfon when they were growing up. Given their later complex relationship which swung from outright dislike and distrust to steadfast and years-long infatuation, at least on Edward's side, it is important to bear in mind that Edward II and Hugh Despenser the Younger must have known each other almost all their lives.

On 2 February 1297, Hugh Despenser the Elder, the bishop of Durham, and Sir Walter Beauchamp, steward of the king's household and Hugh the Younger's great-uncle, were appointed to take oaths in the matter of the proposed marriage between Edward of Caernarfon and Philippa, daughter of Guy, count of Flanders. The three men were to swear on Edward I's behalf that the king would keep the treaty of alliance with Guy and go ahead with the marriage. [15] (It never took place; Philip IV of France (r. 1285–1314) kept the count's daughter Philippa as a hostage in Paris to ensure that it did not.) At this time Hugh the Elder was appointed as 'justice of the forest this side [of the river] Trent,' and had been made constable of the royal castle of Odiham in Hampshire on 12 June 1294, an appointment which his son would also receive from Edward II in 1320. [16] Edward I, at war with his kinsman the powerful French king Philip IV, went on military campaign in Flanders in August 1297. The heir to the throne Edward of Caernarfon, now 13, remained in England as nominal regent. Despenser the Elder is frequently named in Edward I's correspondence in this difficult, crisis-ridden year as one of the king's most important supporters. [17] Hugh the Elder's stepfather Roger Bigod, earl of Norfolk and earl marshal of England, however, had a famous altercation with the king about the earl's unwillingness to go overseas on the king's latest military campaign. Hugh the Younger's grandfather the earl of Warwick claimed poverty and did not take part in the Flanders campaign either. [18] He remained behind in England as a member of the regency council advising Edward of Caernarfon. Earl William had been ill in 1296/7 which would account for him making his will in September 1296 – people generally only made their wills when they thought they were dying – though by mid-September 1297 had recovered sufficiently to be ordered to attend Edward of Caernarfon in London immediately. [19]

Several of Hugh Despenser the Younger's elderly relatives died in the late 1290s and early 1300s. The first was his father's step-grandmother Ela Longespée, who died on 8 February 1297. At this point Hugh the Elder, now almost 36, came into his entire inheritance when the one-third of the Basset lands held by Ela in dower reverted to him. Ela was a link to the remote past: her father William Longespée, earl of Salisbury and an illegitimate son of Henry II, had been born c. 1176 and died in 1226 when Ela was a young child, and her grandfather Henry II himself was born in 1133. Even Ela's second husband, Hugh the Younger's great-grandfather Philip Basset, had been born back in the 1100s or early 1200s, and her first husband Thomas Beaumont died in 1242.

Hugh the Younger's maternal great-uncle Richard FitzJohn, lord of Shere, died childless in August 1297, leaving five heirs: his eldest sister Maud, countess of Warwick and Hugh's grandmother; his great-nephew Robert Clifford, grandson of the second FitzJohn sister Isabel Vipont; his niece Idonea Leyburne, Isabel Vipont's daughter; his nephew Richard Burgh, earl of Ulster, son of his third sister Aveline; and his fourth sister Joan Botiler. [20]

William Beauchamp, earl of Warwick, died on 5 or 9 June 1298 when he was about 60 and his grandson Hugh about nine or 10, and was succeeded as earl by his son Guy. According to the Worcester chronicle, William made his will 'in the absence of all his friends' and on the advice of one Brother John Olney, who persuaded the earl to change his mind and ask to be buried with the Franciscans of Worcester rather than in the cathedral (though in fact Warwick had made his will in September 1296). [21] Warwick had apparently been expecting to die for a few days or weeks before he did, and on 25 May 1298 'in case of his death' Edward I granted the executors of the earl's will free administration of his goods and promised to charge the earl's debts to the Crown, both his own and his ancestors', to Warwick's heirs. [22] As was common at the time, Warwick asked for his heart to be buried separately, wherever his widow Maud chose, and left £200 for his funeral. The Worcester chronicle relates that the Franciscans processed through the streets and squares of the city bearing the earl's body as if carrying the spoils of war, and buried him in a place 'where in winter time he could be said to be drowned rather than buried.' [23] Hugh's last remaining grandparent Maud Beauchamp née FitzJohn, dowager countess of Warwick, died on or about 16 April 1301, and was buried at the Franciscans' church in Worcester next to her husband on 7 May. On 9 August 1298, two months after her husband's death, Maud had been allowed to appoint two attorneys to act on her behalf on the grounds of her 'infirmity.' [24] It is likely that Hugh attended his grandparents' funerals, though we cannot be sure. Countess Maud's only surviving sibling Joan Botiler followed her to the grave two years later. Shortly before 24 May 1302, yet another elderly relative of Hugh's died: his great-great-uncle Sir Matthew Lovaine, younger brother of Hugh's great-grandmother Hawise, who was the first wife of Philip Basset and the mother of Aline, countess of Norfolk. [25] And on 16 February 1303, Hugh's great-uncle Sir Walter Beauchamp, steward of Edward I's household for the last 14 years, also passed away. [26]

On the death of Patrick Chaworth in July 1283, official custody of his daughter and heir Maud, Hugh the Younger's older half-sister, had passed to King Edward I, though she probably remained with her mother Isabella. [27] On 30 December 1291, Edward I granted the rights to Maud's marriage to his brother Edmund, earl of Lancaster and Leicester, and on or shortly before

2 March 1297, Maud married Edmund's younger son Henry of Lancaster, the king's nephew. Maud was then 15, Henry the same age or a little older. [28] This union brought an extremely highly-born young man into Hugh's close family circle. Henry of Lancaster was not only Edward I's nephew, he was the brother-in-law of the powerful king of France, Philip IV. Henry's mother Blanche of Artois, niece of Louis IX of France, married King Enrique I 'the Fat' of Navarre in northern Spain as her first husband. This marriage produced one surviving child, Jeanne I, queen of Navarre in her own right and Henry of Lancaster's elder half-sister. Jeanne was born in 1273 and married 16-year-old Philip of France in 1284; the following year, he succeeded his father Philip III as king. Enrique I of Navarre had died when his daughter was only a baby in 1274, and his widow Blanche of Artois married Edmund of Lancaster, the only brother of the reigning king of England Edward I, in late 1275. And now in 1297, the half-brother of the queen-regnant of Navarre, the brother-in-law of the king of France and the nephew of the king of England had become the brother-in-law of Hugh Despenser the Younger. Henry of Lancaster had an older brother Thomas, born in about 1278. In 1294 Thomas had married the heiress Alice Lacy, who was in line to inherit (and did) the earldom of Lincoln from her father and the earldom of Salisbury from her mother. Thomas and Alice had no children together in their unhappy marriage which ended in separation in 1317, and Henry of Lancaster therefore was his brother's heir and would ultimately inherit Thomas's earldoms and huge wealth. He and Maud Chaworth were to have seven children together, the eldest of whom, Hugh's niece Blanche of Lancaster, was born sometime between 1302 and 1305. The marriage of the king's nephew Henry of Lancaster to his half-sister would have brought Hugh even closer into the orbit of the royal court than he was already, as Henry and his brother Thomas were frequent visitors to their cousin Edward of Caernarfon. In the early 1300s, Hugh the Younger entered his teens. Soon after 3 May 1302, he probably attended the wedding of his elder sister Alina to Edward Burnell. [29] Edward was the son and heir of Philip Burnell, who died in 1294 and was himself the nephew and heir of the wealthy and influential Robert Burnell, bishop of Bath and Wells and chancellor of England, a close ally and friend of Edward I (in honour of whom Edward Burnell was presumably named). In March 1300, Edward Burnell was in the custody of the Kent baron Guncelin Badlesmere, who was said by King Edward I that month to have committed destruction and waste in several of Edward's manors. [30] There was a family connection via marriage to the Despensers: Guncelin's son and heir Bartholomew Badlesmere married Margaret Clare, whose brother Gilbert, lord of Thomond, married Hugh's second sister Isabella Despenser some years later. Edward Burnell came into a large inheritance, with lands

in 10 counties. [31] Hugh the Elder had been granted the rights to Edward Burnell's marriage on 1 January 1296, so had probably been planning the boy's wedding to his daughter for some years. It cost him 1,000 marks. [32]

Hugh Despenser the Elder took part in Edward I's siege of the castle of Caerlaverock in Scotland in July 1300, and came to the attention of a poet: 'the good Hugh Despenser, who loyally on his courser knew how to disrupt a melee.' [33] The rhyming chronicler Piers Langtoft called Hugh the Elder a *baroun renomez*, 'renowned baron'. [34] Despenser the Elder was sent to the 'court of Rome', i.e. the *curia* of the pope, two months later, and was still there at the beginning of 1301. He was back in England by 25 April 1302 when he was appointed – on Edward of Caernarfon's eighteenth birthday – as one of Edward I's 'envoys to treat touching the re-establishment of peace with the king of France.' [35] Edward I had by this point married his second queen, Philip IV of France's younger half-sister Marguerite; the wedding took place in Canterbury on 8 September 1299 almost nine years after the death of Edward I's first queen Leonor of Castile, with Hugh the Younger's uncle Guy Beauchamp one of the guests. [36] Marguerite became pregnant immediately and gave birth to her son Thomas of Brotherton on 1 June 1300, followed by her second son Edmund of Woodstock on 5 August 1301. These two boys, born when their father was in his early 60s, were the half-uncles of Hugh's future wife Eleanor, the king's eldest granddaughter, though were eight and nine years her junior. Edmund often acknowledged Hugh, a dozen years his elder, as his nephew in years to come.

Hugh the Elder's loyal service to Edward I continued in the last years of the king's reign, when the ongoing situation in Scotland dominated much of his business and energy. Edward I's brother-in-law King Alexander III (r. 1249–86) died in March 1286, leaving as his heir his young granddaughter Margaret, daughter of King Erik II of Norway (r. 1280–99). Margaret was betrothed to her cousin Edward of Caernarfon in 1289 when he was five and she six. One day this marriage should have made them joint rulers of Scotland, but Margaret died in the autumn of 1290. The nobleman John Balliol was declared the winner of the ensuing competition for the Scottish throne in 1292, but was removed from power by Edward I, who claimed overlordship of Scotland in 1296 after Balliol allied with Philip IV of France against England. Balliol lost the battle of Dunbar and was imprisoned with his son, and later went into exile on the continent. For a decade there was an interregnum in the northern kingdom, and it was governed by the Guardians of Scotland. Hugh Despenser the Elder and his wife Isabella Beauchamp's first cousin Richard Burgh, earl of Ulster, were the two men sent to negotiate with the important Scottish nobleman John Comyn in February 1304. [37] This was John 'the Red Comyn', lord of Badenoch,

John Balliol's nephew and one of the Guardians of Scotland. That same year, the 19-year-old Edward of Caernarfon, prince of Wales since February 1301, campaigned in Scotland, and one of the men who accompanied him was Hugh the Younger's uncle Guy Beauchamp. Edward met John Comyn of Badenoch on 5 February 1304, and had spent Christmas 1303 at Perth, where his guests included the earl of Warwick, Warwick's brother-in-law Hugh Despenser the Elder, and Warwick's first cousin the earl of Ulster. [38] At this point Warwick and the young heir to the throne were on good terms, though this would not last past Edward's accession.

The correspondence of Edward of Caernarfon survives for the year 1304/5, and reveals that he was on excellent terms with Hugh Despenser the Elder. Edward of Caernarfon was also very close to two of his nobly-born companions, Hugh the Younger's soon-to-be brothers-in-law Piers Gaveston (who would marry his wife Eleanor's sister Margaret in 1307) and Gilbert Clare, lord of Thomond (who would marry Hugh's second sister Isabella *c.* 1306). [39] The prince of Wales sent eight letters to Hugh the Elder in 1304/5, all of them in French, and called him 'our dear and faithful friend.' Hugh the Elder was urged on another occasion to come to Edward with haste, and was described as one of the members of his father's council 'who are our friends.' [40] He managed the very difficult task of remaining close to, and trusted by, both Edward of Caernarfon and his father the king for the last few years of Edward I's reign. His tact and diplomacy, as well as his lifetime of loyal service to two kings, would reap great benefits for his son.

Chapter 3

Knighthood and Wedding

Never give in to melancholy and never think that we do not have the matters which you relate to us much at heart; rather, we are thinking, and will think, how we can further the matters as speedily as we possibly can.

In October 1305 Hugh the Elder again went to the papal court as one of the envoys who were 'to treat with the pope touching a crusade to the Holy Land, peace with the king of France and other things touching the salvation of the king's soul,' and in the same month was appointed as one of the five men who were to arrange the journey to England of the king's granddaughter Jeanne de Bar. [1] Jeanne was the only daughter of Edward I's eldest daughter Eleanor, who had married Count Henri III of Bar in eastern France and died in 1298. Henri III himself died in 1302, leaving his young son Edouard as his heir. Edouard as the future count of Bar remained in France and may never have met his grandfather the king of England, but his sister Jeanne, born in 1295 or 1296, was to spend most of her life in her mother's homeland. Another important royal girl almost exactly the same age as Jeanne de Bar was Isabella of France, only surviving daughter of Philip IV of France and Jeanne I of Navarre (r. 1274–1305), and thus the niece of Hugh the Younger's brother-in-law Henry of Lancaster. Isabella had been betrothed to Edward of Caernarfon since 1299 and officially since 1303. She would have Hugh hanged, drawn and quartered in 1326.

Someone of whom Hugh would have been closely aware throughout his adolescence was the young man who, at Queen Isabella's side, would have him grotesquely executed, the man he considered his hereditary enemy and who was his distant cousin: Roger Mortimer, heir to the lordship of Wigmore in Herefordshire. Roger was a year or two Hugh's senior, born on 25 April 1287, and was the grandson and heir of the Roger Mortimer who had stood at Lord Edward's side at the battle of Evesham in August 1265, where Hugh's grandfather Hugh Despenser the justiciar had fallen. Roger married the heiress Joan Geneville in September 1301 when he was 14 and she 15; she was Hugh's second cousin. [2] The couple, young as they were, had their first child in 1302 or 1303, and ultimately had a dozen children together. [3] Although we do not and cannot know the nature of Hugh Despenser and Roger Mortimer's relationship so early in their lives, given their families' enmity going back at least two generations and their own later deadly mutual hostility, it is probable that they always disliked each other. According to the well-informed royal clerk who wrote the *Vita Edwardi Secundi* (Life of Edward II), Hugh swore to avenge the death of his grandfather at Evesham on Roger and his namesake uncle Roger Mortimer, lord of Chirk. [4] Although Joan Geneville as a bride could not begin to match the royal and noble connections of Hugh's future wife Eleanor Clare, she brought Roger numerous lands in England, Wales and Ireland as her inheritance from her grandparents, including Ludlow Castle in Shropshire. The result of this was that Roger was considerably wealthier than Hugh for many years which surely rankled with the latter. Roger's father Edmund died in 1304 when Roger was 17, and in July that year Edward I granted his wardship to his son Edward of Caernarfon's close friend and companion Piers Gaveston, a nobleman of Béarn in the far south-west of France, whose name was later to become notorious. [5]

The teenaged Hugh was knighted at Westminster on 22 May 1306, the feast of Pentecost. In total, 266 young men were knighted with Edward of Caernarfon, prince of Wales, count of Ponthieu, earl of Chester and duke of Aquitaine, in a ceremony described by one contemporary chronicler as the greatest ceremony in Britain since King Arthur was crowned at Caerleon. [6] The new knights included the earls of Surrey and Arundel; Hugh's nemesis Roger Mortimer of Wigmore; John Maltravers of Dorset, who would be one of Edward of Caernarfon's custodians at Berkeley Castle in 1327 after Hugh had brought down the king and himself; Gilbert Clare, lord of Thomond; Ralph Camoys, who would later also become yet another of Hugh's brothers-in-law; and William Trussell, who may be the man of this name who would pronounce the sentence of hanging, drawing and quartering on Hugh 20 years later. [7] The young men were meant to spend the night before the ceremony at the Templar church in London awake and in prayerful contemplation, but instead, shouted and laughed and blew trumpets all night. Numerous inhabitants of the capital lined the streets to watch and cheer on the young men as they paraded from the city to Westminster Abbey along the Strand the following morning. Edward of Caernarfon had already been knighted by his father in a private ceremony in the palace, and had spent the night before in the abbey church with a few of the more distinguished future knights, who may have included Hugh. [8] A splendid banquet was held in Westminster Hall afterwards, where the new knights were entertained by dozens of performers including the famous acrobat Matilda Makejoy, Pearl in the Eye, who had cataracts, and many musicians.

Piers Langtoft in his rhyming chronicle called Hugh 'among the most noble' of the new knights, and mentioned him in third place behind the earls of Surrey and Arundel, John Warenne and Edmund Fitzalan. Langtoft rather amusingly referred to Hugh as 'Sir Huge, son of Hug, called Despenser.' [9]

On 26 May, four days after the knighting, came an even greater honour for Hugh: marriage to the king's eldest granddaughter Eleanor Clare, daughter of the late Gilbert 'the Red' Clare, earl of Gloucester and Hertford, and Edward I's second daughter Joan of Acre. Hugh Despenser the Younger, though the grandson of the earl and countess of Warwick and the countess of Norfolk, was not himself in line to inherit an earldom, but was of high noble birth, and Edward I selected him as a husband for his granddaughter and paid Hugh Despenser the Elder £2,000 for the privilege. Hugh the Elder received £300 of the payment due to him on 3 June 1307 which came in the form of being granted the custody and marriage rights of the heir of Sir Philip Paynel, tenant-in-chief. He received another 50 marks on 28 June that year 'in part payment of 2,000 pounds granted to Hugh for the marriage of his eldest son,' this time in cash. [10] Precisely when the wedding of Hugh the Younger and Eleanor Clare had been arranged is not clear, but it took place in the presence of the king himself, in his own chapel at Westminster palace. Edward I paid 37 pounds for the minstrels who performed at the wedding, including harpers called Richard Whiteacre and Richard Leyland, and gave Eleanor almost 29 pounds to buy herself jewels and another 10 pounds for robes for her attendants. [11]

On the same day as he attended his granddaughter's wedding, Edward I granted a manor in County Durham to Hugh's kinsman Robert, Lord Clifford, which had once belonged to Robert Bruce, earl of Carrick. The manor was forfeit because of Bruce's 'felony, rebellion and sacrilege, and treacherous slaughter' of John the Red Comyn, lord of Badenoch and nephew of the former king John Balliol. [12] Bruce had stabbed his rival Comyn to death in the Franciscan church in Dumfries on 10 February 1306, and had himself crowned king of Scotland a few weeks later. Bruce's namesake grandfather Robert Bruce had been one of the main Competitors for the throne in 1292, though he lost out to John Balliol; now, finally, a Bruce had taken the throne. Edward I, furious at what he saw as the betrayal of his former ally Robert Bruce and considering himself rightful overlord of Scotland, went on campaign against Robert in 1306 and again in 1307. Edward of Caernarfon swore an oath on 22 May 1306 that he would never sleep more than one night in one place until he had defeated Bruce and avenged the murder of John Comyn, but his inability to do so was to become one of the defining features of his reign. [13] John the Red Comyn's daughter Elizabeth would become one of Hugh's victims in the 1320s; he imprisoned her for about 18 months until she handed over some lands to him and his father.

Piers Langtoft wrote that at the time of the mass knighting, Hugh 'took there to wife the maiden of noble parents, whom Gilbert Clare had begotten on Joan the countess, surnamed of Acre.' [14] It is an extremely common modern misconception that Eleanor's uncle Edward II arranged her marriage to Hugh after Hugh became his favourite, but it is certain that it was Edward I who arranged the marriage and who promised Hugh the Elder £2,000 for it. Hugh did not become the favourite and perhaps the lover of Edward II until about 1319, more than a dozen years after he had married Eleanor, and by the late 1310s the couple had at least six or seven children. The confusion arises because Edward II did arrange the weddings of Eleanor's two younger sisters Margaret and Elizabeth to three of his male favourites, Piers Gaveston, Roger Damory and Hugh Audley, in 1307 and 1317.

Eleanor Clare was the second child and first daughter of Gilbert 'the Red' and Joan of Acre. She was named after her maternal grandmother Leonor of Castile, Edward I's first queen, and her great-grandmother Eleanor of Provence, Henry III's queen and Edward I's mother. She was born at Caerphilly Castle in South Wales, the great stronghold built by her father which was to pass to herself and Hugh in 1317, in October 1292, and was therefore perhaps three or four years younger than Hugh and only 13 and a half when they married. Eleanor's brother Gilbert, heir to their parents, was born in late April or early May 1291 and was the eldest grandchild of Edward I and Leonor of Castile. [15] Gilbert 'the Red' had been vastly wealthy and held lands in England, Wales and Ireland, all of which would pass to his only son Gilbert the younger and make him one of the two or three richest men in the country. A second daughter, Margaret, was born sometime between late 1293 and the autumn of 1294, and the youngest child Elizabeth followed in September 1295 just a few weeks before Gilbert 'the Red' died at the age of 52. He had been the most powerful nobleman in England for much of Edward I's reign, and had previously been married to Henry III's half-niece Alice Lusignan, with whom he had two daughters: Isabel, born in 1262, who was briefly married to Hugh the Younger's uncle Guy Beauchamp, and Joan, countess of Fife, born in c. 1264. These two women, the decades-older half-sisters of Eleanor Clare, were made illegitimate when their parents' marriage was annulled in 1285. In April 1290 when he was 46 and she 18 or almost, Gilbert 'the Red' married his second wife Joan of Acre.

After she was widowed five and a half years later, Joan of Acre was given Bristol Castle by her father for her sustenance and her children's, so Eleanor may have grown up there, and it is also possible that she and her younger sisters spent at least part of their childhoods at Amesbury Priory in Wiltshire. Eleanor's great-grandmother Eleanor of Provence had retired there in the 1280s a few years after she was widowed from Henry III, and made the priory fashionable among the women of the royal family. Edward I's fourth daughter Mary and his niece Eleanor of Brittany were nuns at Amesbury, and in later years so were Eleanor Clare's younger half-sister Joan Monthermer and Hugh the Younger's niece Isabella of Lancaster, one of the six daughters of his half-sister Maud. Joan of Acre caused a scandal in early 1297 little more than a year after she was widowed from Gilbert 'the Red' by marrying an obscure and possibly illegitimate squire named Ralph Monthermer, while her father the king was pressing ahead with negotiations for her marriage to the count of Savoy. Edward I imprisoned Monthermer in a rage, but could not annul the marriage, and thus was eventually forced to accept it and to release his new son-in-law. As for Eleanor Clare, she was Edward of Caernarfon's eldest niece, only eight and a half years his junior, and was closer to him in age than her mother Joan, who was 12 years older than he. Eleanor and Edward were extremely fond of each other, and in the later years of Edward's reign in the 1320s became very close indeed.

Hugh Despenser the Elder witnessed a charter of Edward of Caernarfon, prince of Wales, duke of Aquitaine, earl of Chester and count of Ponthieu, in London on 25 May 1306, the day before his son and heir's wedding. [16] Given that Hugh the Elder was in his company at this time, it seems highly likely that Edward of Caernarfon attended Hugh the Younger's wedding to Edward's niece Eleanor Clare the following day, especially as his father the king and his beloved sister Joan of Acre were present, and as he was always very fond of Eleanor. It is possible that Hugh and Eleanor's marriage was not yet consummated and that they did not live together as husband and wife just yet; their first child was born in 1308 or 1309 when Eleanor was 15 or 16 and Hugh about 20. For Hugh, marriage to such a highly-born and well-connected young woman, a member of the royal family, was the most prestigious union he could have hoped to make. Eleanor's feelings about marrying Hugh can, however, only be guessed at. As the eldest granddaughter of the king and daughter of a great earl, she might have expected or hoped to marry an earl herself. The two available in 1305/6 were 19-year-old John Warenne of Surrey, who married Eleanor's younger cousin Jeanne de Bar the day before her own wedding – this marriage proved to be an unhappy disaster which resulted in separation in or before 1313 – and 20-year-old Edmund Fitzalan of Arundel, whose marriage to Surrey's sister was seemingly happier than Surrey's own, but which began badly when Arundel at first refused to wed Alice Warenne. [17]

Still, the evidence we have suggests that Hugh and Eleanor built a strong and contented partnership. Their marriage proved a fertile one, producing at least 10 children, of whom five girls and four boys survived childhood. Their first child and Edward I's eldest great-grandchild was a boy inevitably named

Hugh (who throughout this book will be called Huchon, the nickname given to him in his great-uncle Edward II's accounts), and their youngest was Elizabeth, born probably in December 1325. Hugh and Eleanor were married for just over 20 years, and of course their relationship must have changed and evolved over time, especially after Hugh became the 'favourite' of Eleanor's uncle the king at the end of the 1310s. Obviously, though, the couple's sexual relations continued even after Hugh became involved in some kind of intense relationship with Edward II, as at least three or four of Hugh and Eleanor's children were born in the 1320s. Eleanor took her husband's name on marriage, and in her own lifetime her name was spelt Alianore la Despensere. Hugh's first name was spelt Hugh, Hughe, Hue, Huwe, Huge, Hug, Hugg and other variations.

As well as his regular sex life with his wife and perhaps also with Edward II in the late 1310s and 1320s, Hugh may have had a mistress named Joan, and a relationship with her which resulted in a son born out of wedlock. An abbot of Westminster called Nicholas Litlington, born around 1312 or 1315, was certainly a member of the Despenser family as he used the Despenser coat of arms, and named his parents as Hugh and Joan. Nicholas, who was appointed abbot of Westminster in 1362 and lived until 1386, was associated with Hugh's grandsons Edward, Lord Despenser and Henry Despenser, bishop of Norwich. As prior of Westminster in 1352, Nicholas distributed alms on the anniversary of Edward II's death. He may well have been Hugh's illegitimate son. It is just possible, though, that he was instead the son of Hugh the Elder, and thus Hugh's much younger half-brother. Hugh the Elder lost his wife Isabella Beauchamp in May 1306 and never married again for the remaining 20 years of his life, so it is possible that he found comfort and companionship in the arms of another woman. [18] The matter remains unclear, and Nicholas's mother Joan cannot be identified; the name was incredibly common in England in the fourteenth century. Edward II fathered an illegitimate son called Adam sometime between 1305 and 1310, and Piers Gaveston, the greatest of the king's favourites besides Hugh himself, had an illegitimate daughter called Amie. Roger Damory, another prominent man high in Edward's favour and Hugh's great rival in the late 1310s, may also have fathered several illegitimate sons. Whatever the nature of Edward's relationships with his male 'favourites', his association with them did not preclude the men's intimate relations with various women.

As Eleanor brought Hugh no lands at all, Hugh the Elder promised Edward I to give the young couple £200 a year in land for the rest of his life (Hugh the Younger would inherit all the Despenser/Basset lands on his father's death). [19] In line with this promise, sometime before early 1310 Hugh the Elder granted his son the income from five or six of his manors for the couple's sustenance. They were Oxcroft (now Balsham) in Cambridgeshire, Kersey and possibly Layham in Suffolk, and North Weald Bassett, Lamarsh and Wix in Essex, most of which had belonged to Philip Basset. Hugh the Elder 'assigned the issues of the said manors to the younger Hugh for his maintenance…the younger Hugh having no other estate.' [20] Hugh the Younger was accused *c.* 1327, after his downfall, of ejecting two sisters called Alice and Avice Boys from the manor of Oxcroft and of imprisoning the elder sister. [21] By 1321 Hugh the Younger and Eleanor held the manor of Bushey in Hertfordshire which Hugh the Elder had acquired by typically dubious means in the early 1300s and which he granted to them, though at an unknown date. Hugh the Elder, also at some point in or before 1321, gave Wix, Lamarsh, Layham, Kersey and Datchet in Buckinghamshire to Hugh the Younger outright. [22] Two historians of the twentieth century claimed that Edward II gave the manor of Sutton in Norfolk to Hugh in May 1309, though in fact this manor belonged to Aymer Valence, earl of Pembroke, and only came under Hugh's control in April 1325. [23]

The fourth week of May 1306, bringing as it did knighthood and marriage into the royal family, was surely the most amazing and memorable of Hugh the Younger's life so far. But at this moment of his triumph, tragedy was to strike. His mother Isabella Despenser née Beauchamp died shortly before 30 May 1306, when the escheator was ordered to take her lands into the king's hand. [24] Historian Natalie Fryde stated in 1979 that Hugh the Younger's mother Isabella 'preferred to endow her daughter [Maud] with Payn [*recte* Patrick] Chaworth with her personal properties' rather than her son Hugh, but cited no source for this claim. The manor of *Herteleye* in Hampshire was given to Isabella by her father the earl of Warwick as her *liberum maritagium* or marriage portion when she married her first husband Patrick Chaworth. This probably means the village of Hartley Mauditt, and it was granted to Isabella's daughter Maud née Chaworth and her husband Henry of Lancaster on 22 July 1306. [25] The dower lands Isabella had held from Chaworth passed to Maud anyway as Patrick's heir, and the Beauchamp patrimony went to Isabella's brother Earl Guy. The 30th of May is almost certainly not the exact date of Isabella's death, but the date when news of it had reached the king's clerks, and she had probably died some days before, perhaps even on the day of her son's wedding. She was only in her early or mid-40s. One of the few things we can say about Hugh's relationship with his mother is that in or after 1320 when he was a powerful royal favourite, he removed the parker of Odiham in Hampshire from his job because the parker had once raised the hue and cry against Isabella after she took five deer from his park without a licence. [26] The parker, William son of Matthew of Odiham, complained about it in early 1327 after Hugh's downfall and execution. Evidently Hugh had a long memory, and was willing to abuse his power to avenge a perceived slight against his mother. The story also reveals that Isabella was a keen hunter and perhaps cared little for legal niceties, a trait her son inherited. Hugh Despenser the Elder was also pardoned by Edward I on 28 June 1307, just days before the king died, for taking a stag in Windsor forest without proper licence. [27]

On 12 April and again on 6 and 25 June 1306, Hugh's maternal uncle Guy Beauchamp, earl of Warwick, was given permission by Edward I to grant Hugh's younger brother Philip all his estate except lands to the value of £400 a year. [28] Earl Guy was now in his mid-30s and still childless, and apparently his marriage to Isabel Clare, the much older half-sister of Hugh's wife Eleanor, had been annulled at some point. Guy and Isabel had been given permission to 'remain in the marriage they have contracted' by Pope Boniface VIII (1294–1303) on 11 May 1297, and any future children they might have were declared legitimate. [29] As Isabel, born in 1262, was about a decade older than her husband and already 35 in 1297, and had been made illegitimate by the annulment of her parents' marriage in 1285, it was rather a peculiar union. Guy instead married Alice, widow of Sir Thomas Leyburne and heir of her brother Robert Toeni, between 5 December 1309 and the early summer of 1310, and had several children with her including his heir Earl Thomas in 1314. [30] These land dealings of 1306 would have made Hugh's younger brother heir to the earldom of Warwick and to lands far more extensive than Hugh himself would inherit from their father. It is hard to imagine that Hugh was delighted about this, and Guy favouring his younger brother over himself as his potential heir, plus of course his mother's death, may have taken the shine off what was otherwise an exciting year. In 1306 Hugh's brother-in-law Gilbert Clare, heir to the earldom of Gloucester, was only 15 and there was every prospect that he would live long and have children, so there must have seemed little if any possibility of Hugh and Eleanor inheriting any of his lands. Hugh therefore would have to wait until Hugh the Elder died before he came into an inheritance.

In 1306, Edward I and his son Edward of Caernarfon went on campaign in Scotland against the new king, Robert Bruce (r. 1306–29). Hugh the Younger did not attend, perhaps still considered slightly too young even though he was now a knight and married. Roger Mortimer of Wigmore, now 19, did go; he, Piers Gaveston, Hugh's brother-in-law Gilbert Clare of Thomond, his cousin Ralph Basset of Drayton and two of his Beauchamp cousins were among the several dozen young knights whose lands and goods were temporarily confiscated by the king when they left the campaign to go jousting overseas without his permission. [31] On or shortly before 6 December 1306, Hugh's step-grandfather Roger Bigod, earl of Norfolk, died in his early 60s. [32] In 1307, Hugh Despenser the Younger went on campaign with the king to Scotland for the first time, as part of his father's retinue of 30 knights and men-at-arms. [33]

Hugh the Elder and his brother-in-law the earl of Warwick were two of the men ordered by the king on 22 March 1307 to accompany Edward of Caernarfon to France, a visit which never took place. [34]

While the English army was at Carlisle just south of the Scottish border, on 23 April 1307, Hugh's mother-in-law Joan of Acre, countess of Gloucester, died hundreds of miles to the south. She was 35 or almost, having been born sometime in the spring of 1272 while her parents were on crusade in the Holy Land. Given the pattern of Joan's childbearing, it is possible though by no means certain that she died of complications in pregnancy, or during or after childbirth. She left eight children: Gilbert, aged not quite 16; Hugh's wife Eleanor, 14 and a half; Margaret, 12 or 13; Elizabeth, 11; and from her second marriage to the obscure Ralph, the four Monthermer siblings Mary, Joan, Thomas and Edward, whose ages ranged from nine down to barely three. Edward I, now almost 68 years old, had lost yet another of his children. He and Leonor of Castile had at least 14 and perhaps as many as 16 children together, and now all but Margaret, Mary, Elizabeth and Edward of Caernarfon were dead (though Edward I's young sons Thomas and Edmund from his second marriage to Marguerite of France were also still alive). Joan of Acre also left her widower Ralph Monthermer, who 11 years later would marry Hugh the Younger's second sister Isabella Hastings. [35] Gilbert Clare, as Joan's eldest son, was her heir as well as his father's. [36] The young future earl of Gloucester had been sent as a 10-year-old in 1301 to live in the household of his step-grandmother Queen Marguerite, who was also granted the rights to the boy's marriage. [37] Edward I heard the sad news of his daughter's death on 6 May 1307, and asked all the bishops of England and five abbots to sing masses and 'other pious works' to 'cause the soul of Joan…to be commended to God.' [38] The king himself had only a few more weeks to live.

On Friday, 7 July 1307 around the middle of the afternoon, King Edward I of England died at Burgh-by-Sands near Carlisle, having failed to reach Scotland or to solve the problem of Robert Bruce. He raised himself from his bed to take some food, and fell back dead in his attendants' arms. Messengers rode to inform his successor, 23-year-old Edward of Caernarfon, who was then staying in or near London more than 300 miles away and who was now Edward II of England. The old king's army and nobles waited in Carlisle for the arrival of their new king, Hugh and his father most likely among them; Hugh's uncle the earl of Warwick was certainly there. Edward II duly arrived in Carlisle on 19 July and took his father's army over the Scottish border, though achieved little besides taking the homage of the Scottish lords loyal to him and soon returned to England. The body of Hugh's grandfather-in-law Edward I was sent south to Westminster Abbey, where his funeral took place on 27 October.

The old king had banished Piers Gaveston from England a few weeks before his death, concerned at the close and perhaps intimate relationship between Gaveston and his son Edward of Caernarfon. According to the Middle English *Brut* chronicle, on his deathbed the old king made the men attending him at his death (including the earl of Warwick) swear not to allow Gaveston to return to England and to lead his son astray. [39] It was already too late.

Chapter 4

The New King

Our lord the king, on the understanding that you do not do anything while in his company which might offend him, would very much like you to come to him.

Edward II's reign began with a considerable amount of hope, and was seen by his subjects as a new dawn after the long reigns of his father and grandfather: between them, Edward I and Henry III had ruled England for 93 years, since 1216. Edward I certainly was mourned, but Edward II was praised as 'equal to or indeed more excellent than other kings.' He had raised the hopes of his future subjects as prince of Wales, when he seemed to be competent both in warfare and potential leadership; unfortunately he would very soon dash these hopes, and his honeymoon period was very quickly over. [1] One huge part of the problem was the excessive favouritism he showed towards his beloved Piers Gaveston.

Perhaps Edward's very first act as king was to recall Gaveston, a subject of the English kings in their capacity as dukes of Aquitaine, who had first arrived in England probably in 1296. Gaveston had been placed in Edward's household in 1300 or a little earlier by his father Edward I as one of the future king's noble companions. At Dumfries on 6 August 1307, Edward II made Gaveston earl of Cornwall. Although this appointment was controversial – previous earls of Cornwall had been born as members of the royal family – all the English earls alive in 1307 set their seals to the charter, with one exception: Hugh the Younger's uncle the earl of Warwick. Edward was already planning to marry Gaveston to Hugh's sister-in-law Margaret Clare, the oldest available female member of the royal family in 1307.

The new king replaced Hugh Despenser the Elder as justice of the forest south of the Trent with Sir Payn Tibetot on 18 August 1307, but restored Despenser to the position on 16 March 1308. [2] Hugh the Elder was high in the new king's favour, and Edward may have seen him as a kind of father figure; he was 23 years his senior. The earl of Warwick was, however, very hostile to the royal favourite Piers Gaveston and by extension to the king, and Hugh followed his uncle's lead. Just months into Edward's reign, battle lines began to be drawn.

In the early years of the reign, it is possible that Hugh the Younger followed his uncle and the other barons hostile to Gaveston as a deliberate strategy; his father was immensely loyal to the young king, so that whatever happened, one of them would be on the winning side.

On 1 November 1307, Hugh was most likely present when his wife's sister Margaret Clare married Piers Gaveston at Berkhamsted, Hertfordshire. The wedding took place just five days after the funeral of Edward I at Westminster Abbey which Hugh probably also attended. Margaret, only 13 years old, became a countess on marriage, and was considerably younger than her new husband. Piers may already have had an illegitimate daughter called Amie, whom he named after his only sister, or Amie may have been born during the early years of his marriage to Margaret Clare. As she was still at the beginning of her teens, it is likely that they did not yet consummate the marriage, and their only child would not be born until January 1312. Gaveston was also involved in some kind of intense relationship with Margaret's uncle the king. Whether this relationship was sexual and romantic or not can only be a matter for speculation, but it is beyond all doubt that Edward II adored Piers Gaveston and was to remember him for the rest of his own life, many years after Gaveston's death. It is possible that Margaret, as the daughter and sister of great earls and granddaughter and niece of kings, felt somewhat disparaged to marry a man of lower birth, as Eleanor had perhaps also felt disparaged on marrying Hugh. It is also possible, though, that the girl was perfectly happy to marry a man who was athletic and a great jouster and soldier, an earl with a large income, and who was 'very magnificent, liberal and well-bred.' [3] Hugh must have known Piers Gaveston very well both before and after 1307, as part of his family circle and as part of the group of young men who had surrounded Edward of Caernarfon for the last few years. Gaveston held a jousting tournament at his castle of Wallingford on 2 December to celebrate his wedding, in which Hugh may have participated; he enjoyed the sport. The young earls of Surrey and Arundel, and the king's brother-in-law the earl of Hereford, were among the great noblemen defeated by Gaveston and his band of 'all the younger and more athletic knights of the kingdom,' who may have included Hugh. [4]

Soon after the wedding, Hugh's brother-in-law Gilbert Clare, lord of Thomond in Ireland and a former close companion of the king (and a first cousin of Hugh's other brother-in-law Gilbert Clare the underage earl of Gloucester and of Margaret the new countess of Cornwall), died at the age of 26. [5] Hugh's second sister Isabella became a widow at the age of only 16 or 17 after what must have been a very short marriage which produced no children. Isabella married her second husband in 1308 or 1309; he was the much older John, Lord Hastings, a plausible competitor for the Scottish throne in 1292.

Edward II appointed Hastings as his seneschal of Gascony in south-west France on 24 October 1309, and Hastings held the position until 24 January 1312. [6] Isabella Hastings née Despenser went to Gascony with her husband; her children Thomas, Hugh and Margaret Hastings were probably born there.

Edward left England first thing in the morning of Monday, 22 January 1308 to travel to Boulogne. Here on the 25th he married 12-year-old Isabella, only daughter of Philip IV, the powerful king of France who was related to Hugh Despenser the Younger through marriage. The wedding was attended by a large number of French and English nobility, including Hugh's father Hugh the Elder and uncle Guy Beauchamp, earl of Warwick, and 20-year-old Roger Mortimer of Wigmore. Edward had left his beloved Piers Gaveston, earl of Cornwall, as his regent of England in his absence. While attending the royal wedding, a group of English barons set their seals to a document called the Boulogne Agreement which separated the two sides of kingship – to the king as a person and to the Crown itself – and stated that the barons' loyalty was due more to the Crown than to the current holder of it. Piers Gaveston was not mentioned and the Agreement probably reflects ongoing issues from Edward I's reign rather than hostility to the new king and his favourite, and Hugh's uncle Warwick was not one of the men who put his seal to the document despite his general stance of opposition to them. Contemporary chroniclers were concerned by their new king's excessive love for and blatant favouritism towards Gaveston. 'I do not remember to have heard that one man so loved another,' wrote the *Vita*, and the *Annales Paulini* added that Edward worshipped Gaveston as though he were a god. [7]

The king and his new queen arrived in England on 7 February 1308, at Dover. Hugh Despenser the Elder was of two men who came ashore with the king in his barge, the other being the lord of Castillon in Gascony. [8] This was a mark of the highest favour. Hugh the Younger's wife Eleanor Despenser was the young queen's principal lady attendant in 1310/11 and 1311/12, and it seems highly likely that she had performed this role since Isabella's arrival in England in early 1308. [9] Two chronicles claim that Hugh and Edward foisted Eleanor on an unwilling Isabella as a kind of jailer and spy many years later in 1324, but in fact the two women had known each other since 1308 and spent considerable time together. Isabella was about three years younger than Eleanor, though was her aunt by marriage. Eleanor Despenser, as the king's eldest niece, was one of the first ladies in England, behind the new queen and Eleanor's aunts Mary, a nun, and Elizabeth, countess of Hereford, the only two of Edward's sisters still alive in England.

Edward and Isabella were crowned king and queen of England at Westminster Abbey on Sunday, 25 February. As usual, there is no information about Hugh the Younger or whether he attended, though his father played an important role, and was one of the four men who carried the royal robes in the procession into Westminster Abbey. The other three were Roger Mortimer of Wigmore; Edmund Fitzalan, earl of Arundel and a cousin of Roger Mortimer; and the obscure earl of Oxford's son. Hugh the Younger's uncle the earl of Warwick carried the third sword behind the earls of Lancaster and Lincoln, and his brother-in-law Henry of Lancaster, the earl of Lancaster's brother (the king's first cousin and the queen's uncle) also took part in the procession. [10] Piers Gaveston played an important role in the whole coronation process and during the ceremony itself, and at the banquet in Westminster Hall afterwards the king offended many by ignoring everyone and laughing and joking with Gaveston.

Parliament began at Westminster at the end of February 1308 three days after the coronation, and a group of barons led by Henry Lacy, earl of Lincoln, demanded Piers Gaveston's exile from England (for the second time), sick of the preferential treatment shown to him by the infatuated king. Lincoln was close to 60 and by far the oldest of the English earls. His son-in-law Thomas, earl of Lancaster, was at this point a staunch ally of his first cousin the king, though that was to change later in 1308 when he moved into the position of strong opposition to Edward he was to maintain for the rest of his life. Edward refused to send his beloved Gaveston away from him, and he and many of the barons spent Easter preparing for war against each other. Hugh Despenser the Elder was as loyal to the king as ever, and was one of the few important men who remained close to Edward in the first few months of 1308. The *Vita* says that 'none of the magnates took Piers' part except the king and Hugh Despenser [the Elder].' Although this is not entirely true, it is indeed the case that few important English noblemen backed the king in 1308, and the chronicler naming Despenser specifically as Edward and Gaveston's only noble supporter demonstrates how close the elder Hugh was known to be to the king. He was almost always at court with the king, and witnessed a large majority of Edward's charters. [11] The *Vita* goes on to say that 'Hugh Despenser [the Elder] was also hateful to all the barons, because he had deserted them as they worked for the common good of the realm and, more from a desire to please and a lust for gain than for any creditable reason, had become an adherent of Piers.' [12] The author may be correct as to Despenser's motives; loyalty to the king would always be rewarded, and with his son and heir Hugh the Younger taking the opposing side, perhaps the two men felt they could not lose.

Edward II even favoured Hugh the Elder over Piers Gaveston on one occasion. Gaveston wrote to his retainer Sir Robert Darcy on 1 April 1308, apologising that he had not been able to secure the custody and marriage rights of the son of Sir John Meriet, a recently deceased tenant in chief, for Darcy, and informed him that Edward had already granted the rights to *Sire Hue le Espenser*. [13] There was no-one else whom Edward would have favoured over

Gaveston in such a manner, and on almost every other occasion the king bent over backwards to help and support his beloved favourite. Anyone else but Despenser the Elder would almost certainly have seen their grant withdrawn and given instead to Piers Gaveston or one of his men. [14] Also on 1 April 1308, Edward paid 20 marks for his niece Eleanor Despenser's expenses while she was staying at the castle of Rockingham in Northamptonshire, and on 8 May paid another 10 marks for her expenses in travelling to see him. She was called 'our very dear niece' by the king at this time. [15]

More royal favours flooded Hugh the Elder's way as the king showed his gratitude for his loyalty. On 12 March and 10 May 1308, Despenser was made constable of the royal castles of Chepstow, Devizes and Marlborough, and on 16 March was reinstated as justice of the forest south of Trent. [16] In May 1308, he received the enormous sum of more than £2,500 in debts owed to him by Edward I and II. [17] Some of this was probably the remainder of the debt owed to him for his son Hugh the Younger's marriage in 1306, though much of it was loans made by Despenser to the king and his father and debts for war service, and in August 1313 Edward again acknowledged that he owed him more than £2,000. [18] Edward tried hard to gain other important allies in his struggle against many of his own barons. On 16 March 1308, the king allowed his nephew Gilbert Clare, Hugh the Younger's brother-in-law, to hold his lands in Wales in exchange for a payment of £1,000 a year, even though Gilbert was not yet 17 and thus more than four years away from attaining his majority. [19] By 12 March 1308 and despite his youth, Gilbert was already being addressed as earl of Gloucester and Hertford, and on that date was given permission to 'marry whomsoever he will,' even though in 1301 the king's father Edward I had granted the rights to Gilbert's marriage to his second queen Marguerite. [20] Marguerite supported the barons against Piers Gaveston in 1308 and even sent them money to further their cause against the unpopular royal favourite; it is likely that her stepson the king never forgave her, and his granting his nephew the choice of his own bride was a punishment of the dowager queen as much as it was a reward (and a bribe) to Gilbert Clare.

On 25 June 1308, Edward was forced, after several months of refusing, to exile Gaveston from England, though ensured that the royal favourite left England in triumph rather than humiliation by appointing him as his lord lieutenant of Ireland. Gaveston sailed for Ireland taking his young wife Margaret with him. Although his earldom of Cornwall was revoked, Edward granted him lands in England and in his native Gascony to the same value so that his income was not affected, and gave him a hugely generous gift of £1,180 shortly before his departure. [21] The king spent the next year scheming to get him back, trying – successfully – to get Pope Clement V (1305–14) on his side, and offering his earls sweeteners so that they would consent to Gaveston's return. It eventually worked: a triumphant Gaveston returned to England a year almost to the day after he had left, and was restored to his earldom on 5 August 1309. [22] On this day, Hugh the Younger must have been near the king for once, although he was not one of the barons summoned to the parliament then being held at Stamford in Lincolnshire, as Edward granted rights of free warren to a man called Peter Gresley at Hugh's request. [23]

A few months earlier, Edward had attended the double wedding of the earl of Gloucester and Gloucester's youngest sister Elizabeth at Waltham Abbey in Essex on 30 September 1308. Elizabeth married the earl of Ulster's son and heir John Burgh, and her brother Gloucester married Maud, one of John Burgh's many sisters. Hugh the Younger may have attended the joint wedding of his brother-in-law and sister-in-law to the Burgh siblings, as Waltham Abbey is only 10 miles from North Weald Bassett; this manor belonged to his father, who had granted the revenues of it to Hugh. Maud, the new countess of Gloucester, was Hugh's second cousin, and may have been named after his grandmother Maud, countess of Warwick, her great-aunt (Maud's paternal grandmother Aveline was the third of the four FitzJohn sisters). Some years later Maud Clare née Burgh would frustrate her kinsman Hugh and his ambitions for years by falsely claiming to be pregnant – for years on end.

At an uncertain date in the spring of 1309 some months before Gaveston's return from Ireland, a jousting tournament was held at Dunstable in Bedfordshire, at least partly as a cover for some of the English magnates to meet and air their grievances against Edward II and discuss possible solutions. It may have been the place where a petition demanding 11 articles of reform, submitted to the king at Parliament in July 1309, was worked out. [24] As a loyal ally of the king, Hugh Despenser the Elder did not take part, but Hugh the Younger did, as did his brother-in-law and Edward's nephew the earl of Gloucester. Gloucester appeared first on the list of the lords, knights and men-at-arms who attended, being the highest-ranked, with 21 men named as members of his retinue, and Edward's brother-in-law the earl of Hereford appeared next with 19 followers. Hugh's uncle Guy Beauchamp, earl of Warwick, Edmund Fitzalan, earl of Arundel, and the king's cousin and new enemy Thomas, earl of Lancaster, also attended. It can be most confusing to try to follow the fluctuating relationships between Edward II and his earls, even his nephew Gloucester; sometimes they were on good terms and sometimes not. Hugh the Younger appears sixty-first on the list of Dunstable participants and was accompanied by 10 knights, including Sir John Haudlo, Sir Ralph Gorges and Sir Robert Echingham. [25] The men with Hugh appear to have been members of the retinue of Hugh's father, rather than his own. At this point, Hugh, with no lands or income of his own, had little if any ability to retain household knights.

Hugh was evidently a keen jouster, and in early 1310 also demonstrated his recklessness and unwillingness to obey rules and even the king's commands. A writ issued on 31 December 1309 stated that the king had heard how some Englishmen intended to go abroad to take part in jousting tournaments, and ordered them not to leave the country. Such bans on tournaments were not uncommon in the thirteenth and fourteenth centuries, especially in Edward II's reign, as they provided cover for armed men to assemble in large numbers and were thus considered dangerous. Edward had also ordered all his sheriffs on 14 June 1309 'to prohibit anyone from tourneying, making bourds, jousting, or doing other feats of arms.' Hugh's brother-in-law Gloucester and uncle Warwick were among the men specifically forbidden to take part in such events on this occasion, almost certainly because Edward knew they had recently taken part in the tournament of Dunstable and used the occasion to plot. [26] The warden of the Cinque Ports and bailiffs of 23 other ports all along the English coast, from Scarborough in the north-east to Bristol in the south-west, were ordered on 31 December 1309 not to permit any man 'to pass the seas to tourney or do other feats of arms, or anything else, without the king's special order.' [27]

Despite this prohibition, Hugh did leave England to joust on the continent, having managed to evade all the bailiffs told to look out for men travelling overseas to tourney and to prevent them from departing. An annoyed Edward had heard of his departure by 9 January 1310, just nine days after his prohibition, when he told 'the escheator this side Trent to take into the king's hand the lands and goods of Hugh Despenser the younger if he find that Hugh has crossed beyond seas without licence contrary to the king's frequent prohibitions…'. [28] Two months later it was realised that Hugh's confiscated lands were not his own, but his father's, and on 10 March they were given back to Hugh the Elder, as he had merely given the revenues of the five or six manors to his son. [29] Hugh left England very early, as the tournament he is known to have taken part in, in the town of Mons, did not take place until July 1310 and he departed from England in early January (in the depths of winter when travel across the Channel cannot have been easy or pleasant). [30] Perhaps he spent six months travelling around Europe to participate in other tournaments and 'feats of arms' for which we have no record. It is possible that Hugh left his wife Eleanor pregnant when he sailed from England. Edward II paid Eleanor's messenger John Chaucomb 20 marks for bringing him news of her on 21 October 1310, though this is not necessarily the day the king saw the messenger, but only the day on which the payment made to him was recorded in the royal accounts, perhaps weeks or months after Chaucomb went to Edward. [31] Edward often paid messengers informing him of children born in his extended family, and it may be that this news related to the birth of one of Hugh and Eleanor's offspring. If so, it may have been their second son Edward Despenser, named after the king and Edward I. Eleanor travelled from Northampton to Berwick-on-Tweed to attend Queen Isabella on 28 November 1310, with 100 marks (66 pounds) from the king for her expenses and another 20 marks as a gift from him. [32] She was high in Edward's favour; her husband was emphatically not.

The tournament of Mons in July 1310 was held by Willem, count of Hainault and Holland – whose sister Alicia was the widow of Hugh's step-grandfather the earl of Norfolk – and celebrated Willem's recent peace settlement with his neighbour Robert, count of Flanders. One hundred ninety-one lords and knights took part, though only two came from England which suggests that virtually all English knights obeyed Edward's command not to leave the country. Hugh's name appears on the list of participants as *Hues Despesier*, place number 121, and the only other English knight was Sir Robert d'Enghien. The jousting area in Mons was located in the market square near the churches of Saint-Germain and Sainte-Waudru, and the so-called 'castle of the counts.' [33]

Hugh returned to England not only to find himself even more out of favour with the disgruntled king he had disobeyed, but perhaps to find his wife heavily pregnant or recovering from childbirth. Eleanor was at court attending the queen and visiting her uncle some of the time, and Hugh's father was also often at court: in 1307/08 and 1308/09, Hugh the Elder witnessed 60 percent of Edward II's charters, and in 1309/10 over a third. This number fell to 4.5 percent in 1310/11, a year the king spent in the far north of his kingdom at Berwick-on-Tweed, but rose to almost 100 percent in 1312/13 and 1313/14. As for Hugh the Younger, he witnessed no charters of the king at all until 1316. [34] It is most unlikely that Hugh spent much time at court in the first eight or nine years of Edward's reign. Despite the king's fondness for Hugh's wife Eleanor and Hugh's father, and despite their later extremely close relationship, for many years Edward showed not the slightest interest in Hugh. Although Hugh was Edward's nephew-in-law, the king never publicly acknowledged that relationship or addressed him as such. He did, however, often call Hugh's hereditary enemy Roger Mortimer of Wigmore 'the king's kinsman,' even though the two men were only quite distantly related. [35] Until 1320, Edward had no reason at all to doubt the loyalty of Mortimer, who was Piers Gaveston's former ward and an ally of the royal favourite in Ireland. Hugh demonstrated no such loyalty to the man who was both his king and his wife's uncle, and therefore Edward felt no need to acknowledge him as his relative. Hugh Despenser the Younger so dominates the story of the last few years of Edward II's reign that it is sometimes hard to grasp how obscure he was and how low in the king's favour for well over half the reign.

Chapter 5

Assaulted and Powerless

It is essential that one is careful about saving money at the right time and never spends it thoughtlessly, because one cannot do anything without money, though on the other hand one should never economise when it can be used to the benefit and honour of the king and to the detriment of his enemies.

Hugh the Younger had no lands or income of his own to support his royal wife and his family, and lived in somewhat straitened circumstances, at least by the standards of his own class if not by those of most of the English population in the early 1300s. Hugh the Elder promised to give his son and Eleanor an annual income of £200, and the five or six manors he assigned to Hugh the Younger might just have reached that amount. [1] This, however, was not much compared to the men around Hugh. As his brother-in-law the earl of Gloucester's income ran to £7,000 per year, and Piers Gaveston's to £4,000, Hugh was comparatively impoverished. [2] Even Roger Mortimer of Wigmore earned about £700 a year just from the lands of his own Mortimer patrimony, and his wife Joan Geneville's extensive estates in England, Wales and Ireland brought him far more. [3] Hugh acknowledged a massive debt of £2,000 to one John Giffard of Weston on 17 April 1315 which would have been 10 years' income for him at the time, so he was living considerably beyond his means – though as that was 10 months after the death of his wealthy brother-in-law Gloucester at the battle of Bannockburn, Hugh may have borrowed the money in expectation of shortly coming into a large inheritance. [4] Although by December 1316 he had apparently been able to lend two men a total of 54 pounds, this was still a comparatively small sum. [5] The couple had a growing family: by 1315 they had at least three children, Huchon, Edward and Isabella (almost certainly named after Hugh's mother Isabella Beauchamp rather than the queen), and probably more. Hugh's very low income in comparison to his peers for the first half of Edward's reign does not justify or excuse his appallingly greedy and lawless behaviour years later after he became the king's powerful favourite, but does perhaps go some way to explaining it.

In 1311, 1313/14 and probably in other years, the king paid the expenses of Eleanor Despenser and her household even when she was not at court. In 1311 she spent time at Northampton, and her uncle paid for it. [6] Edward was particularly generous in late 1313 and early 1314: he gave Eleanor 10 pounds on 10 October, another 10 pounds five days later, five pounds on 27 October and five marks (three pounds and 33 pence) on 29 October, 10 pounds on 7 November, 10 marks on 19 November, four pounds on 11 December and five marks on 4 February. The money was paid out to Hugh as her husband, but was specifically said to be for Eleanor, not both of them. [7] Edward probably did this out of affection for his eldest niece and perhaps also because he did not wish to see her suffer from lack of money, and for years showed conspicuous favour to Hugh the Elder and to Eleanor, while ignoring Hugh the Younger.

Edward spent much of 1310/11 in the far north of his kingdom at Berwick-on-Tweed near Scotland, hoping to meet Robert Bruce in battle and defeat him, an ambition in which he failed utterly. Queen Isabella, who was now probably 15, accompanied her husband and spent the whole period in Berwick with him. Only three earls, however, went north with their king: Edward's nephew and Hugh the Younger's brother-in-law Gilbert Clare, earl of Gloucester; Piers Gaveston, earl of Cornwall, also Hugh's brother-in-law; and John Warenne, earl of Surrey, husband of Jeanne de Bar, another niece of the king. In March 1310 while Hugh was overseas without permission, Edward had been forced to consent to a group of 21 earls, bishops and barons undertaking wholesale reforms of his household and of the kingdom. The men were known as the Lords Ordainer, and included eight of the 11 English earls alive at the time (the exceptions were Piers Gaveston, the nonentity earl of Oxford who played no role whatsoever in Edward's reign, and the earl of Surrey, who for the most part was very loyal to the king). Hugh's brother-in-law the earl of Gloucester was thus one of the Ordainers, though unlike the others did accompany the king to Scotland in 1310/11, and Hugh's uncle Warwick was another. In September 1311 after working on them for 18 months, the Ordainers announced their reforms. There were over 40 of them and they severely limited the power of the king, demanding, for example, that he should not declare war or even leave his kingdom without his magnates' consent. The Ordinance which caused Edward the most personal grief was the one which mandated the exile of Piers Gaveston from all Edward's territories, that is, England, Wales, Ireland, Gaveston's native Gascony, and Ponthieu (a county in northern France Edward had inherited from his mother on her death in 1290). [8] They also demanded that Edward remove several Gascon members of his household. With little other choice, after a few weeks the king was forced to consent to all the Ordinances, and they were published in the churchyard of St Paul's Cathedral in London. Hugh

Despenser the Elder was one of the members of Edward's council who came to St Paul's and announced that the king would accept the Ordinances. [9]

The Ordainers also demanded the removal from court of two men named as Sir Robert Darcy and Sir Edmund Bacon, as well as unnamed others. These men were said to have left court with the specific intention of assaulting Hugh Despenser the Younger. [10] Robert Darcy was an ally and retainer of Piers Gaveston, and the man for whom Gaveston had failed to obtain the custody of John Meriet's heir in 1308 as Edward had already given it to Hugh the Elder, and Edmund Bacon was a household retainer of the king. This probably means that several of the king's closest supporters were furious at Hugh's support of Edward's baronial opponents; Hugh was, after all, Edward's nephew-in-law, and might be expected to support him as his father did. Edmund Bacon as a retainer of the royal household was very close to Edward, so it is even possible that the king knew of or approved his men's actions beforehand (though this is not certain). The nature of the physical attack on Hugh is not stated, nor whether he was hurt, though as he was to be arrested in early 1316 for an assault with his fists on another baron and in 1326 was involved in a fight in Northamptonshire, he was surely capable of giving as good as he got. The statement that the men 'went out of court' to assault Hugh is further evidence that he did not generally live or stay at court. Somewhat ironically, years later when Hugh was a powerful royal favourite, Edmund Bacon wrote to him asking for his help in obtaining a wardship. [11]

Queen Isabella's household accounts for Edward's fifth regnal year, July 1311 to July 1312, fortuitously survive. Eleanor, called *Domina* [Lady] *Alianore la Despensere*, headed the list of the queen's lady attendants that year, ahead of Isabella Vescy, Alice Beaumont and Ida Clinton. The most amusing entry in the queen's extant household account reveals that in late 1311, Isabella had to make alternative arrangements for Eleanor's transportation because 'the lord Hugh Despenser her husband stole away from her her sumpter-horses and other carriage.' [12] Eleanor Despenser, who turned 19 in October 1311, was with Isabella on 31 July 1311, shortly before the royal couple travelled south to attend the parliament which demanded the exile of Eleanor's brother-in-law Piers Gaveston. On that day, Isabella paid 12 pence for ale for the breakfast of the 'Lady Despenser.' [13] Isabella sent a letter to Hugh Despenser the Elder on 11 January 1312, and at Christmas 1311 had also sent one to the countess of Cornwall, Eleanor Despenser's sister Margaret Gaveston. Margaret was heavily pregnant when her husband was exiled from England by the Lords Ordainer in the late autumn of 1311, for the third time. Gaveston was meant to depart from England by 1 November, though in fact left on the 3rd. Even Gaveston's brother-in-law the 20-year-old earl of Gloucester, who had previously been an ally of his (albeit perhaps often reluctantly) pushed for Gaveston's third exile with his fellow Ordainers and closed his ears to his incensed uncle the king's pleas and blandishments. Although it is often assumed that Queen Isabella was hostile to Gaveston and that the two were rivals for the king's affections, there is no evidence to prove that this is the case, and on 29 October 1311 the queen sent letters to her receiver of Ponthieu 'concerning the affairs of the earl of Cornwall,' apparently an order to aid Gaveston financially. [14] Isabella later came to loathe Hugh Despenser the Younger, and some writers have wrongly assumed that therefore she must have loathed Gaveston as well, but the two men were very different and the way they behaved towards Isabella was also very different. Edward gave his wife the palace of Eltham in Kent in late October 1311, perhaps as a reward for her support of Gaveston, and Isabella set off for her new residence immediately with Eleanor Despenser. [15]

In early 1312, Piers Gaveston returned to England after only a few weeks' absence, and Edward travelled to Yorkshire to meet him. Gaveston had perhaps only intended to come back briefly for the birth of his and Margaret's child, who was born in York in early January 1312: a girl they named Joan after her maternal grandmother Joan of Acre, and who was Eleanor and Hugh the Younger's niece. Hugh and Eleanor's eldest daughter Isabella Despenser, probably their third child, was born sometime in 1312 as well. Edward took the matter out of Gaveston's hands by defiantly declaring him 'good and loyal' and restoring him to the earldom of Cornwall. Most of the English barons and some of the bishops were furious, and while the king and his beloved skulked in the north, they met in London on 13 March to discuss Gaveston's fate. Hugh's, and Gaveston's, brother-in-law Gloucester was not one of them, but he agreed to abide by whatever the others decided. For once, Hugh Despenser the Elder was not with the king at this time; he was busy at the other end of the country indulging in reprehensibly lawless behaviour. [16] Despenser sent 100 or more men to abduct a woman called Elizabeth Hertrigg 'with force and arms' from the custody of her guardian George Percy at Wambrook in Dorset on 22 February 1312. Although he is not mentioned, the chances are high that Hugh the Younger was among them and aided his father in this most unpleasant act, and John Berenger, son of the long-term Despenser adherent Sir Ingelram, was later accused of raping the unfortunate Elizabeth during her abduction and was imprisoned. [17] Edward had granted the rights to Elizabeth's marriage to George Percy in December 1309, and around the same time granted custody of the lands of her late father John Hertrigg to Hugh the Elder. [18] This must have been a reason (though of course is not a justification) for Despenser's abduction of Elizabeth, for which he does not seem to have suffered so much as a slap on the wrist, despite her horrific and brutal experience.

Thomas, earl of Lancaster, Edward's first cousin and his worst enemy for much of his reign, travelled slowly north in the early spring of 1312, arranging jousting tournaments on the way as an excuse to assemble armed men. He almost captured Piers Gaveston at Tynemouth, and the favourite and the king had to flee to Scarborough by boat, leaving numerous possessions behind which Lancaster later restored to Edward. Gaveston was besieged at Scarborough Castle by the earls of Pembroke and Surrey, both usually staunch allies of Edward, but by now sick of Gaveston and the king's infatuation with him. They were joined by Hugh's second cousin Robert, Lord Clifford, and the great northern lord Henry Percy, and Gaveston, with little other choice in a castle which was not provisioned for a siege, soon surrendered to them. While Gaveston was being taken south to a parliament which would decide his fate, in the custody of the king's cousin Aymer Valence, earl of Pembroke, Hugh's uncle Guy Beauchamp, earl of Warwick, abducted him from the manor of Deddington early one morning and took him to the dungeons of Warwick Castle. Thomas of Lancaster, Edward II's brother-in-law Humphrey Bohun, earl of Hereford, and the earl of Surrey's brother-in-law Edmund Fitzalan, earl of Arundel, were present as Gaveston was run through with a sword and beheaded a few miles from Warwick Castle on 19 June 1312; the earl of Warwick lost his nerve and remained in his castle during the execution. Gaveston's brother-in-law the earl of Gloucester had refused to help him, and remained deaf to the earl of Pembroke's pleas.

Edward was devastated at the loss of the man he had loved for at least a dozen years, and the country teetered on the brink of civil war as the earls responsible for killing the earl of Cornwall raised an army and took it to the gates of London. In the end, however, war was averted. The earl of Gloucester mediated between his uncle and the earls, and although still only 21 was respected by both sides, as the eldest grandchild of the late king, scion of the ancient noble house of Clare and the richest nobleman in the realm behind the earl of Lancaster. The situation was calmed still further on Monday, 13 November 1312 when the queen gave birth to a son at Windsor Castle. Known as Edward of Windsor after his birthplace, the boy immediately became heir to his father's throne, displacing his 12-year-old uncle Thomas of Brotherton, elder of the king's two half-brothers. The people of England rejoiced at the birth of their future king, especially in London where a public holiday was held on 14 November. Hugh Despenser the Elder was chosen as one of the boy's seven godfathers, a very great honour.

One of the very few references to Hugh the Younger in the first half of Edward II's reign comes during the very difficult and tense period following Gaveston's murder, but has nothing to do with politics. On 8 September 1312,

Edward gave Hugh permission 'to hunt with his dogs by himself…foxes, hares, cats and badgers,' but not the king's great deer. [19] Hugh briefly appears again on 7 April and 3 May 1313, when Edward altered the terms of service on one manor of 'the provost and chaplains of the house of St. Elizabeth by Winchester' at Hugh's request. [20] Hugh had for once been able to reach the king's ear, and on 5 November 1313 Edward ordered the sheriff of Oxfordshire to elect a new county coroner also 'by the testimony of Hugh Despenser the younger.' [21] A petition which probably dates to the autumn of 1313 is a request to Hugh from a Ralph Grendon to help him obtain his release from prison. [22] All the matters were, however, extremely minor, and an indication of Hugh's total lack of influence and power for the first few years of Edward's reign. His father was one of the handful of men present with and advising Edward in London after Piers Gaveston's death and was chosen as godfather of the king's son and heir; his uncle Warwick was the chief mover who had brought about the kidnapping and murder of the royal favourite; and his brother-in-law Gloucester was one of the negotiators trying to avert a civil war. Hugh himself was reduced to asking for permission to hunt and requesting an alteration to the terms of service on one manor. He was about 23 or 24 in 1312, and it may well have seemed to him that until his father died, he would never wield any influence. By 1313, government records generally referred to Hugh the Elder as 'Hugh Despenser the father' rather than simply 'Hugh Despenser' as previously, a tacit acknowledgement by the king and his clerks that Hugh the Younger actually existed, at least.

Hugh's brother-in-law John, Lord Hastings died shortly before 28 February 1313 at the age of not quite 51. [23] Isabella Hastings née Despenser, still only about 22, remained a widow for five years. In May 1313, King Edward II and Queen Isabella went on a long visit to the queen's homeland of France, the first time she had returned since she left her family at Boulogne after her wedding to Edward more than five years previously. The occasion was the simultaneous knighting of her three older brothers, her cousin Philip de Valois, and dozens of other young men; Edward himself knighted his eldest brother-in-law Louis, king of Navarre and many of the others. The king and queen's baby son remained in England, and Hugh the Younger's brother-in-law Gloucester was left as regent in the king's absence. Hugh the Elder was one of the men who accompanied the king and queen on their visit, and he took his elder son with him: Hugh appears first on a list of 17 men attending his father during the French visit, including Despenser stalwarts such as Ralph Camoys (who later married Hugh's youngest sister Elizabeth), Ingelram Berenger, John Haudlo, John Ratinden and Martin Fishacre, all of them long-term knights of Hugh the Elder whom Hugh must have known for most of his life. [24] The king and queen and their large retinue spent two months in France, and returned to

England on 16 July 1313. According to the 1311 Ordinances, Edward was meant to have asked for his magnates' consent before he left his kingdom, but had failed to do so, and he also (as he often did) arrived late for Parliament.

On 18 June 1313 during the extended royal visit to France, Edward's niece and Hugh's sister-in-law Elizabeth Burgh née Clare was widowed when her husband, the earl of Ulster's son and heir John, died in Galway. Elizabeth had given birth to their son William Burgh on 17 September 1312, the day after her seventeenth birthday, and the baby boy was now heir to his grandfather Richard's earldom. Elizabeth had anticipated that one day she would become countess of Ulster; it was not to be, though she remained in Ireland under the protection of her father-in-law for several more years. Hugh the Younger lost two brothers-in-law in 1313, but soon gained another when his third sister Margaret married Sir John St Amand sometime after 4 December 1313. [25] Margaret and John's son Amaury was born around 20 February 1315. [26] Whether Hugh had any kind of relationship with his nephews such as Amaury St Amand, Philip Despenser and Thomas and Hugh Hastings is impossible to say. It is unfortunately also impossible to say what kind of relationship he had with his own many children, other than his eldest son Huchon, who spent a lot of time with him in the 1320s.

In October 1313 Edward finally came to a peace agreement with the barons who had kidnapped and killed Piers Gaveston in June 1312, including Hugh's uncle Warwick, and they submitted to him on their knees in Westminster Hall on 14 October. Hugh Despenser the Elder was, inevitably, at the king's side at Westminster throughout this period, and Edward made him justice of the forest south of the river Trent for life on 11 December 1313, a few days after Despenser arranged the marriage of his daughter Margaret to John St Amand. [27] This was probably a reward for the elder Hugh's unswerving loyalty and his support in the difficult 18 months after Piers Gaveston's death, and for all the previous years of devotion and royal service. On 12 December, Hugh the Elder and the royal cousin the earl of Pembroke were Edward's attendants when the king made a week-long visit to his continental county of Ponthieu and its capital of Montreuil and had meetings with his father-in-law Philip IV of France. [28] The picture was not entirely rosy, however: on 13 July 1315, Edward announced that he 'wishes to be certified of the bearing of Hugh Despenser the Elder' in his capacity as justice of the forest, 'on account of the frequent complaints of acts of oppression alleged to have been committed' by Despenser and other justices. Sixteen men were commissioned to investigate Hugh the Elder's behaviour, and a few months before this – despite supposedly being appointed to the position for life – he had been replaced as justice by Ralph Monthermer, who was the stepfather of Hugh the Younger's wife Eleanor and who in 1318 married Hugh's second sister Isabella Hastings. [29]

Before the Despenser-St Amand wedding took place in or a little after December 1313, tragedy struck the Despenser family. Hugh's younger brother Philip had married the heiress Margaret Goushill in or before June 1308, and on 6 April 1313 in Lincolnshire, Margaret gave birth to their only child, a boy called Philip Despenser after his father. The elder Philip, still only between 19 and 22 years old, died when his son was mere months old, shortly before 24 September 1313. [30] Hugh the Younger had lost his only brother. Margaret Despenser née Goushill married her second husband Sir John Ros fairly soon after losing Philip, sometime before 22 April 1314, though by the conventions of the era might normally have been expected to wait a year before remarrying; later evidence suggests that Hugh was not pleased about this. Hugh's third sister Margaret St Amand also seems, like her brother Philip, to have died at a young age. The date is not known, but there is no record of her receiving any dower when John St Amand died in January 1330, so apparently she had died before then. [31] Hugh's eldest sister Alina lived into her 70s.

Shortly after his only brother's death, on 9 October 1313, came the first real gift Hugh had ever received from Edward more than six years into the king's reign. He was granted custody of the lands of the recently-deceased tenant in chief Sir William Huntingfield, with the marriage rights of Huntingfield's son and heir Roger. [32] Huntingfield had been one of the men knighted with Hugh, Edward of Caernarfon and all the others on 22 May 1306, and died (like Philip Despenser) shortly before 24 September 1313 when his son Roger was only seven or eight years old. [33] This would have meant that Hugh would receive the income from the Huntingfield lands in five counties for 13 or 14 years until Roger turned 21; this equalled £50 of land a year plus £300 for Roger's marriage rights. On 18 October 1313 just nine days after making this rather generous gift to Hugh, however, the king rescinded it and ordered his escheator to take back the lands into his own hand. It transpired that several of Huntingfield's manors had been held of Thomas, earl of Lancaster, not of the king, and the matter was still being investigated as late as June 1316, when Edward admitted debts of £950 to Hugh for his feudal war service and for horses lost while fighting for the king, payable from two Huntingfield manors in Suffolk. [34] Hugh would have to wait a while longer for a decent income.

Chapter 6

A Death is an Opportunity

No man can do anything against the will of God.

More than six years into his reign, Edward still had not solved the Scottish problem, nor come anywhere close to doing so. Robert Bruce was still king of Scotland, and his support had been growing since 1308. His greatest enemy the earl of Buchan had fled to England after defeat to Bruce that year and died there, and although the earls of Atholl, Angus and Fife (Duncan MacDuff, married to Eleanor Despenser's younger half-sister Mary Monthermer) also lived in England by choice, more and more of the Scottish nobility went over to Bruce's side. Bruce's own nephew Donald, heir to the earldom of Mar, had been imprisoned as a child by Edward I in 1306, but in or before 1309 joined Edward II's household and became a friend and staunch ally of the English king. Beginning in 1312, Robert Bruce started taking the English-held castles in his kingdom, destroying them to prevent them being retaken and removing any lingering English influence. Edward Bruce, his only surviving brother, provoked Edward II into taking an army north to relieve Stirling Castle in June 1314, a challenge even Edward could not ignore, and so he raised a massive army and marched north. Hugh and his father Hugh the Elder were among the noblemen and knights who accompanied Edward on the 1314 campaign to Scotland, and fought at the battle of Bannockburn which took place near Stirling on 23 and 24 June 1314.

Over-confidence was a huge problem on the English side. Even though Edward had never met Bruce in battle before, let alone defeat him, both he and many others appeared to think that all he had to do was take an army to Scotland and he would win by default. As part of this over-confidence, on 12 June 1314 at Berwick-on-Tweed Edward promised Hugh the Younger and his wife Eleanor all the lands and tenements in Scotland which currently belonged to Sir John Graham and Thomas Randolph, earl of Moray, a close ally and kinsman of Robert Bruce. [1] Edward was thus presumptuously handing out lands he had not won belonging to men he had not defeated, and Hugh would never hold the lands. The battle of Bannockburn resulted in a huge defeat for Edward's army, although the king himself fought bravely in the thick of battle: his knights on horseback were unable to make any headway against Bruce's *schiltroms*, formations of men holding long pikes. The English cavalry died en masse throwing themselves against these formations, and thousands of soldiers on foot were killed as well. The second-highest ranking English nobleman to fall was Robert, Lord Clifford, Hugh's second cousin and one of the FitzJohn heirs, and Robert Bruce courteously sent Clifford's body back to England with full military honours. Other men who lay dead on the battlefield included Edward's household steward Sir Edmund Mauley and the Scottish nobleman John Comyn, whose father the lord of Badenoch had been stabbed to death by Robert Bruce in 1306.

The greatest shock of all was the loss of Hugh's brother-in-law Gilbert Clare, earl of Gloucester and Hertford. Gloucester, just 23, had quarrelled with his uncle the king the evening before the battle when he suggested that the army, exhausted from its long march in the heat, take a day off to recuperate. Unreasonably taunted as a coward by Edward and competing with the earl of Hereford as to which of them should take precedence as the army advanced, Gloucester rode full tilt at the Scottish *schiltroms* with his men without waiting for an order to do so, and 'was pierced by many wounds and shamefully killed.' [2] The Scottish soldiers did not recognise him; if they had, he would – as a wealthy nobleman capable of paying a huge ransom – have been captured and taken prisoner instead. Robert Bruce treated the body of this greatest of English noblemen, who was his second cousin and who was married to his wife's sister, with the utmost respect and honour. He personally kept an overnight vigil over the body and sent it back to England with full military honours and without demanding payment. Gloucester was buried at Tewkesbury Abbey in Gloucestershire, as Hugh also eventually would be, with his father and other Clare ancestors. After Bannockburn, the king of England was forced to make a long and humiliating gallop from the battlefield to evade capture. He was pursued all the way by Robert Bruce's friend James Douglas, and rode hard towards Dunbar, where his ally Patrick, earl of Dunbar, opened the gates of his castle and let him into safety. Five hundred knights accompanied Edward on this hard and desperate ride of almost 70 miles, one of them Hugh Despenser the Elder. [3] Hugh the Younger was another: the Lanercost chronicler names 'Hugh Despenser' without specifying which one, but describes this Hugh as Edward's 'right eye' after Piers Gaveston, certainly a reference to Hugh the Younger as he calls him the same thing a few years later when Hugh was firmly ensconced as royal favourite. [4]

The earl of Gloucester's premature death was to prove a turning-point in Edward's turbulent reign. Although he was not always his uncle's ally and sometimes sided with the barons against the king, he was generally a moderate voice and was respected by everyone (with the possible exception of Edward's first cousin Thomas, earl of Lancaster, who had been engaged in a feud with the young earl in 1311). [5] Gloucester was the second largest and wealthiest landowner in the realm behind Thomas himself, who held five earldoms. The writ to three escheators – on either side of the River Trent in England and Wales, and in Ireland – to take Gloucester's lands into the king's hands was issued on 10 July 1314, and the earl's widow Maud Clare née Burgh was granted her huge dower, the customary third of her late husband's lands, on 5 December 1314. It amounted to well in excess of £2,000 a year. [6] Royal clerks and juries in the numerous counties and regions in the three countries where Gloucester had held lands began the arduous task of recording all his lands and their value. Gloucester's lordship of Glamorgan in South Wales which would ultimately pass to Hugh Despenser the Younger and Eleanor, was given into the custody of two royal officials on 13 July 1314, one of them the long-term Despenser adherent Sir Ingelram Berenger. [7]

On a personal level, Hugh may well have grieved for his brother-in-law – or perhaps he did not – but the earl's premature death was also a massive opportunity for himself and Eleanor. On 14 July 1314, Edward II admitted that his nephew had died without an heir of his body. [8] In the absence of any children, Gloucester's heirs were his three full sisters, Hugh's wife Eleanor, Piers Gaveston's widow Margaret, and Elizabeth, widow of the earl of Ulster's eldest son John Burgh. This was in accord with contemporary inheritance law in England; primogeniture, where the eldest son inherited everything, did not apply to female heirs, who inherited equally. Maud, the earl of Gloucester's widow, however, soon claimed to be pregnant. This presumed pregnancy and an error by some of the jurors who sat on the earl's Inquisition Post Mortem were to delay the partition of the earl's lands by some years, to Hugh's immense frustration. Some indication of Hugh's new status, as one of the co-heirs (with his wife) of the earl of Gloucester, is demonstrated by his summons to the parliament held in York in September 1314, for the first time. His father and he appear second and third respectively on the list of barons summoned, behind only Henry Percy, from a great northern family who became earls of Northumberland later in the century. [9] Earls and barons were summoned in order of rank, and the Despensers ranked highly among the barons. In Edward II's eighth regnal year which ran from July 1314 to July 1315, Hugh is listed as a knight banneret of the royal household. [10] Bannerets were created by the king as a reward for valour on the field of battle which means that Hugh must have acquitted himself bravely and honourably at Bannockburn. Although Edward himself made Hugh a banneret and must have been impressed by his conduct, the two men were still not at all close.

Gilbert 'the Red' Clare (d. 1295), father of Gilbert, Eleanor, Margaret and Elizabeth, had previously been married to Henry III's half-niece Alice Lusignan, with whom he had daughters Isabel and Joan, countess of Fife. The annulment of Gilbert and Alice's marriage made the two women illegitimate, and they had no claim to the estate of their father or their much younger half-brother Gilbert. Unfortunately, in 1314 some of the jurors of the earl's Inquisition Post Mortem confused his youngest full sister Elizabeth with their much older half-sister Isabel, or simply mixed up the names, and named the earl of Gloucester's three heirs as his sisters Eleanor, Margaret and Isabel. The jurors of five counties (Suffolk, Hertfordshire, Berkshire, Oxfordshire and Devon) called Elizabeth 'Isabel' in error, and the Suffolk jurors also got her late husband John's name wrong and called him 'Thomas Burgh'. The jurors of Suffolk, Worcestershire, Wiltshire and London cautiously added that the earl's three sisters were his heirs only if his widow the countess was not pregnant, and the Gloucestershire, Hampshire and Wales jurors went further and declared that they had heard Maud was indeed expecting a child. Given the huge significance and wealth of the earl of Gloucester's landholdings and his important political position, it was most unfortunate that his Inquisition Post Mortem proved to be something of a mess which left a delicate situation unclear. All of this caused a long delay while the matter was clarified, and further inquisitions had to be held in all the counties which wrongly named Elizabeth as Isabel a year later in August 1315. [11]

The jurors of all the counties in question finally admitted their error and declared that 'there is no Isabel, a sister of the said earl by the same father and mother, who could be co-heir' to Eleanor, Margaret and Elizabeth. This confusion may have prompted the widowed Maurice Berkeley, son and heir of Lord Berkeley, a powerful and wealthy nobleman in Gloucestershire, to marry Isabel Clare in about 1315 or 1316 just in case she did benefit from the division of the Clare estates. Isabel was nine years Maurice Berkeley's senior, and well into her 50s in the mid-1310s. If trying to force himself into a share of the Clare estates was indeed Berkeley's objective, nothing came of it. Isabel Clare had previously been married briefly to Hugh the Younger's uncle Guy Beauchamp, earl of Warwick, who was now married to Alice Toeni and had a growing brood of children. Warwick's son and heir Thomas was born around 2 or 14 February 1314 when the earl was at least 40, and named after the earl of Lancaster, his godfather. [12] As Guy Beauchamp in 1306 had considered the possibility of making Hugh's younger brother Philip his heir and Philip was now dead, and as he was the son of Guy's eldest sister, Hugh may have had some vestige of hope of inheriting the earldom of Warwick one day; but it was not to be. Still, the likelihood of inheriting one-third of the earldom of Gloucester must have been some consolation. Hugh, Eleanor and her sisters Margaret and Elizabeth were ordered on 25 June 1315, a year almost to the day after Bannockburn, to appear before Chancery on 21 July 1315 (though Elizabeth in fact was still residing in Ireland). Eleanor and Margaret appointed lawyers to act on their behalf on 13 July. [13]

In the meantime at the beginning of January 1315, Edward finally had his beloved Piers Gaveston buried, two and a half years after his death, at Langley Priory in Hertfordshire which the king himself had founded in 1308. Several contemporary chroniclers claim that Edward had sworn not to bury Gaveston until he had avenged his death on Gaveston's murderers, but in 1315 the king, shocked and near-powerless after his humiliating defeat in Scotland, still had no prospect of revenge. Hugh the Younger attended the funeral with his father, but few other members of the English nobility, whose hatred of the royal favourite persisted long after his death, did likewise. [14] Hugh had shown no liking for or loyalty to Gaveston during the latter's lifetime, at least that we know of, so one might be tempted to take a cynical view and suggest that his presence was not a matter of honouring his late brother-in-law, but perhaps rather an attempt to impress the king and let Edward see him paying respects to Gaveston, in the hope that Edward would divide the earl of Gloucester's lands. It was not to be, and soon Hugh's frustration was to reveal itself.

Around the middle of May 1315, Hugh Despenser the Younger's first piece of lawlessness took place: he seized control of Tonbridge Castle in Kent which had formerly belonged to the earl of Gloucester. Hugh must have known by this point that Countess Maud could not possibly be pregnant by the earl 11 months after Bannockburn. The jurors who had erred in his late brother-in-law's Inquisition Post Mortem and named the earl's half-sister Isabel as one of his heirs still had not met to discuss and clarify Gloucester's real heirs, and would not do so until August 1315. Hugh, impatient for his and Eleanor's share of her late brother's inheritance, took matters into his own hands. On 20 May 1315, Edward II at Hadleigh in Essex ordered Hugh 'to surrender without delay to the king's escheator the castle and honour of Tunebrigge [Tonbridge] which he has seized...'. Edward told his escheator, John Abel, 'to go in person and take the said castle and honour into the king's hand,' and ordered several men who were in Tonbridge Castle with Hugh – Sir John Penrith, Sir John Haudlo, Sir Walter Haket, Robert Haudle, John Clerk and unnamed others – to surrender possession of it to Abel. On the following day, 21 May, Edward issued a writ of privy seal to his council, asking them to 'ordain speedy remedy and punishment for the outrage.' John Abel returned to the king and his council on the 22nd with the news that Hugh and his men had refused to hand Tonbridge Castle over to him: Abel tried to take possession of it, but Hugh and his associates 'raised the drawbridge, so that he could not enter the castle. But in words he seized the castle.' The incident in fact ended shortly afterwards, when Hugh and his men left the castle on Friday, 23 May, and Hugh went directly to Edward to explain himself in person (Hadleigh, where the king was then staying, was about 40 miles' ride from Tonbridge, crossing the Thames).

Hugh was never punished for illegally seizing Tonbridge Castle, although on 6 July 1315 the sheriff of Kent was ordered to confiscate the goods of his allies Robert Haudle and John Clerk 'for the seizing of the castle of Tonbrugge and other enormities.' [15] Hugh gave up Tonbridge Castle after several days and did not try to stay there for a long time, but left a day or two after the escheator had tried to take it from him and went directly to see Edward. He was not attempting to remain in permanent possession of the castle, but was making a point. Hugh may have chosen Tonbridge because it was the oldest of the Clare honours in England and had some unique rights and privileges, and because of its strategic position close to the River Medway. It was held of the archbishop of Canterbury, not of the king in chief, further complicating matters in 1315. Sir John Haudlo, one of the men inside the castle with him, was a long-term Despenser adherent and had accompanied Hugh to the jousting tournament at Dunstable six years earlier. Sometime before 4 December 1315, Haudlo married Maud, sister and heir of Hugh's brother-in-law Edward Burnell. Edward himself died on 23 August 1315 at the age of only 29; Hugh's eldest sister Alina Burnell was to live as a widow for the remaining 48 years of her life. [16] John Haudlo had been sheriff of Kent from April 1313 to June 1314 which did not dissuade him from taking part in Hugh's lawlessness. [17] The other men present with Hugh at Tonbridge are not so easy to identify and were not members of the Despenser affinity; they may simply have been adventurers or mercenaries of a kind, hired in desperation. In 1979 the historian Natalie Fryde wrote in melodramatic style that Hugh achieved the seizure of Tonbridge with his 'characteristic brutality,' but there is nothing in any source to indicate that anyone was harmed during the episode or that there was anything remotely brutal about it, unless one counts the escheator John Abel having the drawbridge raised against him. Fryde also assumed for her own purposes that the dowager countess of Gloucester Maud Clare was living at the castle at the time and that Hugh seized it from her directly, for which there is also no evidence; none of the entries in the chancery rolls mention her presence. [18] Tonbridge was not one of the many manors assigned to Maud in dower in December 1314 so there is no reason why she would have been living there in May 1315, and given the ongoing pretence that she was pregnant, it might have made more sense for her to be living somewhere more remote than in a town in the busy and well-populated south-east of England easily accessible from London. [19]

Hugh's uncle the earl of Warwick died on 12 August 1315, leaving his 18-month-old son Thomas Beauchamp as his heir. Hugh Despenser the Elder was granted custody of his brother-in-law's lands and of the infant Thomas, for which he would pay 1,000 marks a year. [20] Hugh may have attended his uncle's funeral, though he had much else on his mind: a few days before the earl's death, jurors sat again in the counties which had wrongly named the earl of Gloucester's heirs. This time they established the correct ones, Gloucester's three full sisters Eleanor, Margaret and Elizabeth. By now, over a year after Gloucester had died at Bannockburn, it must have been obvious to everyone that his widow had not given birth and could not possibly be carrying his child; yet still nothing happened, and no attempt was made to divide the lands or parcel them out among the three sisters. Hugh made another effort to claim his and Eleanor's share of her late brother's inheritance in the autumn of 1315. On 16 October, he went to see Edward personally at Impington in the Fens, where the king was taking a month's holiday swimming and rowing with a large company of 'common people.' [21] By this stage, Hugh had had enough of asking politely, and it is recorded that he 'demanded' his and Eleanor's share of the Clare lands and income. The king's councillors advised Hugh that the dowager countess was certainly pregnant and that 'the case was novel and hitherto unseen in the realm, and that a new law could not be made without the assent of parliament.' Letters to this effect were given to Hugh. He replied two days later on the 18th, a letter which does not survive, but in which he set out his reasons for demanding Eleanor's rightful inheritance. The king's councillors, 'for the doubt they see in the business,' stated that they 'dare not finish it nor advise further.'

Their reluctance to deal with the situation is surely because Edward did not want his late nephew's inheritance divided. By contemporary law, because the earl of Gloucester was a tenant in chief who held his lands directly of the king, if he left a child, the king would automatically become the child's guardian and would receive the income of his or her father's lands for 15 years if the child was female or 21 years if male. It was therefore entirely in the king's interests to continue to claim that Maud was going to bear a child to her late husband, as the earl of Gloucester had an enormously high income which would pour into the king's coffers for many years. Perhaps Edward was also keen to keep a third of the Gloucester estates out of Hugh's hands for as long as possible, as he did not like or trust him. Although the lands would be inherited by Eleanor, as her husband Hugh would be the one who performed homage for them to the king and who would control them as long as he lived. As he and Eleanor had children together, by the custom called the 'courtesy of England' Hugh would be entitled to hold his wife's entire inheritance for the rest of his life even if Eleanor died before him. Given his affection for his niece Eleanor, Edward may have regretted keeping her share of her inheritance to himself, yet he continued to do for many more months and even years, and his dislike of Hugh and his desire to hold on to the Gloucester income for as long as possible were surely the reasons. Whether or not the dowager countess Maud herself was complicit in this peculiar situation is not entirely clear; was she really claiming to be pregnant or were the king and his council only pretending that she was. Hugh pointed out at some point, probably in his letter of 18 October 1315, that as the earl of Gloucester had fallen at Bannockburn on 24 June 1314, 'so much time has passed that if the said countess were pregnant, according to the common course of childbirth she could not be said to have been made pregnant by the aforementioned earl.' It was in fact extremely fortunate that the dowager countess of Gloucester did not become pregnant by a lover in 1314 or 1315 which would have made things exceedingly awkward indeed.

As Hugh was of course correct that his kinswoman Maud Clare could not possibly be carrying her husband's child well over a year after his death, he surely thought he had a water-tight case. But he had reckoned without the ingenuity of Edward's lawyers. Gilbert Touthby and Geoffrey Scrope, two chief justices of the King's Bench, told him that the delay 'ought not to harm the case for the pregnancy of the same countess: for they said that she conceived of the aforesaid earl, her late husband, and that from the time of the death of the same earl she felt a living boy in her belly, at the due time and day.' [22] Faced with such an intractable legal defence of something which was obviously impossible, and as he could hardly go to the dowager countess of Gloucester's home and drag her out in public to prove that she was not carrying a child, Hugh could do nothing but gnash his teeth in frustration and continue to wait.

Chapter 7

A Three-Year Pregnancy

*As often as you can, we beseech you to send us news of your
health, and may God make it ever good.*

At some point in about late 1315, a knight of Oxfordshire and
Buckinghamshire called Sir Roger d'Amory or Damory began a meteoric
rise in Edward II's favour. Hugh Despenser the Younger had probably
known Roger for a long time: the Damory manor of Bletchingdon in Oxfordshire
lay just a mile and a half from the Despenser manor of Kirtlington, and Roger
had served in the retinue of Hugh's brother-in-law the earl of Gloucester
since October 1308 or earlier. Like Hugh, Roger took part in the Dunstable
tournament of 1309. [1] Roger's older brother Richard, heir to their father and
probably born in the 1270s, was summoned for military service in 1297 and was
appointed keeper of the peace in Oxfordshire in 1300. [2] Their father Sir Robert
Damory, who died in 1285, was an associate of Edward I's first cousin Edmund,
earl of Cornwall (d. 1300), and their mother or stepmother, Robert Damory's
widow, was called Juliana. [3] Roger Damory also had a sister Katherine, who
married Sir Walter Poer or Poure of Oddington in Oxfordshire, one of the men
knighted with Edward of Caernarfon and Hugh in May 1306; Roger himself
was not among the young knights who took part in that mass ceremony, but
first appears on record, already a knight, in late September 1306. [4] His older
brother Richard Damory was high in Edward's favour throughout the reign,
and Roger himself came to the king's attention at the battle of Bannockburn.
Although his lord the earl of Gloucester was killed, Edward praised Roger for
'his good service against the Scots at Strivelyn [Stirling, i.e. Bannockburn]
and elsewhere' and promised him an income of 100 marks a year. [5] The king
also began to give Damory appointments, lands and gifts. The Damory family
was neither rich nor influential – the author of the *Vita* called Roger a 'poor
and needy knight', though also praised his 'industry and valour' – but had a
noble pedigree stretching back to at least 1138 and probably 1086. [6] Since
the murder of Piers Gaveston in June 1312 Edward had not taken another male
favourite, but dependence on men was a large part of his emotional make-up,
and he became in some way infatuated with Roger Damory, who may – or may

not – have become his lover. Two other men also became 'court favourites' in the mid-1310s. They were Sir William Montacute from a noble Somerset family, a renowned soldier who had been knighted with Edward and Hugh in May 1306; and Sir Hugh Audley, who had become a household knight of Edward's in late 1311, and who came from a noble family of Oxfordshire. All three of these men were knights from good families and certainly not nobodies, although Edward's strong feelings for them and his granting them lands, income, favours and much more began to incur almost as much criticism as his favouritism towards Gaveston had. Despite his new obsession with Roger Damory and to a lesser extent with William Montacute and Hugh Audley, the king maintained intimate relations with his wife the queen; his and Isabella's second son John was conceived around November 1315 while the couple were staying at the royal manor of Clipstone in Nottinghamshire, and was born on 15 August 1316. Their first daughter Eleanor of Woodstock was born in June 1318.

Hugh made arrangements regarding lands for his second son Edward Despenser – who was now somewhere between two and five years old – on 23 November 1315. Hugh's mother's first cousin Idonea Leyburne, daughter and co-heir of Isabel Vipont (younger sister of Hugh's grandmother Maud, countess of Warwick) and her second husband Sir John Cromwell, were childless, and Idonea consented to several manors she owned in five counties passing to Edward Despenser after her death. [7] Several manors in Rutland, Northamptonshire, Bedfordshire, Buckinghamshire and Wiltshire did pass to Edward in October 1334 after Idonea's death, as unlike his later land grabs when he was the king's favourite, Hugh carried out the deal perfectly legally and legitimately. [8]

The charade surrounding the earl of Gloucester's inheritance continued in early 1316. Parliament began at Lincoln on 27 January, though proceedings were delayed for more than two weeks by the failure of Thomas, earl of Lancaster, to arrive on time. Since Edward's heavy defeat at Bannockburn in June 1314, his wealthy kinsman Lancaster had been virtually his co-ruler, but the two first cousins loathed each other and could not co-operate. Lancaster finally arrived in Lincoln on 12 February and Parliament at last could begin properly. Hugh attended the parliament, and unable to stand the wait any longer, went to the king on 27 January, the first official day of proceedings. Once again he asked Edward and his council for the division of his late brother-in-law's lands to take place, reminding them that in the Magna Carta of 1215 'it is contained that the lord king ought not to deny or delay granting right or justice to anyone.' Hugh once more faced the justices Gilbert Touthby and Geoffrey Scrope, who repeated that he and Eleanor, and her sisters Margaret and Elizabeth, should not yet receive any of their lands on the grounds that 'the said countess [of Gloucester], after the death of the aforementioned earl her late husband, at the due time according to the course of nature, felt a living boy, and that this was well-known in the parts where she lived, and that although the time for the birth of that child which nature allows to be delayed and obstructed for various reasons, is still delayed, this ought not to prejudice the aforesaid pregnancy, at least while nature does not suppress the same pregnancy, but supposes a future birth.'

Hilariously, the king's lawyers were pretending that Maud Clare might still be expecting her husband's child 19 months after his death and that she somehow knew it was a boy, the pregnancy being unaccountably 'delayed' by nature. Furthermore, they added

'the said Hugh could, and ought to, if he thought it would help him, according to the law and custom of the realm, and the course of chancery used in such cases, have sued out a writ of the lord king's chancery to have the belly of the aforesaid countess inspected by knights and discreet matrons, that is to see whether the said countess were pregnant or not: and if so, then when she was expected to give birth. And since the aforementioned countess was always prepared to undergo such an examination, and the said Hugh and Eleanor had not observed that due process, their negligence ought not to prejudice the said pregnancy, but rather to redound to the harm and prejudice of the same Hugh and Eleanor.'

The whole business, 'on account of its difficult and unusual nature,' was postponed again until 25 April 1316 (Edward II's thirty-second birthday), when Hugh and Eleanor were ordered to appear before the council. On this date it was postponed yet again until 13 December 1316, a full two and a half years after the death of the earl of Gloucester. Although it is sometimes stated in modern books that Hugh had become the king's favourite by the time of Bannockburn in June 1314, he certainly had not, or Edward would have done everything in his power to grant Hugh and Eleanor their rightful lands as soon as he could rather than thwarting Hugh at every turn for years on end. At the very least, he would have given Hugh appointments, income and any wardships which fell vacant to tide him over until Gloucester's lands were ready to be divided and handed out.

Edward's determination to keep the vast Clare inheritance in his own hands for as long as possible was probably strengthened by what happened in Bristol in early February 1316. He had ordered his widowed niece Elizabeth Burgh née Clare back from Ireland in late 1315. She was staying at Bristol Castle when on 4 February 1316 she was abducted and married, possibly forcibly, by the baron Theobald Verdon, justiciar of Ireland and the brother-in-law of none other than

Roger Mortimer of Wigmore, Hugh's hereditary enemy. [9] Mortimer himself was present at Lincoln and perhaps grimly amused at Hugh's predicament, and the abduction and marriage of one of the Clare co-heirs almost certainly increased the king's determination not to partition the lands quite yet. Verdon would, as Elizabeth's husband, also now receive a third of the estate, and although he was probably not an enemy of the king as such, he was an ally of the earl of Lancaster, who certainly was. His wealthy niece marrying a man he could not trust or rely on was one of Edward's worst nightmares.

Aggravated beyond endurance at the ludicrous farce and at the intransigence of the king and his councillors and lawyers, Hugh was out for blood, and unfortunately for the baron John Ros, he became the target of his rage. Ros had married Margaret Goushill, widow of Hugh's brother Philip, in or before April 1314, only seven months or less after Philip's death. He compounded this grievance by arresting (for an unexplained reason) Sir Ingelram Berenger, one of Hugh the Elder's retainers, a man Hugh the Younger had known for most of his life. Hugh came across Ros on 22 February 1316, and lashed out. He punched him in the face over and over until Ros bled, careless that they were standing in the middle of Lincoln Cathedral, that it was a Sunday, careless even that the king himself was standing nearby. As well as the relentless punches, Hugh 'inflicted other outrages' on Ros, who was forced to draw his sword to defend himself. Hugh was a hot-headed young man, and it was fortunate that things did not go even further. Both of them were arrested, and Hugh was handed over to the official custody of the earl marshal, Nicholas Segrave. He was subsequently questioned by the chief justices Gilbert Touthby and Geoffrey Scrope, the lawyers who were thwarting him in the matter of the inheritance which surely made him even more furious. Hugh claimed that he happened to see John Ros in the cathedral and politely asked him to act more prudently in the manner of Ingelram Berenger's arrest. His testimony stated that

> 'the aforesaid John, scorning the words of the aforesaid Hugh, heaping outrageous insults on the same Hugh taunted him with insolent words, and putting his hand to his knife he menaced the same Hugh, and made a rush towards the said Hugh as if he wanted to strike him with his knife, and the same Hugh, so that the aforesaid John would not hit him, stretched out his hand between himself and the aforementioned John, by which he touched John in this way on his face.'

John Ros contradicted Hugh's amusingly implausible tale that he had merely stretched out his hand to defend himself and accidentally punched Ros in the face many times, and stated that 'the aforementioned Hugh approached him, and assaulted the same John with his fist, striking him on his face until he drew blood, because of which the same John, fearing that danger threatened him from this quarter, drew his sword in self-defence.' Hugh was fined the staggeringly large though purely nominal sum of £10,000, of which he never paid a penny, and four years later after he had become the king's great favourite, Edward cancelled the fine. [10] Neither was he punished in any way for the seizure of Tonbridge Castle a few months before, either because Edward was wary of offending him too much or because Hugh the Elder or Eleanor Despenser had interceded with the king and persuaded him to show Hugh leniency. Hugh was released though was still officially retained in the custody of the earl marshal, and six lords and knights stood as his mainpernors (guarantors) and promised to produce him before the king and his council when the latter decided what to do with him. One of the lords was Roger Mortimer of Wigmore's namesake uncle Roger Mortimer of Chirk; two were Hugh's cousins Ralph Basset and William Ferrers; a fourth was the earl of Angus in Scotland, Robert Umfraville; the fifth was the man who had just married Hugh's sister-in-law Elizabeth Burgh, Theobald Verdon; and the last was Robert Hastang. Hugh got off lightly: a man called John Ingwardby was imprisoned in the Tower of London for an unspecified long time for 'maliciously drawing a knife in the king's great hall at Westminster.' [11]

The royal officials appointed to rule the late earl of Gloucester's lordship of Glamorgan in South Wales were corrupt and unjust. To make matters even worse, a terrible famine raged in northern Europe in the mid-1310s after years of endless rain flooded the fields and destroyed crops, and the people of South Wales suffered as much as anyone. The Welsh lord Llywelyn Bren launched a rebellion in January 1316, aimed not so much at Edward II personally as at the officials causing suffering to the local people, and attacked Caerphilly Castle in Glamorgan, built by Gilbert 'the Red' Clare a few decades before. Edward sent a group of men to put down the rebellion, including his first cousin and Hugh the Younger's brother-in-law Henry of Lancaster, Roger Mortimer of Wigmore, and Hugh Audley, Roger Damory and William Montacute, the three newly prominent courtiers and 'favourites'. Although Hugh Despenser and his wife Eleanor would end up inheriting Glamorgan, Hugh was not one of the men sent there by the king; Edward still did not trust him an inch. The campaign against Bren was over quickly, and he and others were sent to imprisonment at the Tower of London.

At Easter 1316, Eleanor Despenser was one of the privileged few who received green cloth lined with expensive miniver fur from her uncle the king, along with Queen Isabella; Edward and Isabella's three-year-old son and the heir to the throne Edward of Windsor; the king's sister and Eleanor's aunt Elizabeth, countess of Hereford; Eleanor's sister Margaret Gaveston, dowager countess of

Cornwall; and Hugh the Younger's aunt by marriage Alice, dowager countess of Warwick. [12] Elizabeth, countess of Hereford died on 5 May 1316 following the birth of her tenth child, and Edward attended her funeral in Essex on the 23rd; Hugh and Eleanor may also have gone to her aunt's interment. Hugh witnessed his first ever charter of Edward II at Westminster on 14 May almost nine years into Edward's reign which demonstrates that he was at court on this occasion, at least. Roger Mortimer of Wigmore and his uncle Mortimer of Chirk witnessed the same charter, and Hugh witnessed his second two months later. [13] On 18 October 1316, he made a contract with Edward to serve him in war for two years with 30 men, for an annual payment of 400 marks (later raised to 600 marks for 'staying near the king'). A few of the other English magnates were doing the same thing. [14]

At a meeting of his council at Westminster on 13 December 1316, Edward acknowledged that Hugh and Eleanor and her two younger sisters Margaret and Elizabeth were the earl of Gloucester's heirs. Four days later, however, he was still pretending that his late nephew's lordship of Glamorgan was in his custody because of 'the minority of the heir.' [15] Elizabeth's second husband Theobald Verdon had died on 27 July 1316 less than six months after abducting her from Bristol which can only have pleased the king, but Verdon left Elizabeth expecting their child; in mid-December 1316 she was about six months pregnant. She had now been widowed for the second time, and her elder sister Margaret had also been a widow since the execution of Piers Gaveston four and a half years earlier. Edward wished to arrange their marriages to men who would hold and control their wives' lands, men whom he could trust. He did not trust Hugh, but was unable to annul his marriage to Eleanor and therefore had to live with it, though he could at least ensure that the two younger Clare sisters were given husbands he knew were his allies. Accordingly, even by December 1316 the lands were not parcelled out and were given into the custody of two knights and a clerk called William Aylmer (who was Hugh Despenser the Elder's steward at his manor of Soham in Cambridgeshire) until Trinity Sunday in June 1317. Another petition from Hugh to the king is recorded on 27 February 1317 when Edward sent it to his chancellor and royal council ordering them to look at it and 'make reasonable writs accordingly;' its contents are not recorded, but surely related to the ongoing inheritance situation. [16] By the end of 1316, Hugh was 27 or 28 and he and Eleanor probably had five or so children already, and yet he still had no lands of his own and was dependent on his father as much as he had ever been.

Finally on 17 April 1317, Edward held another council meeting at Westminster, and after considerable preamble admitted that his three nieces were the heirs of their brother and 'it was agreed that they are to be admitted to the inheritance which belonged to the aforementioned earl.' Yet one issue remained before the lands were delivered to the heirs: Margaret and Elizabeth were not yet married safely, and so on 28 April 1317 Edward attended the wedding at Windsor of Margaret and Sir Hugh Audley, one of the three current court favourites. Around the same time, Elizabeth married Sir Roger Damory, the most influential of the three men, with whom her uncle Edward appears to have been, in some way, infatuated. [17] The third court favourite Sir William Montacute was already married hence could not be rewarded with a Clare bride, though he received the wardship of Joan Verdon, the eldest of Elizabeth's three stepdaughters, and Joan's wedding to Montacute's son and heir John (who died a few months later) took place at Windsor also on 28 April 1317. [18] The marriages of the two younger Clare sisters to men he liked, and whom he had raised up from positions of minimal influence, satisfied the king, and the division of the late earl of Gloucester's lands could at last go ahead. Hugh Despenser the Younger and his wife Eleanor were about to become rich; the Clares owned lands in almost every county in the south of England, the lordships of Glamorgan, Usk and Caerleon in Wales, and the lordship of Kilkenny in Ireland.

On 12 May 1317, Edward ordered his chancellor to divide the Clare lands, and to 'put all possible aid and counsel that it be made reasonably and in good and courteous manner and without riot, and hasten it as much as can reasonably be done.' [19] It took time for three royal officials to divide the Clare inheritance; six months, in fact. Four other men, including Roger Damory's older brother Richard, were appointed to 'enquire into the true value of the lands etc,' with more than 20 men all over England and Wales ordered to assist them. Edward took the homage of Hugh Despenser the Younger, Hugh Audley and Roger Damory for their wives' lands at Windsor on or shortly before 22 May 1317. [20]

The partition was finally ready on 15 November 1317, and the escheators and keepers were ordered to deliver the lands to the heirs. [21] Hugh and Eleanor Despenser received lands worth more than £1,415 a year, and by far the larger part of their lands lay in Wales, with a value of £1,276 a year, with only £138 in England. As husband of the eldest sister, Hugh had first pick of the estates, and chose the third which included the rich lordship of Glamorgan in South Wales. Hugh had always been of high rank, and now had an income commensurate with his status. He and Eleanor were to become even richer in 1320 when the dowager countess of Gloucester died and the third of her husband's estate she held in dower was shared out among the three sisters and their husbands. Margaret and Hugh Audley received most of the Clare lands in Kent and Surrey; Elizabeth and Roger Damory's lands were mostly centred in the east of England, and they also received the rich Welsh lordship of Usk on the death of the dowager countess in 1320. Via Elizabeth, Damory also controlled much of the estate of her late husband Theobald Verdon, and was granted the marriage rights of her stepdaughters Margery and Elizabeth Verdon. [22]

Elizabeth's heir was her son William Burgh, who was five years old in late 1317 and who was also the heir of his paternal grandfather the earl of Ulster, an ally of Edward. Margaret's heir, at least until she and Hugh Audley had a son (which, as it turned out, they did not), was her daughter by Piers Gaveston, Joan. The king arranged Joan Gaveston's betrothal to another grandson of the earl of Ulster, John Multon, on 25 May 1317. [23] With his two younger Clare nieces well married and with their inheritance due to fall to his ally's grandson and his beloved Piers Gaveston's child, Edward had good reason to feel pleased with himself in late 1317. Perhaps the only fly in the ointment was Hugh Despenser the Younger, a man he had known most of his life, but never liked nor trusted. One bright spot at least was that Hugh and Eleanor's share would ultimately pass to their son Huchon, who was Edward's eldest great-nephew. Perhaps recognising the need to put his long-term dislike of Hugh to one side and learn to work with him, Edward granted Hugh the remainder of a large fine owed to him by a woman named Katherine Giffard, and custody of the lands and co-heirs of a tenant in chief Edmund Deyncourt with the right to their marriages, on 21 March and 20 April 1317. It may be, though, that something of the shine was taken off these gifts for Hugh when Edward gave Roger Damory his houses at Brokenwharf in London, and custody of the lands and heir of Sir Robert Willoughby, at the same time. [24] Hugh himself received the Lincolnshire manor of Carlton and the Northamptonshire manor of Glapthorn in 1317, both of which had been forfeited by his wife's much older half-sister Joan Clare the dowager countess of Fife and her second husband Gervase Avenel because of their faithfulness to Robert Bruce. Joan's son Duncan MacDuff, earl of Fife, was (most confusingly) married to Eleanor Despenser's younger half-sister Mary Monthermer, and returned to Scotland and to the allegiance of Robert Bruce in 1315. [25] Edward also granted Hugh the castles of Dryslwyn and Dinefwr and the lands of Cantref Mawr in South Wales on 18 November 1317, in payment of the 600 marks due to him 'for staying with the king.' [26] Until 1282, Dinefwr had been the principal seat of Deheubarth, one of the three ancient native kingdoms of Wales. The king was, therefore, bestowing a location of great prestige on Hugh. Six months later Hugh leased the two castles to Rhys ap Gruffudd (a loyal supporter of Edward II for many years, even after his deposition) for 500 marks a year. They were valued at 300 marks a year, so he made a nice profit. [27]

The lordship of Glamorgan included the great stronghold of Caerphilly, the town and castle of Cardiff, and the castles of Llanblethian, Kenfeg, Neath,

Llantrisant and Whitchurch. Grants to Hugh in Glamorgan alone totalled close to £2,000 a year. [28] For a man who had previously been entirely dependent on the income of five or six of his father's manors, here were rich pickings indeed. Even this, though, did not suffice for Hugh. He decided to try to take over the county of Gwynllŵg (Newport) which had once been part of the lordship of Glamorgan, but it had been given to Margaret and Hugh Audley. Hugh took the homage of some of Audley's tenants before Audley had a chance to do so himself, sometime before 12 December 1317 when news of it reached the king's ears at Windsor. [29] On 30 January and 4 March 1318 Edward told his officials to regard the oaths of fealty to Hugh Despenser as 'of no effect' and that he did not accept them, and that the officials were to take Gwynllŵg into his own hands for the time being. Hugh appeared before the king and his council and pretended to agree, stating untruthfully that he had acquitted the men of their oaths and subsequently 'withdrew wholly from such occupation.' [30] The king's actions here are more evidence that as late as 1318, Hugh was not yet in his favour. Hugh, however, persisted in his attempts to gain Gwynllŵg, and on 28 December 1318 Margaret and Hugh Audley gave up the fight and agreed to exchange it for some of Hugh Despenser's English manors and properties, of much lower value. [31] In fairness, Hugh was not the one who tried to claim more lands and titles; Margaret and Hugh Audley themselves audaciously tried to claim the earldom of Cornwall in 1319 as Margaret's dower from her late husband Piers Gaveston. This was refused. [32] They also claimed a stake in Gwynllŵg when a sulky Audley asserted as late as November 1321 that Gwynllŵg actually belonged to him and his wife, but by then Edward was so besotted with Hugh Despenser that he had none of it. [33] Hugh Despenser cared little for his English lands, at least before 1320 when he and Eleanor inherited far more from the late Maud Clare's dower, and wished to build up an extensive power base in South Wales. This brought him into conflict with Roger Damory when he and his wife Elizabeth inherited the Welsh lordship of Usk which Hugh also desired. Always a man with a great talent for quarrelling with and annoying people, Hugh soon began feuding with William Braose, lord of the Gower peninsula which bordered Glamorgan, and John Giffard of Brimpsfield, whose lordship of Cantref Bychan bordered Hugh's possession of Cantref Mawr. On 3 August 1318, the king ordered Hugh and Braose 'not to do anything in breach of the king's peace by reason of the dissensions' between them. [34] This was but a taste of things to come.

In the summer or autumn of 1318 came a great promotion for Hugh the Younger, a promotion which enabled him to become as great a royal favourite as Piers Gaveston had been. He was appointed as the chamberlain of Edward's household, replacing Sir John Charlton. The exact date of the appointment is not recorded, but Hugh was confirmed as chamberlain at the York parliament of 1318 which began on 20 October, and he was certainly already acting in the role by 6 December. [35] The records of the parliament state that 'the king agrees by counsel and at the request of the magnates that Sir Hugh Despenser the son remains his chamberlain.' [36] Pope John XXII (1316–34) wrote to Hugh as chamberlain possibly on 2 October 1318, 'enjoining him to be watchful in the king's service, and to continue to be as faithful and diligent as heretofore' (though the year is not given in the letter and it might belong to 2 October 1319 or 1320). [37] It is interesting to note that Hugh was appointed 'at the request of the magnates.' Even in 1318, months after he had begun his attempts to take Gwynllŵg from his sister-in-law and thus shown a hint of his ruthlessness, greed and overweening ambition, the English magnates still wished to place him in an incredibly important and influential position where he would work with the king on a daily basis. Edward had finally come to terms with his cousin Thomas, earl of Lancaster, on 9 August 1318, and Hugh was one of the men who negotiated the Treaty of Leake which made peace between the two. [38] Lancaster did not object to Hugh's appointment as chamberlain, though he had long hated his father and wished to bring him down. [39] Perhaps he did not see Hugh, as the nephew of the late earl of Warwick who had been his close ally, and always previously on the barons' side, as a potential enemy. Hugh's itinerary demonstrates that from around late 1316 onwards he spent more time at court than had previously been the case (as far as can be ascertained), yet in 1318 does not seem to have been viewed by Lancaster as part of the royal faction, in the way his father was.

The person of the chamberlain was hugely important as he controlled access to the king in person and writing, and over the next few years Hugh was to exploit this power to the hilt. As chamberlain, he also automatically became a member of the king's council. It seems highly likely that Hugh, and perhaps his wife and father too, had schemed furiously to reach this position; Hugh Despenser was not the kind of man to whom things simply happened, and he was highly intelligent, manipulative and determined to get what he wanted. Hugh abused his office by demanding bribes of cash or large gifts before he allowed people to see the king. He only permitted people to talk to Edward when he himself was there, and answered the petitioners himself or told the king what to say. [40] One petition states that when one John Pateshull was arrested in 1322 and taken before Edward, Hugh 'whispered to the king' and that Edward did Hugh's bidding by committing Pateshull to prison. [41] This was Hugh's way of gaining power; to give answers to petitioners on the king's behalf and to let Edward see his competence and his willingness to do the hard work. Edward himself, though certainly not unintelligent or lacking ability, was not interested in the daily grind of government and business, and therefore was only too happy to let Hugh take care of it for him. Before too long, says the *Anonimalle* chronicle, the king did not want to do anything against Hugh's own wishes. [42] Hugh's behaviour as chamberlain was widely known in England, and many people realised that the best way to reach the king's ear was to speak or write to him. The prior of Christchurch, Canterbury, for example, wrote to a courtier begging him to speak to and plead with Hugh, in order to ascertain the king's wishes on a certain manner. [43] Hugh soon became massively unpopular, especially when he demanded bribes from petitioners. The *Anonimalle* thundered that he was covetous, greedy, proud and haughty (all of which is certainly true), more inclined to wrongdoing than any other man, and 'full of wickedness and perfidy.' The author added that

> 'Hugh's instructions were carried out and put into effect everywhere according to his will, and everyone feared him and hated him from the bottom of their hearts. Nevertheless they did not dare say anything…there was not in the land any great lord who, against Sir Hugh's will, dared to do or say the things he would have liked to have done.' [44]

Chronicler Geoffrey le Baker wrote a few years later that many people considered Hugh to be

> 'another king, or more accurately ruler of the king…in the manner of Gaveston, so presumptuous that he frequently kept certain nobles from speaking to the king. Moreover, when the king, out of his magnanimity, was preoccupied with many people addressing him about their affairs, Despenser threw back answers, not those asked for but to the contrary, pretending them to be to the king's advantage.' [45]

Hugh in fact acted in a very different way from the previous great royal favourite, Piers Gaveston, who enjoyed the riches which came from being the beloved of the king, but who had no interest in government or in ruling through Edward. Some of the English magnates had killed Gaveston to remove him from the king's side, because they were so sick of the excessive favouritism; they had merely opened the door to someone far more dangerous.

Chapter 8

Power at Last

As a result of your good conduct the king and ourselves may discuss continuing our good will towards you.

Following the abortive rebellion of the Welsh lord Llywelyn Bren in Glamorgan in early 1316, Bren himself, his wife Lleucu, his sons and five others were imprisoned at the Tower of London and allowed three pence a day for their maintenance (Bren and Lleucu) or two pence (the others). By June 1317 all the prisoners had been released except Bren and his sons Gruffudd and Ieuan, who now all received three pence a day. [1] According to Hugh's baronial enemies in August 1321 when they were spitefully demanding his and his father's exile from England and their perpetual disinheritance, Hugh and Hugh the Elder

> 'took the said Thlewelyn [Llywelyn] and sent him to Cardiff...and seizing jurisdiction by their conspiracy where in this case they could have no jurisdiction according to reason, feloniously caused him to be there drawn, hanged, beheaded and quartered...and so seizing royal power and jurisdiction that pertained to the crown, in disinheritance of the crown, dishonour of the king and of the said lords of Hereford and Mortimer [who had 'promised him grace'].' [2]

If Hugh and his father really did murder Llywelyn Bren (as they had no authority to execute him, it was indeed murder), it was an atrocious act and is impossible to defend or justify. It seems a little curious, however, that few if any contemporary chroniclers held them responsible for Bren's death. Even the *Vita*, whose author was associated with the earl of Hereford who, along with Roger Mortimer of Wigmore, considered himself an aggrieved party in the matter, gives a long account of the campaign against Bren in early 1316, but is utterly silent on his execution. [3] The Bridlington chronicle *Gesta Edwardi de Carnarvon* written a few years later does say the two Despensers had Bren executed, but is only repeating the charges issued against them at the parliament of August 1321 in exactly the same order, so is not an independent source. [4] The Tintern version of the chronicle *Flores Historiarum* gives a brief description of the unfortunate Bren's execution by hanging, drawing and quartering under the year 1318 and says that the parts of his body were displayed throughout Glamorgan to strike fear into other traitors, but does not mention the Despensers or say they were in any way responsible for the execution. [5] Tintern Abbey is only 30 miles from Cardiff, and Hugh's great rival Roger Damory was its patron, so if the Despensers really did have Bren executed, one might expect the Tintern chronicler of all people to mention the fact. A writ to the keeper of Glamorgan early in Edward III's reign (1327–77), when a veritable flood of petitions complaining about Hugh poured forth, states that Hugh fraudulently disinherited Bren's sons, but not that he had Bren executed. Nor was Bren's execution mentioned at Hugh's trial in 1326. The records of Edward II's government are also silent on the issue, and although in the 1320s Edward was certainly excessively forgiving of Hugh's appalling behaviour, it is hardly likely that he would have let the matter of the Despensers' murder of a nobleman pass without so much as a mention, especially as Hugh was not yet particularly in his favour in 1318. In 1326, Hugh's enemies were to accuse him of torturing a noblewoman called 'Lady Baret' into insanity, a story which finds no confirmation in any chronicle, petition or government source. [6]

The torture of Lady Baret and the awful execution/murder of Llywelyn Bren are the two central planks in the popular modern notion that Hugh Despenser the Younger was little more than a vicious psychopath. This notion is perpetuated by additional claims that he raped Queen Isabella which is simply an invention of the twenty-first century. Yet the only evidence for both the murder and the torture is the biased and frankly somewhat dubious statements of Hugh's enemies, firstly in 1321 when they were trying to exile him and his father permanently from their homeland because of their rage that Hugh and the king had stepped on anachronistic Marcher lord privileges, and secondly in 1326 when a list of accusations described by historians as 'an ingenious tissue of fact and fiction' and a 'piece of propaganda' was used to condemn Hugh to death. [7] Edward II in November 1326 was depicted in public as Hugh's puppet and Hugh as the prime mover in everything that had gone wrong in the last few years, because even at that late stage in the reign, those who had invaded Edward's kingdom did not yet dare to apportion blame to the king himself for his failings and errors. Perhaps something similar happened in 1321 and Bren had been executed at Edward's own command, but Hugh and his father were blamed instead because the earl of Hereford and Roger Mortimer could not publicly demonstrate their anger at the king for executing a man to whom they had promised leniency. [8] It seems likely that Llywelyn Bren was executed sometime between June 1317 and August 1321 in Cardiff – perhaps in 1318 as the Tintern *Flores* states – but at the command of the king himself, not the two Hugh Despensers. Although Hugh certainly did threaten, blackmail, imprison and take lands from numerous men and women and was never going to win a prize as England's nicest person, it seems probable that in the matters of Llywelyn Bren and Lady Baret later writers have been rather too keen to take the word of his enemies at face value without checking, and probable that the charges of murder and torture against him are exaggerated, if not outright invented.

On 20 November 1318 during the York parliament which confirmed Hugh as chamberlain, the king learned that Hugh's sister Isabella Hastings had married Ralph Monthermer, widower of Edward's sister Joan of Acre and father of four of his nieces and nephews, without his permission. Edward ordered the escheator to seize Isabella's and Monthermer's lands into his own hand, as was customary, and finally pardoned the couple on 14 May 1321 in exchange for a fine of 1,000 marks. [9] Somewhat peculiarly, the stepfather of Hugh's wife Eleanor had now become his brother-in-law. Hugh had made a contract with a knight called Peter Ovedale on 30 August 1316 in which Ovedale promised to serve him with 10 men, and 'should the said Peter take to wife the lady Hastings, the said Hugh's sister, he should pay the said Hugh 400 marks.' [10] Apparently Isabella was not willing to marry Ovedale; perhaps she thought him beneath her, as a mere knight.

Hugh was one of the four men who formulated a Household Ordinance for the king's household on 6 December 1318, with the steward Bartholomew Badlesmere, the treasurer Roger Northburgh and the controller Gilbert Wigton. The 1318 text, known as the York Ordinance, is the second oldest royal household ordinance in existence in England, after one made in 1279 during the reign of the king's father. [11] It was written in French and specified all the jobs and responsibilities within Edward's household and the rates of pay which were generous by the standards of the time. The staff were provided with all food, drink, clothes and shoes as well as their pay, and were allowed to take leave to visit their families on occasion with the king's permission. Officers of the court were ordered to search for and remove anyone who was not permitted to be there and yet who was eating at the king's expense, on a weekly basis; clearly this was a common problem, and it must have been easy for intruders to insert themselves among the many hundreds of royal servants without being noticed. As the chamberlain, Hugh Despenser received wages of 200 marks a year plus an annual allowance of 16 marks for clothes. He had three squires assisting him who were also entitled to eat in the king's hall, and his own chamberlain; Hugh's chamberlains were Alan Tesdale and Clement Holditch. [12] He was also entitled to his own chamber with 12 candles, three torches, bedding and firewood, plus a food allowance, wine and ale.

Somehow, over the months and years following October 1318, Hugh Despenser the Younger used his close proximity to the king to make himself indispensable (to coin a bad pun) to Edward. The king became dependent on Hugh in some way, and even infatuated. We cannot know what happened between them in private, but from Edward's behaviour over the next few years it is apparent that they became extremely close and perhaps intimate, and that Edward grew to love his chamberlain. It is possible that Hugh used sex to climb his way into Edward's affections; perhaps he calculated that the best way to gain power and wealth was to seduce his wife's uncle and to take advantage of the king's strong emotional (and perhaps sexual) need for a man in his life. He turned Edward's previous dislike and distrust of him into affection and trust, then love and infatuation, to the point that the king refused to send Hugh away from him in 1326 even when his throne depended on it. As they were together so much of the time Edward came to appreciate Hugh as he never had before, and where Hugh's itinerary can be established, his location almost always coincided with Edward's between 1319 and 1326. However, Roger Damory, Edward's previous great favourite, was also determined to hold onto the king's affections, and there must have been furious politicking and jockeying for power and position which is not visible in the contemporary records. Thomas of Lancaster had been demanding the removal of Damory, Hugh Audley and William Montacute from court for a long time, and they do seem to have left by late November 1318. [13] Surprisingly Edward consented to the three men's removal, as he would never have done with Piers Gaveston, or later with Hugh; perhaps he had already tired of them. [14] Their departure was a great favour to Hugh, leaving his way to Edward more or less clear, even though Damory remained in Edward's favour for some time afterwards.

According to the *Anonimalle* chronicle, 'the king loved [Hugh] dearly, with all his heart and mind, above all others,' and Geoffrey le Baker wrote much later that Hugh had enchanted Edward's heart. [15] One annalist in 1326 called them 'the king and his husband' which indicates that some people at least believed them to be an intimate couple. [16] The *Scalacronica* says 'the great men had ill will against [Edward] for his cruelty and the debauched life which he led, and on account of the said Hugh, whom at that time he loved and entirely trusted.' [17] This was written decades later, but its author Sir Thomas Gray was the son of a man of the same name who served in Hugh's retinue in the 1320s. [18] The *Lanercost* chronicle wrote on two occasions that Hugh was Edward's 'right eye,' and the Westminster chronicle *Flores Historiarum* that he led Edward around as though he were teasing a cat with a piece of straw. [19] The *Vita* says 'confident of the royal favour, [Hugh] did everything at his own discretion, snatched at everything, did not bow to the authority of anyone whomsoever,' and that

Edward 'promoted Hugh's designs as far as he could.' [20] The later chronicler Jean Froissart, who knew Hugh's grandson Edward Despenser well, wrote about Hugh that 'without him nothing was done, and through him everything was done, and the king trusted him more than any other.' [21] It is remarkable that the king had come to love a man he had known most of his life and never previously liked which suggests that Hugh as chamberlain worked very hard to ensure Edward's affection for him. Geoffrey le Baker even wrote that the king had once hated Hugh, though this is probably an exaggeration. [22] Still, Edward's closeness over the years to Hugh's father and wife, while ignoring Hugh, suggests he was at least indifferent to him and perhaps that he actively disliked him. In the absence of direct evidence we can only surmise what happened between the men in private and how Hugh turned the king's feelings about him around so completely. It is even possible that Edward was, in some ways and on some levels, frightened of Hugh, as well as obsessed with and dependent on him. As virtually everyone who knew Hugh feared him, even the great English magnates and certainly Edward's queen Isabella, perhaps Edward did too, and it is curious that he never punished Hugh for his illegal seizure of Tonbridge Castle or his assault on John Ros even before Hugh worked his way into royal favour.

Hugh's father Hugh the Elder went overseas on Edward's business in February 1319 and appointed Hugh and Sir Ingelram Berenger as his attorneys while he was away, which he expected to be until late September. [23] The reason for Hugh the Elder's embassy is not entirely clear, but one of the countries he would visit was Spain. Edward asked his cousins Infante Don Pedro and Infante Don Juan, respectively the grandson and son of Edward's uncle Alfonso X of Castile and two of the regents for the seven-year-old king Alfonso XI (r. 1312–50), to 'aid and counsel' him. [24] The author of the *Vita*, who did not have a lot of time for Hugh the Elder, says that he 'craftily took refuge in subterfuges to gain time and keep out of danger.' He added that rumours were current that the elder Hugh had gone on pilgrimage to Santiago in northern Spain to avoid the earl of Lancaster, but the rumours were wrong; there is no evidence that he intended to go there, and various entries in the chancery rolls make it clear that he was going abroad on the king's business and with a sizeable retinue including his son-in-law John St Amand and John Haudlo. [25] Hugh the Younger was with the king at Kirkham in Yorkshire in April 1319, when the prior of Ogbourne near Marlborough in Wiltshire, William Pont l'Evêque, acknowledged that he owed Hugh the vast sum of £2,220. [26] Hugh used his new influence with the king to complain about the archbishop of Canterbury, Walter Reynolds, excommunicating some of his officials in Wales for arresting a renegade monk of Ogbourne and delivering him to Pont l'Evêque. Edward immediately ordered

Reynolds on 10 April to revoke the sentence of excommunication. [27] This is one of the earliest examples of Hugh's newfound favour with the king. His rival Roger Damory witnessed his last-ever royal charters on 4 February, 25 May and 19 July 1319; his disappearance from court and from Edward's favour is visible in the records. [28]

Another sign of the king's newfound affection for his chamberlain comes on 28 July 1319, when the court was at Durham on the way to Berwick-on-Tweed on the north-east coast. Edward ordered an inquisition into the lordship of Gower, to discover which parts of it William Braose (the neighbour in South Wales with whom Hugh had been feuding for the last year or more) and his ancestors had held of the king and might have transferred to others without licence, 'to the king's damage and in his contempt.' He gave instructions to take such lands into his own hands if necessary. Edward believed that such transfers might have been concealed from him, 'whereat the king is much disturbed.' It is possible that as early as the summer of 1319, Edward was seeking a way to ensure that Hugh gained possession of Gower, as one of the inquisitors was Sir John Inge, sheriff of Glamorgan, a close ally of Hugh who did what Hugh told him. [29] Certainly the king had never shown the slightest concern for Gower, let alone been 'much disturbed' by transfers of land there, until Hugh Despenser demonstrated an interest in it.

Robert Bruce, king of Scotland, had captured the vital port of Berwick-on-Tweed in April 1318. It was so vital for the English to retake the port that even Thomas, earl of Lancaster, who generally preferred to stay away from his hated cousin the king and his court, co-operated with Edward in September 1319. Predictably, given Edward II's and his advisers' incompetence – no-one even thought to take along siege-engines – the English failed entirely to recapture Berwick. A Scottish army invaded England and came close to seizing Queen Isabella, and the earl of Lancaster left the port in disgust. Edward had ominously announced that after the siege was over, he would 'turn his hands to other matters,' as he had not forgotten the wrong that was done to his 'brother Piers,' i.e. Gaveston. [30] This was a clear threat aimed at Lancaster.

While at Newcastle with the king after the failure of the siege, Hugh wrote a long letter in French to Sir John Inge, sheriff of Glamorgan and his close ally. [31] Hugh informed Inge that the Scots had invaded England and that Thomas, earl of Lancaster, 'acted in such a way that the king took himself off with all his army, to the great shame and grievous damage of us all. Wherefore we very much doubt if matters will end so happily for our side as is necessary.' [32] Lancaster was suspected of conspiring with the Scots to capture his niece the queen, and in an attempt to deflect criticism, accused Hugh instead. This hardly seems probable, and Hugh had no reason to wish for the queen to be taken prisoner by Robert Bruce, who would demand a huge ransom for her return. [33] Although he and Isabella came to detest and fear each other in later years, there are no grounds to suppose that there was any conflict between them as early as 1319.

Hugh often wrote (or dictated) long, articulate and detailed letters to John Inge which show that he micromanaged his affairs in his South Wales lordship and took a deep interest in them wherever he happened to be in the country. He had some kind of ongoing vendetta against the abbot of Glastonbury in Somerset, and told Inge in this letter of September 1319 to continue behaving towards him as he had already been instructed to do until Hugh decided what to do about him, so that 'the said abbot may be aware that we have the power to harm him.' He was not a man scared of making threats to get people to do what he wanted or indeed of making good on his threats, and given Hugh's later behaviour, the abbot, Geoffrey Fromond, got off lightly. Fromond paid Hugh 200 marks 'in respect of certain disputes' between them in Wales. In later years Hugh Audley tried unsuccessfully to force the abbot to pay the same amount to him; Hugh Despenser had no monopoly on greed, but was better at threatening and extorting people than his rivals. [34] Adam Sodbury, however, who became abbot of Glastonbury in 1323, concealed Hugh's ally Robert Baldock and Hugh's treasure after Queen Isabella invaded her husband's kingdom in 1326 with the intent of bringing Hugh down, so evidently Hugh had not continued his feud with Fromond's successors and indeed was on excellent terms with Abbot Sodbury. [35] Hugh also told Inge in this letter to harm and harass a man called Roger Seyntmor as much as he possibly could, on the grounds that Seyntmor had always been an enemy of Hugh's lordship. Sir Roger Seyntmor or Seymore may have been the Gloucestershire knight of this name who was released from prison in Oxford in March 1285 after committing homicide, and who sometimes witnessed charters of Hugh's step-grandfather Roger Bigod, earl of Norfolk. [36] Apparently in the belief that Inge might balk at 'harassing' a knight, Hugh ordered him to do it, 'on the faith which you owe us.'

Hugh talked about a debt to himself of £3,000, of which £1,000 remained to be paid after 29 September and £2,000 due to his treasury at Cardiff. He was very keen to know on which day he could expect to receive the outstanding sum, and told Inge to take the £2,000 under safe guard to the treasury at Tewkesbury in Gloucestershire. He also told him to make overtures towards Llywelyn Bren's wife and her sons to see if he could get more money out of them than the £100 they had already given Hugh as a gift. If he and his father had, indeed, had Bren executed, Hugh did not mention it in the letter, nor is there any hint of guilt or remorse. He referred to Lleucu as 'the wife of Llywelyn Bren,' not 'formerly the wife' as one would normally expect if Bren was dead. Hugh briefly referred to William Braose, the lord of the Gower peninsula with whom he had been feuding, and told Inge to act in this matter as he would regarding all of Hugh's affairs, i.e. to increase his profit and honour, 'so that we can achieve our aims and desires, one of these days, and that with your help.' Hugh's aims and desires were not explicitly laid out in this letter, but he expressed them in later correspondence to Inge: he wanted to be rich. Hugh added 'take our affairs completely to heart as you have always done well until now, and henceforth all our trust will be given to you.' In 1321, Sir John Inge would specifically be named as one of the three closest allies of Hugh and his father, with Ralph, Lord Basset of Drayton, who was Hugh's cousin, and Ralph, Lord Camoys, who became Hugh's brother-in-law in about 1316. [37]

In September 1319, Hugh evidently already held considerable influence over Edward, even though his rival Roger Damory was still more or less in the picture. The letter to John Inge opened with Hugh announcing that he wished the advancement of Inge's brother within the Holy Church 'for love of you' and that 'we will put this wish into effect as soon as we can, with God's help.' The brother had previously been given a church by the king at Hugh's request. However, Hugh wrote he had since found out that the church was of little value, and therefore he would tell the king this 'and arrange with him, in every way we can, that the first good church' which Edward was able to obtain would be given to the brother instead. The statement that Hugh would plead with the king using every way he could suggests that he was still learning the best methods to curry Edward's favour. In this letter Hugh referred to Edward simply as le Roy, 'the king', rather than as 'our lord the king' as was conventional and as he always did in later correspondence. Calling him merely 'the king' was rather indecorous, and perhaps reveals Hugh's rather dismissive or even disrespectful attitude towards Edward. Nor was Hugh any more respectful towards his Welsh tenants. He told Inge to keep an eye on the woodland throughout his jurisdiction in case dangers occurred there, 'bearing in mind how the people of those parts are often of frivolous resolve and reckless character.' For Hugh to condemn anyone for being 'reckless' was very much a case of the pot calling the kettle black.

From 1318 to 1321, Hugh was closely associated with Bartholomew Badlesmere, a baron of Kent who became steward of the royal household when Hugh was appointed chamberlain. Badlesmere was married to Eleanor Despenser's first cousin Margaret, whose brother Gilbert Clare, lord of Thomond, had rather briefly been the first husband of Hugh's sister Isabella Hastings until his premature death in late 1307. Badlesmere had been a retainer in the household of Hugh's brother-in-law the earl of Gloucester until June 1314 (as had Roger Damory), and was alleged to have betrayed his lord to his death on the battlefield of Bannockburn. Despite this, and despite inciting a rebellion against himself in Bristol in the 1310s and allowing the king's niece Elizabeth Burgh to be abducted from Bristol Castle in early 1316 when it was under his command, Badlesmere was an important politician at Edward's court in these years and a close ally of Aymer Valence, earl of Pembroke. Hugh was one of the men appointed on 1 December 1319 to treat for peace with envoys of Robert Bruce, alongside the earl of Pembroke, Badlesmere, and the bishop of Ely. He had come a long way since the days of 1312 and 1313, when he was only able to ask the king to grant minor favours, and only very rarely. Hugh, Pembroke and the others met the Scottish emissaries at Newcastle-on-Tyne sometime after 7 January 1320, when they were given safe-conducts to come to England. [38] They extended the truce for another two years.

The closeness of Hugh's relationship with Bartholomew Badlesmere is further hinted at in 1319, when Badlesmere's wife Margaret suffered a deeply unpleasant situation. Sometime before 6 December 1319, she and her servants were attacked by a large group of armed men and women at Cheshunt in Hertfordshire, and besieged overnight inside a house. They demanded £100 from her. Several entries on the Patent Roll relate that on the following day 'Hugh Despenser the younger rescued them.' [39] Sadly, there are no further details of Hugh's heroics on this occasion, or how he happened to be there to save the day. The king spent the entire period from October 1318 until February 1320 in the north of England, so it is a little curious that Hugh was so far from court during a period when he was working himself into Edward's favour. Cheshunt is 180 miles from York, where Edward spent most of 1319.

Hugh and Bartholomew Badlesmere were jointly involved in some deeply shady business in 1319/20, concerning a man called John Lashley (this may have been the reason why Hugh left court and returned south). Lashley was one of a large group of men who broke into the manor of Lindsell in Essex, where a lady called Jacomina Merk lived, sometime before 12 February 1319. They stole goods worth about £1,000, including two swans, six horses and timber. [40] Peculiarly, John Lashley was the owner of Lindsell and Jacomina held it from him, and he was committed to prison in Colchester for this theft of goods from his own manor by Ralph Giffard, sheriff of Essex. Hugh removed him from there and incarcerated him in his own prison – the location of Hugh's prison is not stated, though Colchester is just 10 miles from his manor of Lamarsh – until Lashley agreed to release the manor of Lindsell to him and his heirs. Hugh subsequently handed over the person of John Lashley to Badlesmere. [41] The grant of Lindsell to Hugh was recorded on 10 April 1320, and six months later, Hugh gave the manor to Badlesmere. [42] Hugh stated that the sheriff of Essex 'entrusted the said John Lashley to me at my request, to be his custodian.' [43] Judging by Hugh's later behaviour, any of his so-called requests would have been impossible to refuse, even by a sheriff. There was already some history between Hugh and John Lashley: as early as 17 December 1316, Lashley acknowledged a debt of 21 pounds to Hugh. [44] Bartholomew Badlesmere later turned against Edward and Hugh and ended up being executed, whereupon the king granted the manor of Lindsell back to Hugh. [45] John Lashley also joined the 1321/22 baronial rebellion against the king and his chamberlain, and was summoned before court as a result, but 'through the malice and persecution of Sir Hugh Despenser the son, who wished him to be drawn and hanged,' did not appear and was thus outlawed. [46] Hugh's removal of a man from prison was 'contrary to the law of the land' and deemed serious enough to be raised against him during the parliament of August 1321 which exiled him and his father, as he had 'usurped royal power' by doing so. [47]

Chapter 9

War, Exile and Piracy

*If you knew the great suffering which the king takes to heart
and the deep anxiety he has.*

On 22 February 1320 Hugh was appointed constable of the royal castle of Odiham in Hampshire, replacing a man called Robert Lewer or le Ewer, a thuggish member of Edward II's household who had once murdered his mistress's husband. [1] Hugh's brother-in-law Ralph Camoys was appointed constable of Windsor Castle on the same day, perhaps as a result of Hugh's influence. [2] It must have been sometime in or after 1320 when Hugh abused his position by removing a parker of Odiham from his job because he had raised the hue and cry against Hugh's mother Isabella Beauchamp many years earlier for hunting in the park. [3] As for Robert Lewer, he was to rebel against Hugh and his father some years later, and apparently was deeply angry about his replacement as constable of Odiham and not reluctant to shout about it, as in August 1320 Edward ordered his arrest on the grounds of his 'trespasses, contempts and disobediences.' The charming Lewer declared that if any royal officials tried to seize him, he would 'slay them and cut them up limb by limb wherever he should find them,' even in front of Edward. [4] Despite this, and despite the furious king's description of him as 'so vile a person,' Lewer was reconciled with Edward somewhat later, at least for a little while before he acted against the Despensers in 1322 and lost his life as a result. Hugh was made constable of Portchester Castle in Hampshire on 22 August 1320; Lewer had also previously been its constable, so Hugh's appointment was a very pointed decision by Edward made just days after he ordered Lewer's arrest. [5] The king stayed at Odiham from 24 to 27 August 1320, and Hugh was surely also there at the castle for which he was accountable. Yet another appointment came on 1 October 1320 when Hugh was made constable of Bristol Castle, replacing Bartholomew Badlesmere. [6] On the 16th of that month, Hugh and his wife Eleanor granted two manors to Hugh's father for his life; quite a turn-around from the days when they had been dependent on the income he gave them. [7]

The king was in Canterbury on 5 and 6 March 1320 with Hugh, and Hugh's wife and Edward's niece Eleanor Despenser was with them (she may almost always have been with them, but her itinerary is difficult to establish). Eleanor sent a courteous letter to John Inge, sheriff of Glamorgan which demonstrates that she took a keen interest in the affairs of the lordship, her own inheritance and birthplace, and which could hardly be more different in tone from the hectoring, menacing manner of her husband's letters to Inge. [8] Between 19 June and 22 July 1320, Edward went to France to perform homage to his brother-in-law Philip V for the lands he held there, the duchy of Aquitaine (or rather Gascony, as the English kings no longer held the entire duchy), and the county of Ponthieu in northern France which the king had inherited from his mother. Hugh the Younger and his father were two of the many English nobles who accompanied Edward, as did Roger Damory, still just about clinging to royal favour though he had mostly been edged out by his rival. Hugh appointed Ralph Camoys to act as his attorney in his absence. [9] While they were away, Maud Clare the dowager countess of Gloucester died, still only about 30 years old or younger, and the huge dower lands she had held – one-third of the Gloucester estates – were divided among her three sisters-in-law and their husbands. Hugh and Eleanor became richer by more than £900 a year, and inherited far more lands in England. They owned manors in 10 English counties and in London. [10]

By this time Hugh was starting to annoy the Marcher lords, the men who held lordships in Wales and along the English-Welsh border. The Marchers had always held extra privileges in return for their extra responsibilities to hold the border, such as the right to administer their own laws and to build castles without royal licence, and although after Edward I's conquest of North Wales in the early 1280s these were no longer justified, the lords continued to demand they retain their traditional privileges and rights. Chief among Hugh's Marcher enemies were Humphrey Bohun, earl of Hereford and widower of the king's sister Elizabeth (and thus technically Hugh's uncle by marriage); Roger Mortimer of Wigmore and his uncle Roger Mortimer of Chirk; John, Lord Mowbray; Roger, Lord Clifford; John, Lord Giffard; Roger Damory; and Thomas, earl of Lancaster, the king's cousin, whom the Marchers considered their leader. Hugh's attempts to gain control of more of Wales brought him into conflict with these men, especially Roger Damory. The Tintern version of the Westminster chronicle *Flores Historiarum* says that Hugh tried to gain control of Damory's lands in South Wales, but that Damory managed to resist him. [11] Hugh's enemies claimed in August 1321 that he was plotting to take Damory's lands in order to have the entire earldom of Gloucester, a statement which also appears in the *Lanercost* chronicle and the *Vita*. [12]

After the visit to France, trouble broke out over the Gower peninsula in South Wales which Hugh lusted after and which belonged to William

Braose. [13] Braose's son-in-law John Mowbray took possession of Gower probably in the autumn of 1320, though Braose was still alive. Hugh persuaded Edward that, as Mowbray had not received a royal licence to enter the lands, Gower should be forfeit to the king. [14] Edward, naturally, agreed, and on 26 October 1320 ordered Gower to be taken into his own hands, presumably with the aim of granting it to his beloved chamberlain. [15] However, the sub-escheator of Gloucestershire, Richard Foxcote, was unable to take possession of it thanks to the 'large multitude of armed Welshmen' who prevented Foxcote 'executing the mandate, so that he could do nothing therein without danger of death.' [16] One of the four men subsequently sent as a commissioner of *oyer et terminer* ('to hear and to determine') relating to 'resistance to the king's writ' in Gower was Hugh's father, and Richard Foxcote was Hugh's steward, so the men were hardly neutral. [17] On 13 November, Edward ordered the escheator south of Trent once again to take Gower into royal hands, and to imprison in Gloucester anyone who resisted him, declaring himself to be 'much astonished and disturbed' that Foxcote had been unable to execute his order. [18] He told the justice of Wales, Roger Mortimer of Chirk, on 1 January 1321 to arrest Master Rhys ap Hywel, whom Despenser the Elder and the others had found guilty of obstructing Foxcote. [19]

In early 1321, probably on 13 January, there is a reference to a son of Hugh and Eleanor Despenser in Edward's wardrobe accounts: the king paid for one piece of gold and silk tissue for him. [20] From the context, it is apparent that the boy was dead, and that the cloth was intended to lie over his coffin or tomb. The child is not named, presumably because he had been stillborn or died shortly after birth at the end of 1320 or beginning of 1321, and was not given a name. Eleanor Despenser was ill in 1320, when her uncle the king paid an apothecary for medicines for her. [21] Perhaps this illness related to pregnancy or childbirth, though this is only speculation. If Hugh was grieving for the death of a child, it is not apparent from one of his frequent letters to Sir John Inge, sheriff of Glamorgan which he sent on 18 January 1321. In it he acknowledged, or boasted, that envy was growing among the magnates against him, because 'the king treats us better than any other.' Honest about his ambitions, he ordered Inge to 'watch over our affairs so that we may be rich and may achieve our aims, of which you have a good understanding, and this will not readily occur without great effort and diligence by you.' Hugh was aware of the discontent and unrest growing against him, and told Inge that if he heard of any secret assemblies among Hugh's tenants – he always spoke of *noz Galeys*, 'our Welshmen' – or any alliance or movement against himself or the king among the Marchers, he must be informed immediately. [22] Hugh was right to be concerned. A letter written at Newcastle-on-Tyne on 27 February 1321, addressed to Edward II by an unknown correspondent, warned the king that the earl of Lancaster and other magnates had begun causing mischief in Wales and that Edward should 'command Despenser the son, that he be so prepared and arrayed in his lands that he may be able to counteract these evils.' The anonymous writer added that 'great ambushes are set for Bartholomew Badlesmere in the south and in the north against his coming.' [23] Edward later sent Badlesmere, his steward, to Yorkshire as a spy when the Marchers met the earl of Lancaster. Badlesmere switched sides and joined them, presumably because he sympathised with their growing anger against Hugh and because he had close family ties to some of them. This decision would lead to Badlesmere's atrocious death in April 1322.

On 9 February 1321 at the royal manor of Havering-atte-Bower in Essex, Hugh attended the wedding of his eldest daughter Isabella to Richard, son and heir of Edmund Fitzalan, earl of Arundel, and nephew and heir of John Warenne, earl of Surrey. It was a marriage of two children: Isabella was eight and Richard seven. [24] Edward also attended his great-niece's wedding and paid two pounds to be distributed in alms, and bought a cloth to be spread as a veil over the young couple during their nuptial mass. [25] The earl of Arundel had been present at the execution of Piers Gaveston in June 1312, but now had come over to the king's side, and for the rest of Edward's reign would be a staunch ally of him and the Despensers. A petition to Edward dated 22 February 1321 was endorsed by a royal clerk with the words 'I am forbidden on behalf of the king by Hugh Despenser from executing this writ without first consulting the king,' a sign of Hugh's involvement in government. [26]

In early March, the king and Hugh set off for Gloucester to meet the Marcher lords, alarmed at the growing unrest and burgeoning hatred towards the royal favourite. Queen Isabella remained in the south-east as she was pregnant with the royal couple's fourth child, following Edward of Windsor, John of Eltham and Eleanor of Woodstock. Joan of the Tower, future queen of Scotland, would be born on 5 July 1321 at the Tower of London. She would be the royal couple's last child; perhaps this was a result of the declining fertility of one or both of them, or perhaps it indicates that Hugh had already begun to intrude into and damage their intimate marital relationship. There is no reason to suppose that Edward's previous associations with men such as Piers Gaveston and Roger Damory had affected his relationship with his wife, and the king and queen spent most of their time together and corresponded frequently on the rare occasions when apart. Isabella even bought Damory gifts and appears to have helped Gaveston financially during his third exile in late 1311, and if she was hostile to either man there is no sign of it. In late 1325, however, Isabella was to complain that Hugh Despenser had come between her husband and herself, and this may have begun as early as 1321. Edward's relationships with his previous male favourites did not affect his wife's access to him, either politically, personally or sexually. His relationship with Hugh Despenser did, and Isabella was not a woman to tolerate it.

On 6 March 1321 at Fulmer in Buckinghamshire (a manor which belonged to his father; Hugh held nearby Datchet), Hugh sent another letter to the sheriff of Glamorgan John Inge, enclosing two letters from his ally Robert Baldock, archdeacon of Middlesex. Hugh told Inge that

> 'we have been given to understand by several of our friends that all this plotting by certain magnates is planned to begin and do damage to us in our said lordship [Glamorgan], to cover themselves that it is not done against the king, and with the intent that he will interfere in the matter and thereby take sides.'

Somewhat amusingly, Hugh asked Inge if he could 'in a subtle manner' take hostages from each commote of Glamorgan, as this would 'ease our heart.' How Inge was supposed to take hostages subtly was not explained. Hugh wrote sarcastically 'it seems a great marvel to us that you so rarely send us news of our affairs,' and added 'we have so often sent you our letters on this matter that we are entirely weary of it.' He stated that he had kept a copy of this letter, word for word, to take action against Inge with it later if the sheriff made any error, 'which God forbid.' This was typical of Hugh, both the threat and the making a copy of his correspondence. [27] Two weeks later, however, when Hugh wrote Inge yet another long letter from Cirencester in Gloucestershire where he and the king now were, he took a more conciliatory tone, and told Inge he would inform him of certain things orally when Inge came to him in person. [28] For all his wish to gain control over as much of Wales as possible, Hugh's disdain for the Welsh people, made apparent in a previous letter, also revealed itself here. He ordered Inge to take 24 'of our Welshmen…the greatest of our land' to send to Hugh to 'remain with us for a while,' and added that he did not want any of the men to ride a horse, but to be forced to travel to him on foot.

In addition to his fight over Welsh lands, Hugh also tried to, and ultimately did (in June 1322), seize control of Lundy Island in the Bristol Channel, and commented in this letter that he was very hopeful of doing so and that 'the king is making every effort on the matter.' [29] By now, Hugh was supremely secure in the king's favour, and knew that Edward would do almost anything he could to help Hugh and advance him. His letters to Inge in 1321 often contained the phrases *molt nous plait* and *nous plait bien*, 'it pleases us well (or much),' which gives a good indication of his state of mind and that he was happy about the high position he had reached and felt things were going his way. Yet even Hugh had to admit that all was not well. He reminded Inge to watch over his castles and towns day and night and for commanders to guard his border with the earl of Hereford's lordship of Brecon so that his people would not create a disturbance, 'which would displease us much.' Despite this, Hugh was not merely enormously confident, he was over-confident. He told Inge that his brother-in-law Hugh Audley was threatening to harm the 'good people' who were serving Hugh in the Gloucestershire manor of Thornbury (which had been given to Audley and Margaret in the 1317 partition), and wrote 'do not doubt that neither [Audley] nor any of his allies have the power to hurt any of us.' A few weeks later, he would be proved horribly wrong. Sir Henry Spigurnel, a justice of the assize and a man then around 60 years old, was appointed to try Hugh Audley on 2 April 1321; Hugh already knew this would happen when he wrote to Inge on 21 March. Audley was accused of having sworn an oath in writing to 'assist the king in all things all his life' and not to leave Edward's company without permission to do so. He was also accused of ignoring Edward's frequent commands to attend him. [30] Much had happened in the four years since a besotted king had married Audley to his niece Margaret, and Audley had now moved into a position of hostility towards Edward. Hugh Despenser wrote that he could not believe that the justice Henry Spigurnel 'would like to be against us nor against any of our friends,' and that therefore Hugh had sent him letters on the matter. He added that it would not be convenient if Audley felt too secure about Spigurnel's help. This was surely a veiled threat that if Spigurnel was found to be too lenient with Audley, he would displease the king. On the other hand, Hugh had to tread carefully, because a man of Spigurnel's stature – a powerful commissioner, keeper of the peace and royal justice – was not someone who could easily or lightly be intimidated, even by the king's favourite. Spigurnel and Edward's half-brother the earl of Norfolk, however, duly pronounced a sentence of forfeiture on Hugh Audley on 8 April, and the following day, the king ordered sheriffs all over the country to confiscate all Audley's lands and goods. [31]

In this letter to Inge, Hugh also provided some insight into the character of Edward's brother-in-law Humphrey Bohun, earl of Hereford and one of the disgruntled Marcher lords: in 1321, Hugh wrote, Hereford was 'even more gloomy and thoughtful than usual, and it is hardly surprising if he is, as he has turned his countenance against his liege lord who has done him so much good and honour, that he might well have much to think about.' Hugh claimed that he had been warned of the Marchers' intentions early enough to have sufficient armed men to be able to 'protect ourselves against our adversaries of the said earl [of Hereford] and others.' An anonymous correspondent in Hugh's retinue sent a letter at this time and in the same handwriting, almost certainly to John Inge. It asked him to apply himself diligently and honourably to Hugh's affairs and to make efforts to ensure that Hugh received the £1,000 which were in arrears, apparently a reference to the money he had been expecting 18 months earlier. The writer added 'understand for certain, sire, that he [Hugh] loves you…and believe in your heart that no knight ever had a better lord than you have, and be sure that great good will come to you and yours in his service… thanks to God, his reputation and honour is increasing every day.' [32] Hugh's 'love' for John Inge did not prevent him committing Inge to prison later and forcing him to pay a large amount (to Hugh) for his release. And for his part, Edward II was also suffering from a bout of over-confidence in 1321. He wrote to his friend Sir William Aune on 10 April 'know that all things go peaceably and well at our wish, God be thanked,' and on 4 May 'we have nothing but good news in front of us.' [33] On this very day, the Marcher lords began attacking Hugh's lands in Wales.

Edward's half-brothers Thomas of Brotherton, earl of Norfolk, and Edmund of Woodstock, soon to be made earl of Kent, were with the king and Hugh at Gloucester, as were Hugh Despenser the Elder and Edmund Fitzalan, earl of Arundel, when the king tried unsuccessfully to reconcile the Marchers. [34] Thomas of Brotherton and Edmund of Woodstock were 20 and 19 in April 1321 (they were born in June 1300 and August 1301) and were the uncles of Hugh's wife Eleanor, though a few years younger than she. The two men were now old enough to play a role in politics, and were both – especially Edmund – entirely loyal to Edward in the 1320s until Hugh's dominance of the king and his government pushed them into opposition. On 13 April and 1 May, Hugh, the earl of Hereford, Roger Mortimer, Roger Damory and others were all ordered not to attack each other (Hugh being added to the list in a transparent attempt by the king to look as though he was not taking sides). Thereafter, Edward returned to London 'with his own Hugh always at his side,' a statement in the *Vita* which hints at intimacy. [35] They arrived at Westminster on 7 May.

Edward's pleas were in vain. On 4 May 1321, the Marcher lords began a massive all-out assault on Hugh Despenser the Younger's lands and castles in South Wales which spread to his lands in England and to his father's manors as well. [36] Hugh holds the dubious distinction of being one of the very few men in history who has a war named after him: the Despenser War. Although sometimes presented in modern writing as a noble and heroic enterprise by brave men fighting a tyrannical king and his favourite for their rights, the Despenser War was simply an orgy of terrible destruction, violence, plunder, murder and mayhem carried out across a large part of the country by disgruntled noblemen and their followers. It was not only the Despensers who suffered as a result, but the thousands of people who lived on their lands and who saw their homes, crops, livestock and goods burned or stolen, or who were imprisoned. The

Middle English *Brut* chronicle says 'when the king saw that the barons would not cease of their cruelty, the king was sore afraid lest they would destroy him and his realm.' [37] Ten of Hugh's castles and 23 manors in South Wales were sacked, and some of his officials and servants were killed, such as the constable of Neath Sir John Iweyn and his servant Philip le Keu ('the cook'). Iweyn was decapitated on the orders of John, Lord Mowbray. Matthew Gorges and 15 unnamed Welshmen were also killed, Philip Joce was 'maimed', and numerous others were taken prisoner. [38] Roger Mortimer of Wigmore captured the Despenser adherent Sir Ralph Gorges and was still holding him captive many months later. He also took the opportunity to seize and occupy his cousin the earl of Arundel's castle of Clun in Shropshire. [39]

The *Vita* says that 30,000 of Hugh's tenants told the barons 'we have never liked the lordship of Hugh Despenser' and would renounce their homage to him. [40] After his downfall, the 'English community of Glamorgan' were to complain of his oppressive, harsh and arbitrary lordship, though in fairness this was a common complaint aimed at their lords by tenants in this era. [41] Disavowing his lordship was surely a way for Hugh's tenants to spare their lives and their livelihoods, as those who refused to swear allegiance to the Marchers were imprisoned until they ransomed themselves, and their houses and goods burnt. [42] The Marchers destroyed all of Hugh's papers and documents they could find which ultimately worked in his favour, as a year later the king pardoned him and Eleanor all debts and arrears at the exchequer going back to Edward I's reign because the Marchers had burned his memoranda. [43] They took the king's sergeant-at-arms Guy Almavini prisoner, and stole the treasure Edward had stored at Neath, one of Hugh's castles. [44] *Lanercost* says 'they seized the king's castles in those parts…and removed the king's arms and standard from the same,' which tends to negate the Marchers' pretence that they were acting out of loyalty to Edward. [45] Hugh surrendered his lands into the king's own hands in an unsuccessful attempt to keep them safe. [46] Edward considered sending him abroad for his own protection, and issued safe-conducts for him, his ally Robert Baldock, archdeacon of Middlesex, his kinsman Sir Walter Beauchamp (son of Hugh's great-uncle of the same name, once steward of Edward I's household), and his barber Robert Torksey. [47]

Parliament opened in London on 15 July 1321, 10 days after Queen Isabella gave birth there to her and Edward's youngest child Joan of the Tower. The Marcher lords arrived two weeks late, having pillaged their way down the country from Yorkshire, where they had met their leader Thomas, earl of Lancaster. John, Lord Mowbray, Sir Stephen Baret and Sir Jocelyn Deyville, all executed in 1322, robbed a church in Yorkshire and stole livestock and goods from townspeople, and the earl of Lancaster's adherent Sir Robert Holland chased the 'poor people' of the elder Despenser's Leicestershire manor of Loughborough out of their homes for three months. [48] In South Wales, the convent of Brecon told Edward that the attacks had 'greatly impoverished' them, and the 'poor people' of Swansea also petitioned the king for help: it was the innocent who suffered most as a consequence of the Marcher lords' brutal vindictiveness, and the Marchers looted and plundered numerous towns and villages that did not even belong to the Despensers. [49] Hugh did not help matters by accusing the 'poor people' of Swansea of aiding John Mowbray in stealing the king's goods from Neath Castle, and he imprisoned them and forced them to pay him a ransom. [50] Hugh was also accused of keeping Sir John Iweyn's great-niece and heir Alice Ragoun out of her rightful inheritance. [51]

The Marcher lords set their armies around the walls of London to prevent the king leaving the city, though the annalist of St Paul's says that Hugh sailed up and down the Thames between Westminster and Gravesend in Kent urging Edward not to reach an agreement with them. The Marchers, whose solution to every problem was destructive violence and slaughter, threatened to burn down the city between Westminster and Charing Cross if Hugh did not desist. [52] When Parliament finally began, they demanded the permanent exile of Hugh and his father from England, and the perpetual disinheritance of them and their heirs. The two Hughs were accused of usurping royal power and 'plotting to distance the affection of our lord the king from the peers of the land, to have sole government of the realm between the two of them.' The magnates had to admit that Hugh had been elected as the king's chamberlain and thus did have a right to be next to the king, but said that he had 'drawn over to his cause Sir Hugh his father,' who did not have this right. The execution of Llywelyn Bren supposedly (though most probably not) by the Despensers was another issue raised, as was Hugh's removal of John Lashley from prison in Colchester the year before. The Marchers also 'set free without any mandate or authority' several prisoners during the Despenser War, yet remained blithely unperturbed by any concept of hypocrisy. They accused Hugh of being 'angered against the king' and of forcing Edward to do his will under duress. [53]

Hugh and his father were not given any chance to speak in their own defence. [54] The author of the *Vita* criticised the Despensers severely, pointing out the younger Hugh's malice and greed and the elder Hugh's harshness, brutality and corruption, and added that therefore some people believed 'this misfortune fell upon them justly.' He also wrote:

> 'Yet in the judgement of some worthy persons the barons went too far in their persecution. For even if they found just reasons for banishment, they did not justly seize their goods. Why did they destroy their manors,

for what reasons did they extort ransoms from their retinues? Though formerly their cause had been just, they now turned right into wrong.' [55]

Edward had little choice but to agree to the Marchers' demands. He entered Westminster Hall flanked by his cousins the earls of Pembroke and Richmond, and announced that the Despensers would be exiled. He retired to his chamber looking 'anxious and sad,' though in truth he was coldly furious: he told his ally Hamo Hethe, bishop of Rochester, that he would avenge his defeat in such a way that 'within half a year the whole world would hear of it and tremble.' [56] The *Brut* and *Anonimalle* chronicles both say that Hugh the Elder cursed his son 'and said that for him he had lost England,' and immediately went abroad (precisely where is not known). [57] The Despensers were ordered to leave England by 29 August 1321 from Dover and nowhere else, as Piers Gaveston had been likewise ordered 10 years before when he was exiled for the third time.

One Canterbury chronicler gives the peculiar story that after the Despenser War, but apparently before his official exile, Hugh the Younger disguised himself in the habit of a monk of Langdon Abbey in Kent (William Digepit, abbot of Langdon was a close friend of Edward II). He crossed to France and arrived in Paris, but soon returned to England because Aymer Valence, earl of Pembroke, was spreading rumours about him at the French court. Pembroke was in Paris in June and July 1321. [58] It is hard to imagine that he would have publicly behaved in such a manner; even if he loathed Hugh, as he might well have done, he would have known that treating the king's beloved in such a fashion would bring Edward's wrath down on his head. The story is most implausible, though in fact Hugh does seem to have been in Paris at some point, perhaps on an embassy to the French court on the king's behalf in the second half of 1320: an undated payment was made to him to there by the Italian bankers the Bardi sometime before November 1321. [59] Hugh did not flee in 1326 when Queen Isabella and her allies came to bring him down and is most unlikely to have fled anywhere in 1321 either, and certainly not to the French court where he had few if any friends.

Edward left Westminster on about 27 August and made his way through Kent to the island of Thanet, where he stayed until 11 September. He sent most of his household away, and on 6 September ordered the bailiffs of Hugh's manors of Tewkesbury and Hanley to pay the wages of Hugh's parkers and foresters there and appointed William Beauchamp keeper of Tewkesbury park and two of Hugh's hunting chases. On 8 September, Edward ordered Hugh's manors of Wix, Lamarsh, Layham, Kersey and Datchet to be given into the hands of one of his clerks. [60] This all suggests that Hugh had remained with him. Edward was at Harwich in Essex from around 12 to 20 September while most of his household was at Faversham and Gravesend in Kent (the king must have travelled there by water). The royal clerk and chronicler Adam Murimuth says that Hugh was with the king at Harwich while they plotted revenge on their enemies and that he did not leave England until a little before the feast of St Michael, i.e. 29 September, a month late. [61] This seems highly likely. Edward was at Hadleigh in Suffolk on 22 and 23 September, just two miles from Hugh's manors of Kersey and Layham, and finally returned to Westminster on 25 September. On this day, he ordered his former favourites Roger Damory and Hugh Audley to deliver Hugh's lands of Glamorgan and Gwynllŵg into his own hands (and repeated the order on 28 November, declaring the men's excuses for failing to do so 'altogether insufficient and derisory'). [62] Just a few days later on about 2 October 1321, the king sent Queen Isabella to Bartholomew Badlesmere's castle of Leeds in Kent deliberately as a *casus belli* and as the first step in a clever strategy against his and Hugh's enemies. Badlesmere's wife Margaret fell into the trap and refused to admit the queen, thus enabling Edward to feign outrage at the insult to his wife and besiege Leeds, whereupon the Marcher lords brought their armies to Hertfordshire in support of Badlesmere. This move provided the king and Hugh with the excuse to go after their enemies; surely a plan devised by Hugh himself, or by him and the king jointly.

If the Marcher lords hoped that Hugh would take himself off quietly and obediently abroad somewhere like his father, these hopes were soon dashed. Hugh became a pirate in the English Channel, a 'sea-monster…he was master of the seas, their merchandise and chattel, and no ship got through unharmed.' [63] Numerous fourteenth-century chroniclers talk of Hugh's piracy, and one of the charges against him at his trial in 1326 was that he had robbed merchant ships and thus made things difficult and dangerous for English merchants sailing to other countries. [64] Edward placed Hugh under the protection of the men of the Cinque Ports, and wrote to them on 27 November 1321 to thank them 'for keeping [Hugh] amongst them at the king's order from the manifold toils prepared for him by reason of his service to the king, and for honouring the said Hugh in many ways.' [65] The words 'at the king's order' are significant, and demonstrate that Edward had no intention of sending his beloved into exile abroad, whatever he had told the Marchers during Parliament. Hugh's fellow pirates may have included Robert Batail of Winchelsea in Sussex, a baron of the Cinque Ports and one of Edward's admirals, Batail's associates Stephen and Robert Alard also of Winchelsea and possibly their relatives Henry, Reginald and Gervase Alard (the Alards were a well-known Winchelsea sailing family), and others called Peter Bard, John Baddyng, John Dyne and Andrew Sely, all sailors of the Cinque Ports. These men were firmly on the king's side in 1321, and on 2 October that year attacked the ship of a group of Dorset merchants on the grounds that they were adherents of Roger Damory. Robert Batail led as assault on the port of Southampton on 30 September and 1 October 1321 'in conspiracy with Hugh Despenser the son' because the townspeople were taking the earl of Lancaster's side. [66] These incidents took place just a few days after Hugh and Edward had probably finally parted, and Edward had returned to Westminster and told his queen to go to Leeds Castle as the first step of his and Hugh's plan to avenge themselves on the Marchers.

On 6 May 1322 Edward pardoned Batail and the Alard brothers for 'all offences committed on land and sea.' Just 10 days later the Alards were accused of plundering a ship, this time off Harwich, and in May/June 1322 committed yet more acts of piracy off Sandwich and Skegness. Not yet finished, Robert Batail, Stephen Alard and nine named relatives and associates of theirs were accused in late 1323 of pursuing a Gascon merchant ship towards the port of Sandwich, entering it, assaulting the merchant and stealing his goods. [67] Hugh Despenser cannot have been involved in these incidents which took place after his return to court, but on 1 March 1322 Edward wrote to the barons, bailiffs and sailors of Winchelsea thanking them for their advice and promises of aid 'lately given to the king on the water.' [68] When Edward met the sailors of Winchelsea on the sea is unclear as the port does not appear in his official itinerary of 1321/22, and probably he secretly met Hugh again in their company; Hugh was said in 1326 to have returned to England illegally during his exile. Pope John XXII asked Edward on 27 April 1322 to restore a vessel and goods to some merchants of Pisa, 'of which they have been despoiled by certain of the king's subjects in Sandwich.' [69] Edward III paid compensation in July 1336 to a Genoese merchant called Juan Luciani and his colleagues because Hugh 'plundered their ship at the Dunes of Sandwich' and took goods worth more than 14,300 marks. He admitted that Hugh was 'upon the seas with the late king's ships,' thus holding his father partly accountable for Hugh's piracy. [70] Peter Bard, a bailiff of Sandwich and possibly one of Hugh's associates, was sent 'on the king's affairs' in a ship on 2 March 1322, the day before Hugh and his father openly re-joined Edward. [71] Hugh himself was officially pardoned for his piracy, as well as for 'all trespasses' going back to the time of Edward I, on 1 June 1325. Edward II granted the pardon on the dubious grounds that 'while [Hugh] was exiled by diverse magnates of the realm, contrariants against the king, he through fear of death adhered to diverse malefactors at sea and on land, and stayed with them to save his life, while they perpetrated depredations and other crimes,' as though Hugh had merely been a passive observer and not a participant. [72] Making money was always Hugh Despenser the Younger's number one priority, and in late 1321 he had found an exciting new source of revenue.

Chapter 10

Executions and Extortion

We are very worried about having some reason for which we might be prepared to harm you.

Around 30 November 1321 – about nine days after Edward wrote to the men of the Cinque Ports thanking them for protecting him – Hugh sent a petition to the king asking for his sentence of perpetual exile and disinheritance to be annulled and for Edward do him justice in accordance with his coronation oath and Magna Carta. Edward granted him a safe-conduct on 8 December and another on 9 January 1322, and issued one to his father on Christmas Day. [1] As he had done with Piers Gaveston several times, Edward bestirred himself to great action to bring the Despensers back. Although it was the depths of winter, the king set off on a military campaign against the Marchers shortly after Christmas with a large part of the English nobility including the earls of Norfolk, Kent, Pembroke, Richmond, Arundel and Surrey and the Scottish earls of Atholl and Angus. The Marchers fled rather than face him, burning the bridges over the River Severn as they went to prevent him crossing. Hugh Audley's father Hugh Audley the elder, Maurice, Lord Berkeley, and Roger Mortimer of Wigmore and his uncle Roger Mortimer of Chirk submitted to the king in late January and early February and were imprisoned, presumably to Hugh Despenser's great satisfaction, especially as he loathed the Mortimers. Hugh Audley himself, Roger Damory, Bartholomew Badlesmere, Roger Clifford, John Mowbray and others fled to Pontefract in Yorkshire to the protection of Thomas, earl of Lancaster, their last hope. Lancaster had once accused Damory of trying to kill him, so the two made peculiar bedfellows. Badlesmere was also loathed by Lancaster, and owing to his betrayal of Edward, his name was now anathema to the king as well. Edward issued safe-conducts to other Marchers, or 'Contrariants' as he began to call the baronial rebels to come to meet him, but pointedly excluded Badlesmere by name. [2]

When Hugh and his father returned to England is not clear. Hugh sent his petition on or around the feast of St Andrew, 30 November 1321, and 'hereupon, the said Hugh the son came, and surrendered himself into the king's wardship as a prisoner, praying that the king would receive him into his protection.' [3] How much time that 'hereupon' involved is a matter for speculation, but it is not impossible that Hugh was already back in England by Christmas 1321 and that his supposedly permanent exile from his homeland had lasted only two or three months. Perhaps piracy had begun to pall; the English Channel in winter would have been rough and unpleasant.

An entry on the Close Roll suggests that Hugh was with Edward at Weston Subedge in Gloucestershire on 25 February 1322, and he and his father openly joined the king at Lichfield on 3 March with a large force of troops. [4] Hugh's petition set out very crisply the five errors he believed had been made in the judgement against him in August 1321. If he formulated the petition himself, it would imply that he had an excellent knowledge of the law, and it is worth remembering that his grandfather was justiciar of England.

In early March 1322 the king, the Despensers and all their allies followed the Contrariants to Pontefract, capturing Tutbury in Staffordshire which belonged to the earl of Lancaster, as they went. Here Roger Damory was condemned to death on 13 March 1322. Edward respited the punishment because he had loved him well in the past and had given him his niece in marriage, but Damory seemingly had died anyway the day before (chroniclers give 13 or 14 March as the date of his death, but his widow Elizabeth Burgh kept his anniversary on the 12th), from wounds sustained fighting in a skirmish against the royal army. [5] He and Hugh had long been rivals for the king's affection, a battle Hugh had convincingly won with Damory's death. As Edward and his party were about to cross the River Trent at Burton-on-Trent, Hugh dismounted from his destrier and prostrated himself flat on the ground in the snow in front of the king, arms outstretched, and made a formal speech:

'Show restraint, lord, show restraint to your people, and for God's mercy, let regal clemency, not might, guide your impulsive actions; my lord king, do not strive to weaken the realm's nobles. They are your vassals, and not led by prudent council but rather spurred by youthful fervour, they put their hand to unwarranted deeds of might, and if your banner, my lord king, shall be unfurled, war among all of us will perturb all the land, everywhere, and only with great difficulty will you be able to bring harmony to your times. Therefore, let your royal highness proceed with what you began, so that, if they see fortune strongly against them, they may be penitent and, with the help of God from the beginnings, they may come to their senses.' [6]

The reference to an 'unfurled banner' was a declaration of war; Hugh meant that a state of open war would exist between the king and his nobles and that common law would be temporarily and partially suspended, with potentially dire consequences. Thomas of Lancaster, Roger Damory, Bartholomew Badlesmere, Henry Wilington, Henry Montfort and other Contrariants were alleged to have displayed their banners in 1322, and thus openly declared themselves Edward's enemies. Hugh's advice was shrewd, and would prevent the Contrariants from claiming that their king had gone to war against them. [7]

On 16 March 1322, Sir Andrew Harclay, sheriff of Cumberland, defeated the Contrariant army at the battle of Boroughbridge in Yorkshire, and just nine days later the king rewarded him with the earldom of Carlisle. [8] Edward's brother-in-law Humphrey Bohun, earl of Hereford, was killed at Boroughbridge, and his cousin Thomas, earl of Lancaster was captured and taken to his own great castle at Pontefract. Edward and Hugh were waiting for him there, with the king's allies: his half-brother the earl of Kent, nephew-in-law the earl of Surrey, cousins the earls of Pembroke and Richmond, the Scottish earls of Angus and Atholl, and Hugh's father Hugh the Elder. According to the *Anonimalle* chronicle, Hugh the Younger threw malicious and contemptuous words in Lancaster's face on the earl's arrival. [9] Lancaster was condemned to death in his own hall for treason, as he and other Contrariants had invited a Scottish army into England to help them defeat their king. He was made to kneel facing Scotland and beheaded with an axe on 22 March. Edward deliberately arranged his execution as a parody of Piers Gaveston's. Although Hugh and his father were later held solely responsible for Lancaster's execution by Queen Isabella and her allies, six earls and a royal justice also condemned him to death, as well as the king.

About 20 other noblemen and knights were executed in March/April 1322 after the failure of the Contrariant rebellion, including the unfortunate Bartholomew Badlesmere. He was the only one given the full horrors of the traitor's death, near Canterbury on 14 April. John, Lord Mowbray, who had robbed a church in Yorkshire and ordered the beheading of Sir John Iweyn and his cook, was hanged in chains at York on 23 March. Another man executed was John, Lord Giffard of Brimpsfield, a neighbour and rival of Hugh in South Wales and keeper of Glamorgan in 1316 before Hugh inherited it. Another was Sir William Fleming, appointed keeper of Glamorgan in 1317 and Gower in 1320. Presumably Fleming angered Hugh in some way, though on 16 April 1321, when Hugh was with him, Edward had given Fleming a gift of 20 pounds, and still thought he was loyal as late as 14 February 1322. Just six days later he ordered Fleming's arrest. [10] Edward sent Hugh's adherents Sir John Inge and Sir Thomas Marlebergh to pronounce judgement on Fleming at Cardiff on 26 March 1322. [11] Inge and three others were also sent to render judgement on one Stephen Baret, an adherent of John Mowbray, at Hugh's town of Swansea on 28 April. [12] Presumably Baret was executed shortly after his trial. A few dozen other men were imprisoned and given three pence a day for their sustenance; many were released on acknowledgement of a large fine which was a form of political blackmail. A handful of men fled to the continent. Edward II's seemingly arbitrary and capricious decisions in 1322, the way some Contrariants were executed, others imprisoned and others pardoned, have often puzzled historians. Sir Henry Wilington, for example, was hanged, but his brother John merely imprisoned, although John was one of the men accused of treacherously negotiating with the Scots against Edward – by far the most serious charge against the Contrariants – and Henry was not. It may well be what the executed men had in common was that they had offended Hugh Despenser the Younger.

In 1326, Hugh was accused, almost certainly with massive exaggeration, of having his mercenaries (or rascals; *ribaudes* was the French word used) torture one 'Lady Baret' into insanity and break her limbs. This lady was presumably Stephen Baret's widow, whose name was either Joan Gynes or Joan Mandeville; she was so obscure that even royal clerks in 1324 did not know her name for certain. Her three manors in Suffolk, Staffordshire and Leicestershire were in Edward's hands in July 1324 and were not given to Hugh which makes it hugely unlikely that he had her tortured, as his only aim in doing so might have been to gain control of her lands. [13] Bartholomew Badlesmere's widow Margaret née Clare, whom Hugh had rescued when she was besieged in a house in Cheshunt in 1319 and who was his wife's first cousin, was released from the Tower of London on 3 November 1322 and went to live at the convent of the Minorites at Aldgate, where Edward paid two shillings a day for her expenses. [14] The wife of Sir John Maltravers, who fled from England and returned with Roger Mortimer and Queen Isabella in 1326, received a pitiful five pounds a year for her sustenance, though the widows of the executed Sir Henry Tyes and Sir Warin Lisle fared considerably better: Edward granted each of them £200 yearly on 6 April 1322, and they were not imprisoned. [15] Roger Mortimer of Wigmore's wife Joan was sent to Southampton with a small household on 4 March 1322 and remained in custody until the end of Edward's reign, although the escape of her husband in August 1323 was surely a factor in Edward's decision not to release her. Edward granted Joan 62 marks annually for the sustenance of herself and eight servants. [16]

Thomas of Lancaster's widow Alice Lacy became a victim of the king and Hugh, even though she was a great noblewoman who had inherited two earldoms: on 26 June 1322, Alice was forced to acknowledge a huge debt of £20,000 to Edward, a typical way for the king and the Despensers to bind people to them, and signed over many of her lands to both. Alice handed over her great North

Wales lordship of Denbigh to Hugh the Elder. [17] Supposedly Hugh and his father told Alice that she had caused the death of her husband, from whom she had in fact been separated since 1317, and threatened that she would be burned alive for this crime. [18] This would certainly not be the last occasion when Hugh threatened a woman to get what he wanted. He was a highly intelligent man, not a dim-witted and ill-educated thug, and knew exactly what he was doing which makes his behaviour even more reprehensible. Not only women were his targets, however. Even the king's half-brother Thomas of Brotherton, earl of Norfolk, assigned lands to Hugh in August 1323, surely not entirely voluntarily: his castle and manor of Chepstow in South Wales, and all his lands between the rivers Severn and Wye. Hugh would pay a yearly rent of £230 and hold the lands for his lifetime, when they would revert to the earl. [19] In November 1324 the earl released Hugh of all rent in exchange for a one-off payment of £800, and so ended up getting the better part of the deal as Hugh was executed two years later. [20]

Parliament opened at York on 2 May 1322, and Edward summoned representatives from the Cinque Ports for the first time, presumably because of their support of Hugh, and from North and South Wales. The king finally revoked the hated Ordinances of 1311 and annulled the judgement of exile and disinheritance on the Despensers. [21] Hugh the Elder was made earl of Winchester on 10 May, an appointment which attracted little criticism from contemporaries, perhaps because he was a highly-born nobleman and the title did not seem undeserved. [22] Hugh the Younger resumed his former position as the king's chamberlain and acted as such until his downfall, and all his lands were restored to him on 7 May with the issues received from them for the last year. [23] On 10 July, Edward gave him custody of yet more castles and lands in South Wales, and the manors forfeited by the Contrariants given to Hugh 'for good service rendered and to be rendered' ran into the dozens. [24] With the lands lavished on him by the king, Hugh became the wealthiest man in the country after Edward himself. He had achieved his aims, expressed to John Inge in September 1319 and more explicitly in January 1321, of becoming rich and of ruling over much of Wales. One wonders if he had deliberately antagonised the Marchers and the earl of Lancaster over Gower to push them into open rebellion and treason so that he could persuade the king to give him many of their forfeited lands. He was surely ruthless, calculating and manipulative enough.

In May 1322, Hugh's elder half-sister Maud née Chaworth died at the age of 40, leaving her widower Henry of Lancaster who was the heir to his childless late brother the earl of Lancaster, and her six daughters and one son. Edward sent a cloth of gold and jewels for her burial. [25] Maud's son Henry, Hugh's nephew, became the first duke of Lancaster in 1351, and was the grandfather of

Henry IV, king of England, and Philippa, queen of Portugal. On 2 May 1322, Edward II ordered his niece Margaret Audley née Clare to go to Sempringham Priory with only three attendants, and ordered the prior 'to cause her to be guarded safely, not permitting her to go without the gates of the house.' [26] Edward had always been on good terms with Margaret, especially when she was married to his beloved Piers Gaveston, but now her second husband had rebelled against him and – whether she had anything to do with it or not – he was infuriated with her. He allowed her to plead with him to spare Hugh Audley's life, probably against the wishes of Hugh Despenser, and Audley would be the only one of Edward's favourites to survive the reign. He escaped from Nottingham Castle in or before 1326. [27] If Eleanor Despenser attempted to intervene for her sister, there is no record of it, though she and Queen Isabella wrote almost identical letters on behalf of Roger Mortimer's wife Joan on 17 February 1323, asking for the money allocated to her to be paid promptly. [28]

Hugh's sister-in-law Elizabeth Burgh, sister of Margaret Audley and Eleanor, became one of his primary victims. Perhaps the king was furious at what he saw as Roger Damory's treachery and took it out on Damory's widow (as with Margaret), but that is no excuse, and he not only made no effort at all to protect his niece, he actively colluded in Hugh's disinheritance of her. Elizabeth, according to her own testimony and various entries in the chancery rolls, was captured at Usk in Wales with her children even before Damory's death. She was sent to Barking Abbey where she heard of her husband's demise, and released some months later. [29] Edward paid £74 for her sustenance at Barking, a generous enough amount, but, again as he did with her sister Margaret, ordered the prioress not to let her out of the gates. He restored her lands to her on 25 July and 2 November 1322. [30] Elizabeth was still at Barking on 29 June that year when she granted, after a considerable amount of coercion, her rich lordship of Usk and Caerleon to her sister Eleanor and Hugh Despenser. [31] Edward granted the peninsula of Gower which had caused the Despenser War in the first place to Hugh and Eleanor on 9 July, and they gave it to Elizabeth in exchange for Usk. [32] Usk was far more valuable than Gower, so the exchange was considerably in the Despensers' favour, as had also been the case when they exchanged some English manors for the lordship of Gwynllŵg with Margaret and Hugh Audley in 1318. Edward gave Hugh Despenser all the 'corn, hay, grass, animals and goods' in Usk and Gower, and from other manors recently granted to him, thus permitting him to keep all his own goods, crops and livestock in Gower and also to take Elizabeth's in Usk. [33] Giving Usk to Hugh and Eleanor was the price Elizabeth paid for her freedom and to have the rest of her lands restored to her. It is notable that in the records of this grossly unfair land deal in the chancery rolls, Eleanor Despenser is called the 'king's niece,' but Elizabeth is not; Edward's partiality for Eleanor over his other nieces had always been apparent, and especially now that her husband was so high in his favour. As for Hugh, his greed for lands and his desire to build a massive power base in South Wales far outweighed any sense of loyalty to or concern for his wife's sisters, and he was not a man who cared much about marital ties.

Elizabeth, who in 1326 bravely wrote a document detailing what her uncle the king and brother-in-law Hugh had done to her, was invited or rather ordered to spend Christmas 1322 with the king. Edward threatened his niece and separated her from her councillors in an attempt to get her to do what he wanted, that is, what Hugh wanted. This resulted in her fleeing from York and an incensed king seizing all her English lands again on 7 January 1323. [34] On 1 April 1324, the former lord of Gower William Braose acknowledged a staggeringly large debt of £10,000 to Hugh, who forced him to take legal action against Elizabeth Burgh to recover Gower from her. By June 1324 this had worked, and Braose granted Gower to Hugh Despenser the Elder, who, in turn, granted it to his son. And so did Hugh the Younger deprive his sister-in-law of both Usk and Gower. [35] Aline Mowbray, daughter and co-heir of the hapless William Braose and widow of John, Lord Mowbray, hanged as a Contrariant in March 1322, later made her feelings about Hugh clear: she called him 'the evil traitor Hugh Despenser the son.' [36] Aline herself had been imprisoned in the Tower of London in February 1322, and was released in June 1323 into the custody of Hugh Despenser the Elder. While she was imprisoned, she was forced to grant the reversion of her lands to Hugh the Elder, i.e. that after her death and her father's they would pass to Despenser and ultimately to Hugh the Younger. [37]

Hugh sent a long letter to his sheriff of Glamorgan Sir John Inge in about October 1322, though it is undated. [38] He ordered Inge to maximise his profit in the land and move any goods of his which remained there (the letter told Inge to 'take care of our profit,' always his top priority, three times) before Hugh gave it to Elizabeth, whom he called *la dame de Burgh* or 'the Lady Burgh'. This was a rather cold, albeit courteous, way of referring to her without acknowledging her relationship to him as his wife's sister. For her part, Elizabeth called him 'Sir Hugh Despenser the son', and Hugh in his letters also often referred to himself as 'Hugh Despenser the son'. [39] Neither of them acknowledged their relationship as would have been usual and conventional – it was common in written documents of the era to refer to one's brother-in-law or sister-in-law as one's own brother or sister – though both carefully used the other's correct title. (Hugh even punctiliously referred to his archenemy Mortimer of Wigmore as 'Sir Roger Mortimer' in a letter of October 1324, a year after the latter sent men to kill him and his father, whereas Edward II and others referred to him as 'the Mortimer'.) [40] With reference to Elizabeth, Hugh wrote in the letter, with his usual hauteur, 'regarding the lady's wet-nurses, we have been requested that they be moved from Usk to Gower or elsewhere, and we have permitted this and wish it to be so.' Perhaps it was Hugh's wife Eleanor who had intervened for her sister, though Hugh did not clarify.

Robert Lewer, the man whose arrest Edward had ordered in 1320 when Lewer threatened to dismember his officers, had been reconciled to the king and commanded the infantry at the battle of Boroughbridge. In 1322 Lewer again grew discontented, not with Edward so much as with the Despensers, and left the king without permission and returned to his native Hampshire. Edward ordered his arrest on 16 September. [41] Lewer went to some of the elder Despenser's manors – though not Hugh the Younger's – and plundered them, and took the food and other things he had stolen to the manors of the executed Contrariants Sir Henry Tyes and Sir Warin Lisle and ostentatiously distributed them as alms. Hugh the Elder, in the belief that Lewer would attack him physically, sought refuge at Windsor Castle. [42] In his very long letter to John Inge of *c.* October 1322, Hugh the Younger informed him about Lewer, and ordered him to take as many men as necessary to capture and destroy him and the 'evil ones' with him because they wished 'harm to my lord our father and to us,' meaning himself. Hugh told Inge that if he managed to capture Lewer he would be doing something extremely pleasing to the king, and that Edward would reward him and Hugh would increase this reward to such an extent that 'you will deem your work well worth it.' Hugh's preoccupation with Lewer is apparent from the many lines he devoted to him in the letter, and when he wrote that he wanted him and his adherents destroyed, he meant it literally. He also told Inge that he was following up the matter of Iscennen, a manor in Carmarthenshire forfeited by his executed rival John Giffard, and on 6 November 1322 the king, inevitably, granted Iscennen and its magnificent castle of Carreg Cennen built by Giffard's father to Hugh. [43] This was a useful gift as it enabled Hugh to link Cantref Mawr with Gower and Glamorgan. [44]

Hugh was a hard man to please and serving him was a thankless task, and the letter included not particularly amiable phrases such as 'we do not wish to receive any excuse from you' and 'understand for certain that if any disgrace or damage happens to us [in Glamorgan], we will proceed against you.' He also wrote seemingly casually in the middle of the letter before he moved on to Lewer:

> 'And know that we trust you more the more you advise us, but we are very worried about having some reason for which we might be prepared to harm you in some way, or for which we might lose the good will which we have for you.'

This threatening missive is the last known letter Hugh sent to him, though Inge was still in his favour on 6 December 1322. [45] At some point probably in 1323, Hugh went so far as to imprison John Inge in Southwark prison because of 'his rancour towards him.' He made Inge and six guarantors promise to pay him a ransom of £300 for Inge's release, and they had handed over £200 of it by the time of Hugh's death. Inge acknowledged a debt of £400 to Hugh on 6 July 1323, either as his ransom or for another reason, and he and three others acknowledged a joint debt to him of over £236 on the same day. [46] Hugh and the king were in York on 6 July 1323, though had spent the period from 25 March to 25 April in and around London. Other than the acknowledgement of these debts to Hugh, Inge does not appear on record after 23 March 1323 until 21 November that year. [47] John Inge was pardoned at the beginning of Edward III's reign in 1327 for having adhered to Hugh, though it would hardly be surprising if he breathed a sigh of relief at the latter's downfall and execution. [48] In 1338 Inge took part in a commission of *oyer et terminer* with Hugh's son Huchon, lord of Glamorgan, regarding a break-in at a manor of Hugh's sister Alina Burnell. [49] He was lucky to have survived: Hugh also imprisoned a man called Thomas Langdon because he was a member of Inge's council, and Langdon died in prison. A petition about Langdon also talks of Hugh's 'anger' towards John Inge, though what the poor man had done wrong is uncertain; whatever it was, Hugh punished his associates for it too. [50] Inge's messenger to Hugh, bearing letters to which Hugh's long last letter was the response, was Thomas Shirugg of Devon. [51] It may not be a coincidence that Shirugg was imprisoned at Pontefract Castle sometime before 1 October 1323 and appeared before Hugh's ally Robert Baldock in chancery on 13 October, when he was released on recognition of a debt of £200 to the king. [52] It is easy to understand why many people, even the great English magnates, were scared of Hugh, and he had the levers of government at his disposal to make good on his threats. If this was the way he treated people who gave him years of faithful service, one can only imagine how he treated those unlucky enough to be deemed his enemies.

Chapter 11

Magical and Secret Dealings

Apply yourself to procuring, encouraging and protecting the honour of our lord the king, to the detriment of his enemies, in every way you can, because in doing so you will find the much heavy and deadened hearts of several people pricked to action and awakened.

Edward attempted an invasion of Scotland in the late summer of 1322 which predictably failed utterly, and the king suffered a personal loss when his teenage illegitimate son Adam died during the campaign and was buried at Tynemouth Priory on 30 September. Adam was born when Edward was in his early to mid-20s, around 1305 to 1310, to a mother whose identity is unknown to historians. [1] Robert Bruce launched a counter-invasion of England, and took Edward completely by surprise while he was staying at Rievaulx Abbey 30 miles north of York in mid-October 1322. Edward's cousin the earl of Richmond, John of Brittany, lost the battle of Byland nearby and was captured. Edward, with his half-brother Edmund of Woodstock, earl of Kent, Hugh, and John, Lord Cromwell among others, had to flee, most humiliatingly, for Bridlington on the coast, leaving many of his precious goods behind at Rievaulx. [2] The appreciative Scots kept them. John Cromwell had been one of the knights who fled with Edward after Bannockburn, and it is hardly surprising that he later joined Queen Isabella when she rebelled. [3]

The king's latest military failure also almost led to disaster for Queen Isabella, who was staying at Tynemouth Priory far to the north of her husband's position. Somewhat inexplicably, she remained there even after the Scottish forces had come into England rather than leave for the safety of York, and came quite close to capture herself; she and her household had to sail down the coast to avoid the Scottish forces, and according to one French chronicle, two of her female attendants died during the flight (though no English chronicler mentions the incident). Isabella blamed Hugh for her predicament, though Hugh's wife Eleanor was with her at the time and even if he cared little for the queen's safety, he would hardly have deliberately put his wife in danger. [4] Isabella was angry and distressed, and even a few years later was still blaming Hugh for 'falsely and treacherously counselling the king to leave my lady the queen in peril of her person.' Eleanor Despenser herself remained on perfectly good terms with her husband and evidently did not blame him, and they conceived another child shortly after the debacle.

Defiantly, Edward made Hugh 'superior keeper' of the castles of Gloucester and St Briavels and of the Forest of Dean in Gloucestershire on 2 November 1322, as though rubbing his wife's nose in his affection for the other man and his refusal to accept Hugh's culpability for Isabella's predicament. [5] Edward had made Roger Damory keeper of these places in October 1317 and June 1318; Hugh's chief rival for the king's affections was now dead, and Hugh held his former positions and his (or rather Elizabeth Burgh's) rich lordship of Usk. [6] His triumph over his foe was complete. Parliament was supposed to begin in York on 14 November 1322, but Edward and Hugh arrived a week late. Given the latest humiliation of the king's near-capture at Rievaulx and the expensive failure of his campaign in Scotland, he probably dreaded facing Parliament, and travelled to York very unhurriedly. Edward hated attending parliaments at the best of times and often arrived late, and in May 1322 specifically asked his councillors to 'set free the people coming to parliament as soon as possible.' [7] The *Vita* commented in about 1325 that 'parliaments, colloquies and councils decide nothing these days…whatever pleases the king, though lacking in reason, has the force of law.' [8] Edward only wanted a compliant group of men to agree with whatever decisions he and Hugh had already made.

Eleanor Despenser gave birth on or just before 2 August 1323, so she must have been in the company of her husband around this time to conceive their child, not long after she had been with the queen at Tynemouth. Edward spent 20 November standing by a river near Doncaster 35 miles south of York, watching men fish, and paid 30 shillings for wax for Hugh's household. After this pleasant little interlude while dozens of men waited for him to appear before Parliament, the king and Hugh went to Cawood, a manor of the archbishop of York – who was William Melton, a close friend and ally of Edward – and from there travelled into the city of York by water. Edward gave 100 shillings as a gift to John Bentley, keeper of Hugh's 'great horses', for his diligence in looking after them in Kelfield. [9] That Hugh now owned great horses is a measure of his wealth; in the years when he had only a small income from five of his father's manors, he could never have afforded them, and in 1311 was reduced to stealing his wife's sumpter-horses, i.e. packhorses. Among Hugh's possessions in Glamorgan stolen by the Contrariants in May 1321 were 40 destriers or war-horses, or so he claimed. [10] Destriers were hugely expensive, and this is the medieval equivalent of owning 40 high-performance sports cars. Edward's own great horses accompanied them by water from Cawood to York, and on 4 December 1322 he gave Hugh 'the king's stud' in seven towns in Wales and England. [11] While in York Edward gave 100 shillings to his eldest great-nephew, Hugh and Eleanor's first son Huchon, 'to buy himself various necessities.' [12] Edward had sent Huchon, now 13 or 14, to take 'fat venison' in the royal forests, parks and chases in 23 counties in July and October 1322. [13] The king and presumably Hugh and Eleanor left York on 5 December and travelled to the royal manor of Cowick; on this day Edward gave his almoner Richard Bliton, a Carmelite friar who may already have been Hugh's confessor (and certainly was by 1325) eight shillings and four pence to feed 50 poor women. On another occasion, the king gave six pence each in alms to 40 'poor pregnant women' in London. [14]

The renegade Robert Lewer was still at large on 28 November 1322 when Edward heard that he had plundered the king's own manor of Itchel in Hampshire and had tried to seize control of Odiham Castle, where Hugh had formerly been constable. [15] Good news came on 19 December that Lewer had finally been captured. [16] He refused to plead and so was subjected to the terrible ordeal inflicted on those who did so, *peine forte et dure*: being slowly crushed to death. He died on 26 December 1322. [17] Edward later granted Lewer's manor of Westbury, Hampshire to Hugh's youngest sister Elizabeth and her husband Ralph Camoys, to pass to their son Hugh Camoys. [18] Also on 19 December 1322, Edward received letters from Queen Isabella – their relationship may have been deteriorating after she was left at Tynemouth, but they did at least keep in touch – and gave 20 shillings to Richard Bliton to distribute for the soul of Hugh's barber Robert Torksey, 'who has been commanded to God.' [19] Christmas 1322 was spent at York, though Queen Isabella was most probably not with her husband. On 23 December, the king announced that his wife was 'going on pilgrimage to diverse places throughout the realm,' and on the 26th gave a safe-conduct to her clerk William Boudon who was going to the great pilgrim site of Santiago de Compostela in northern Spain on her behalf to fulfil a vow the queen had made. [20] The tale of the pilgrimage around England appears to be a fabrication, as Isabella was living in the Tower of London for least some of the period January to March 1323 and not visiting shrines, and may be a cover story to hide a crisis in the royal marriage: that Isabella had angrily left her husband's company or that Edward had ordered her away. It is not clear when she took the vow to go to Santiago, but perhaps it reveals that she was so livid with Edward for taking Hugh's side over the Tynemouth affair that she swore to leave the country during a quarrel. Edward and Hugh, as far as the latter's itinerary can be determined, were always together during this period and long afterwards which can only have angered and upset the queen. Whether it was fair or reasonable for Isabella to blame Hugh for Tynemouth, she certainly did and it was still preying on her mind even four years later, so that her husband's insistence on keeping Hugh constantly with him surely felt like a deep betrayal to her. Isabella had always been active in politics and was a frequent intercessor with her husband, but after 1322 rarely appears on record, and Hugh's influence with the king was a major cause. The two men stayed in Yorkshire for most of the first three months of 1323, and on 7 January listened to four musicians playing 'interludes' for them in the hall at the royal manor of Cowick. Edward spent three shillings playing dice on the same day. [21] This sounds like a very pleasant and relaxing occasion, except that also on this day the king seized his niece Elizabeth Burgh's English lands because she and her household had fled from his angry threats. [22]

Elizabeth's sister Eleanor Despenser, about three and a half months pregnant, was attending Queen Isabella at the Tower of London on 17 February 1323 when they sent near-identical letters on behalf of Joan Mortimer née Geneville, asking that the allowance owed to her by the Exchequer be paid promptly. [23] On 5 March Eleanor's uncle the king ordered 'various horses' of hers to be transported from Knaresborough (where he and Hugh were) to London, so presumably she was still with Isabella. [24] Eleanor and the queen appear to have been on excellent terms; Isabella would hardly have kept Eleanor as her attendant for so many years if she had not thoroughly enjoyed her company, and whatever rage and loathing the queen felt for Hugh, she still voluntarily kept his wife close to her even after Tynemouth, and the two women continued to spend much time together. Eleanor's sisters Margaret and Elizabeth never acted as the queen's attendants, whereas Eleanor did so regularly, as far as can be ascertained, from 1310 or earlier until 1325. Edward II's other adult niece, Jeanne de Bar, countess of Surrey, accompanied Isabella to France in March 1325, but seems not to have attended the queen otherwise. Eleanor Despenser was in charge of the household of her cousin John of Eltham (born August 1316), younger son of the king and queen, at least on occasion, starting on 3 July 1322 or earlier. [25] One writer in the late 1970s invented a story that Edward and Hugh cruelly removed Queen Isabella's children from her in September 1324 when the king confiscated her estates, but this is untrue. [26] It is often assumed that the queen loathed Eleanor Despenser because the latter helped her husband and uncle take away her children and was appointed as a kind of jailer and spy over her in 1324, but there is no reason to suppose this is true, nor that Isabella was anything but perfectly happy for Eleanor to take care of her second son sometimes. If she was not, she had plenty of time to protest before she left England in March 1325, given that Eleanor had been appointed to the position in July 1322 or earlier.

Both the king and queen enjoyed Eleanor's company which suggests that she was pleasant and entertaining, and good fun to be around. The king certainly enjoyed Hugh's, and doubtless Hugh was more than capable of turning on the charm when necessary, though also demonstrated extreme callousness towards anyone who did not please him or who had what he wanted, and could be a difficult man to get on with. Edward owned a ship named after his niece, *La Alianore la Despensere*, which is mentioned between 1323 and 1325, as well as another one called *La Despenser* in Hugh's honour. *La Despenser* was supposedly a gift from Hugh to Edward, but the £130 cost came out of Edward's own purse. The king did not have any ships named after his other nieces or his sisters, or even, for that matter, his children (he did have one called *La Isabele* after the queen). Edward was hugely fond of Eleanor to the point where one Flemish chronicler even claimed they were lovers – supposedly Hugh gave his wife to the king for sex – and that Eleanor was imprisoned in late 1326 in case she was pregnant by Edward. [27] It is impossible to know whether this is true or not, and as the relationship would have been incestuous we should give them the benefit of the doubt in the absence of any firm evidence, but their closeness as demonstrated by Edward's accounts over the years and especially in the 1320s can lead one to understand how some people might have thought uncle and niece were lovers. In Edward's extant chamber accounts Eleanor is the only woman besides the queen assigned the honorific title *ma dame*, 'my lady'. Her cousin the countess of Surrey, also a niece of the king, Edward's sister-in-law the countess of Norfolk, and his daughters were not called *ma dame*. [28] Eleanor's itinerary in the late 1310s and 1320s can only rarely be established, but where her location is known it coincided either with the queen's or (much more often) with Hugh's and the king's, or at least she was just a few miles from them and they kept in touch with her and sent gifts. Edward often gave Eleanor large sums of money, and on 1 November 1324 and 3 December 1325 she sent him gifts of clothes which seems oddly intimate. [29]

There is no evidence that Eleanor disapproved of her husband's behaviour in the 1320s, even towards her sister Elizabeth Burgh, and the couple spent much time together. Hugh and Eleanor seem to have had significant physical desire for one another, as they had at least 10 children born over a period of about 16 or 17 years and continued sleeping together and producing offspring for many years after they had produced the requisite 'heir and the spare'. At least four of their children were born in and after 1320, after Hugh became the royal favourite. We do not and cannot know for sure whether Edward and Hugh had a physical relationship, though it seems beyond doubt that Edward loved Hugh, and it would hardly seem surprising if they did go to bed together. Queen Isabella's statement in 1325 that Hugh had come between her husband

and herself and was trying to break their marriage bond strongly implies that she believed their relationship to be intimate. Hugh's feelings, given that he gained so much from his familiarity with the king, are impossible to ascertain; whether he loved Edward as his sexual and romantic partner, or genuinely cared for him as a good, loyal and extremely useful friend, or was using him in a calculating manner for power and wealth, is difficult to say.

Andrew Harclay, earl of Carlisle, was growing ever more impatient and frustrated with Edward II's inability to protect the north of England or to resolve the Scottish situation, and in early 1323 met Robert Bruce without any authorisation and negotiated a peace settlement. Although it is easy to sympathise with Harclay's frustration, there was no doubt this was treason, and on 3 March 1323 the unfortunate man suffered the traitor's death at Carlisle which he had staunchly defended against Scottish raids for many years. He had been earl of the town for less than a year. The St Albans chronicler says that Harclay hated Hugh which cannot have helped his situation; if he had cultivated Hugh as an ally, doubtless the chamberlain and royal favourite could have saved his life. Not long after Harclay's atrocious execution, Edward himself negotiated a 13-year peace settlement with Robert Bruce. Several of Bruce's envoys came to England, and Hugh's eldest son Huchon was one of the noblemen sent to Scotland as a sort of hostage to assure Bruce of the safe return of his envoy and kinsman Thomas Randolph, earl of Moray. The others included Thomas, Lord Wake, John, Lord Hastings (stepson of Hugh's sister Isabella), and Henry, Lord Percy. [30] At Bishopthorpe near York on 30 May 1323, the treaty was finalised by Edward and his council, including Hugh.

Hugh's nemesis Roger Mortimer of Wigmore escaped from the Tower of London on 1 August 1323, and fled to the continent. Mortimer sent assassins into England later in 1323 to kill Edward's 'counsellors', meaning Hugh and his father, Edmund Fitzalan the earl of Arundel, and probably Hugh's protégé Robert Baldock, now treasurer of England. [31] Edward retaliated in early 1324 by sending three of Mortimer's eight daughters to convents, though they were not veiled as nuns, with a pittance for each to live on, and Mortimer's wife Joan remained under house arrest for the rest of the reign. Mortimer and his uncle Mortimer of Chirk had been condemned to death in 1322, but Edward commuted the sentence to life imprisonment. As Hugh loathed both men and had sworn revenge on them for the death of his grandfather at the battle of Evesham almost 60 years earlier, Edward's decision to spare them was certainly against his own wishes, and demonstrates that Hugh did not always get his way with the king. And now one of the most dangerous Contrariants was at large. Edward at Kirkham in Yorkshire heard of Mortimer's escape five days later, on

6 August; Hugh was almost certainly with him. The news threw them into deep alarm, and the king made attempts to recapture Mortimer, but it was too late.

Eleanor Despenser gave birth to another child on or just before 2 August 1323 (perhaps even on the day of Mortimer's escape) at Cowick, on which date the king gave £100 to Hugh's clerk Godfrey Rudham for the expenses of 'her childbed'. [32] This infant was almost certainly the Despensers' fourth daughter Margaret, who on 1 March 1327 was said to have lived for more than three years with Thomas Houk with a nurse and a great household. [33] Sir Thomas Houk(e), Huke or Hook was a knight of Yorkshire. [34] The timing fits – the girl must have gone to her new home not too long after birth – and Thomas Houk's manor of Hook lay about eight miles from Cowick, so this fits too. As well as often paying for Hugh and Eleanor's household items and frequently giving them hugely generous gifts of cash even after they became rich – £100 in 1323 is several hundred thousand in today's money – the king also sometimes paid the expenses of their eldest daughter Isabella, who turned 11 in 1323. [35] On Wednesday, 1 June 1323, Pope John XXII issued a dispensation for the future marriage of Hugh and Eleanor's second daughter Joan Despenser and John FitzGerald, eldest son of the earl of Kildare in Ireland and yet another grandson of Richard Burgh, earl of Ulster. [36] John was born in 1314 and was probably about the same age as his fiancée, but died later in 1323 before the wedding took place, and Joan became a nun probably in 1327 after her father's execution. The Despensers' third daughter Eleanor was betrothed to Laurence Hastings (born 1321), future earl of Pembroke, in 1325, a marriage which did not take place either. In April 1325 Hugh's sister Isabella Hastings was said to be the *mestresse* of her niece Eleanor, meaning the woman in charge of her household, and Eleanor was looked after by Lady Hastings' damsel Margaret Costantyn. [37] Isabella Hastings was also in charge of the household of the king's daughters Eleanor of Woodstock (born 1318) and Joan of the Tower (born 1321), who presumably were at least partly raised with their cousin Eleanor.

Although Hugh did not know it until later, a meeting took place in Coventry on 30 November 1323 when 27 merchants and craftsmen went to visit a famous necromancer of the town called John of Nottingham. According to the testimony of the necromancer's assistant Robert Marshall, they complained that they could no longer tolerate the harshness which the prior of Coventry was imposing on them with the support of the king and the two Hugh Despensers. They asked John of Nottingham to kill Edward II, Hugh and his father, the prior of Coventry, and two of the prior's servants. They promised him a huge sum of money to do so, £35, and a week later paid the first instalment. On Monday, 12 December 1323, Nottingham and his assistant Marshall went to an 'old house' half a league from Coventry, having purchased seven pounds of wax and two ells of canvas to form images of the men (the king's bore a crown). For the next six months, they worked their magic there on a wax image of a local resident called Richard Sowe, presumably as a test case, and one Friday night in June 1324 drove a sharpened feather two inches into the forehead of Sowe's image. When they went to his house the next day, the unfortunate Sowe had gone out of his mind and was unable to recognise anyone, and could only cry out *Harrou!*, an expression of distress in fourteenth-century English. Some days later when Nottingham and Marshall plunged the sharpened feather into Sowe's image where the heart would be, he died. Before they could attempt to murder Edward, Hugh and his father, however, the assistant Robert Marshall was seized by an attack of conscience and gave the game away to the authorities. The case was heard before the coroner of Edward's household on Wednesday 31 October 1324, and John of Nottingham was to die in prison. [38]

It appears that Edward, although he could be superstitious and even gullible in matters of religion, laughed this off, but Hugh took it seriously enough to write to the pope complaining that he was 'threatened by magical and secret dealings.' John XXII wrote the notably unsympathetic response that Hugh should 'turn to God with his whole heart and make a good confession,' and that no other remedy was necessary. [39] This was perhaps a result of Hugh's extortion of various English bishops: on 8 August 1324, he extorted the staggeringly large sum of £1,000 from John Stratford, new bishop of Winchester and a future archbishop of Canterbury. This was mere weeks before the pope wrote to Hugh about the magical dealings. Two years later Stratford acknowledged a debt of £2,000 to Hugh, who was livid, as was Edward, that his ally Robert Baldock had not been elected to Stratford's bishopric of Winchester. Stratford was also forced to acknowledge an impossibly large debt of £10,000 to Edward. [40] Roger Northburgh, bishop of Coventry and Lichfield, one of the three men with whom Hugh had devised the Household Ordinance in 1318, gave Hugh £100 in November 1324, and on another occasion paid him £376. [41] Hugh demanded 1,000 marks from John Eaglescliff, bishop of Llandaff, in order for him to be allowed to enter into his new diocese, though in fact Eaglescliff never paid it. Even though Eaglescliff was a Dominican friar and Edward II was a huge supporter of the Dominicans (and vice versa), the king also demanded the money from him, or so the bishop claimed. [42] John XXII often sent letters to Hugh in the 1320s, asking him to intercede with the king: in Avignon the favourite's power at the English court was well known, and in January 1324 the pope wrote to Hugh 'as one able to influence the king.' [43] Edward was feuding with several of his bishops, notably Henry Burghersh of Lincoln, who was the executed Bartholomew Badlesmere's nephew, and Adam Orleton of Hereford, whom the king accused of supporting the Mortimers in 1321/22. He asked

John XXII to translate them to offices outside England; John refused, and asked Hugh to persuade the king to reconcile with the men.

Edward II spent Christmas 1323 and New Year 1324 at Kenilworth Castle in Warwickshire, presumably with both Queen Isabella and Hugh (who was certainly there with the king on 30 December and 2 January). For a few days in January 1324, the king and perhaps the queen were guests of Hugh at his Worcestershire castle of Hanley, where the king himself was paying for repairs and restoration after it had been sacked by the Marchers in May 1321; he spent more than £1,500. During this visit, the king gave a bonus of two pounds to 12 carpenters for building a new perimeter wall, drawbridge and hall, described as the 'finest in the land.' [44] Edward and presumably Hugh also visited Gloucester, where Edward would one day be buried in St Peter's Abbey (now Gloucester Cathedral), and nearby Tewkesbury, a manor belonging to Hugh and Eleanor and where they and several of their descendants would be buried in the abbey. Hugh's brother-in-law the earl of Gloucester had been interred there in 1314, and Edward placed a green and gold cloth on his tomb.

Sometime after the visit to Hanley, a man called John Steven sent a petition directly to Hugh, addressing him as 'the noble and wise man, Sir Hugh Despenser'. He asked to be pardoned for 'certain trespasses' he had committed, because he had served the king's justices for four days and delivered their verdicts at Hanley while Edward was visiting. Sadly, Hugh's intercession with Edward failed (assuming he ever tried), and Edward refused to pardon John Steven. The justices were trying to ascertain who had been responsible for burning Hanley Castle during the Despenser War in May 1321. [45] Royal justices had also been ordered to investigate a break-in and theft at Hugh's manor of Frampton in Lincolnshire when all his manors were in the king's hands in 1321/22. One member of the gang of thieves was Richard of Furness, parson of the church of Frampton, who did not appear before the court when summoned and was outlawed. Edward withdrew the sentence of outlawry against Richard of Furness on 9 April 1324, because he 'has satisfied Hugh for the trespasses, as Hugh has testified personally before the king.' [46] One dreads to think what Hugh demanded from the parson to 'satisfy' him for the break-in and theft. Another of the gang was a knight called Roger Pedwardyn, who on 12 April 1325 acknowledged a debt of 40 pounds to Hugh, and another was Ascolf or Hasculph Whitewell, who himself often acted as a royal justice and in later years was the attorney of Edward III's wife Queen Philippa (c. 1314–69). [47]

Trouble was brewing in 1324. Edward's brother-in-law Philip V of France had died on 2 January 1322 at the age of only 30, and was succeeded by Charles IV, the third and last of Queen Isabella's brothers. Edward now owed homage to his overlord for his French lands of Gascony and Ponthieu, yet again. Charles courteously invited him to present himself in France for this purpose between April and July 1324, but Edward made excuses and did not go. A series of mishaps and the French king's annoyance with his brother-in-law led to Charles IV ordering his uncle Charles de Valois to invade Gascony in August 1324, and Edward found himself at war with France, a short and little-known conflict known as the War of Saint-Sardos. His cousin Aymer Valence, earl of Pembroke, went to the French court as an envoy shortly before war broke out, but died suddenly on 23 June 1324 before he could reach Paris. As Pembroke left no legitimate children from either of his marriages, his heirs were his nephew John, Lord Hastings and his nieces the Comyn sisters Joan, countess of Atholl and Elizabeth. [48] Elizabeth became Hugh's next victim.

Elizabeth Comyn stated later that even before her uncle Pembroke's death, Hugh Despenser the Younger moved against her. In about April 1324, she said, he captured her at the manor of Kennington in Surrey with his father the earl of Winchester (who had been granted Kennington by the king on 4 April 1322) and the help of Sir Nicholas Sudington, William Staunford and John Hasselegh. On another occasion, however, Elizabeth claimed to have been captured at Hertingfordbury in Hertfordshire which was her own manor. [49] This mix-up is hard to explain; Elizabeth must have known whether she was captured at a manor she herself owned or one of the elder Despenser's. The Despensers took her firstly to Woking and then to Pirbright, two Surrey manors which also belonged to Hugh the Elder. There, Elizabeth stated later, they kept her in captivity for a year or more until 20 April 1325, when she finally agreed to grant her manors of Painswick and Goodrich Castle to the elder and the younger Hugh respectively after they threatened that she would never leave prison unless she did so. She was then kept imprisoned for another half year until October 1325, and finally released. On 6 April 1325 she was given permission by the king to grant Goodrich Castle and Painswick to Hugh and his father, and on 20 April at Pirbright she duly released the manors to the two men. On 8 March, she had acknowledged a huge debt of £10,000 to the elder Hugh. [50]

Elizabeth also released her Kent manor of Swanscombe to Edward II, and the deed was witnessed by Hugh the Younger and Elder and their close ally Sir Ingelram Berenger. Edward gave it to the two Hughs on 5 July 1325. [51] Even the king colluded in Elizabeth's disinheritance and mistreatment, and his itinerary puts him at Pirbright on 6 and 9 August 1324; he must have known Elizabeth was being held there. One small bright spot came out of this deeply unpleasant situation: Hugh the Younger's household knight Sir Richard Talbot 'secretly married' Elizabeth at Pirbright. (The couple became the ancestors of the later Talbot earls of Shrewsbury.) Talbot was in Gascony between August and November 1324 or later, was in England on 11 July 1325, had returned to Gascony by 4 November, and was back in England by 27 December 1325. [52] It seems likely that he saw Elizabeth in captivity at Pirbright either before he left for Gascony in 1324 or in the spring or summer of 1325, and the couple kept their marriage hidden for a good few months: on 9 July 1326, Edward gave Talbot a gift of 10 marks because he was 'very poor' and because he had secretly married Elizabeth. [53] The king had clearly just found out about it. Hugh lent Talbot – lent, not gave, typically of him – another 10 pounds on 17 July. [54] Their gift and loan of money to Talbot might be a sign of a guilty conscience, at least on the king's part; whether Hugh was capable of guilt and remorse is uncertain. On 21 August 1324, Elizabeth Comyn's cousin and the earl of Pembroke's co-heir John, Lord Hastings acknowledged that he owed Hugh £4,000, and two days later Hugh acknowledged that he owed Hastings £1,000. [55] The reasons behind this are unclear, but given Hugh's dealings with the Pembroke heirs, he is likely to have had some nefarious motive (though he is not known to have taken any action against Elizabeth Comyn's sister and brother-in-law Joan and David Strathbogie, earl and countess of Atholl). John Hastings died in early 1325, and custody of his lands and his four-year-old son Laurence was, inevitably, given to Hugh on 12 February. Hugh betrothed Laurence (his sister Isabella's step-grandson) to his third daughter Eleanor by 27 July 1325. [56] John Hastings' executors complained after Hugh's downfall that he had ransacked the goods on Hastings' lands to a value of more than £773 and left hardly anything behind, and that he owed them £1,000. [57] During the minority of Laurence Hastings, Hugh held the county palatine of Pembroke and the lordships of Abergavenny and Cilgerran, and he also held the lordship of Brecon during the minority of Edward's nephew John Bohun, heir to the earldom of Hereford. Hugh now ruled over virtually all of South Wales, from Pembroke to Chepstow. [58]

The royal favourite's greed was insatiable. By the time of his downfall in late 1326, Hugh held estates worth over £7,150 a year, and thus was even wealthier than his enormously rich brother-in-law the earl of Gloucester had been. Even this huge figure is incomplete as the income from his Welsh lands is impossible to calculate, and they were far more extensive than his English estates. He owned goods worth over £3,000 on his English lands alone. [59] By 18 November 1321 he was already rich enough to have deposited £2,170 with the Italian banking firm the Bardi, and between March and mid-November 1324 deposited at least £4,122 with the Bardi and another banking firm called the Peruzzi. By the end of 1324 he had close to £6,000 on deposit with the Peruzzi alone, and withdrew almost £2,000 from his bankers between 31 October and 14 November 1324 and another £1,000 on 3 December that year. [60] By early April 1324, the king owed Hugh £1,325 and Hugh owed the king £2,244. [61] At some date, two merchants transported '15 iron-bound barrels full of gold and silver of the treasure of Sir Hugh Despenser' in a ship from the Tower of London to Hull, though to what purpose is unclear. [62] In modern terms, Hugh was a multi-millionaire. In March 1324 he was able to make a loan of £400 to Hugh the Elder, and in May 1325 lent his sister Isabella Hastings 100 marks. [63] Even when it came to close family he made loans, not gifts to them which is quite revealing of his character.

For all his wealth, Hugh paid his bills tardily: the chamberlain of South Wales had to petition the king for 60 pounds he had paid to the keepers of Hugh's castles at Dinefwr and Dryslwyn after the Despenser War, but had received no recompense from Hugh. One of Edward's clerks, perhaps rather nervously, endorsed the petition 'to be sent to Sir Hugh Despenser so that he might advise himself of the contents.' [64] Hugh paid the 208 marks he owed to the executors of William Huntingfield in June 1325, also extremely tardily given that Huntingfield had died in September 1313. [65] In April 1324, Hugh had not yet paid the 'relief', i.e. a kind of inheritance tax, on Eleanor's lands given to them in November 1317. [66] And by 1326 he owed Queen Isabella £1,200 from the revenues of Bristol for the previous six years, but never paid her a penny. [67]

When even a woman who was the granddaughter and niece of kings (Elizabeth Burgh), and another who was the great-niece of two kings (Elizabeth Comyn, of Henry III and John Balliol), could be treated in such fashion, clearly people farther down the social scale were even more vulnerable to Hugh's machinations. To detail all his extortions and crimes would require several chapters, but here are a mere handful of examples to give a flavour of his methods, in addition to others cited throughout the book. I have chosen petitions which are supported by other evidence, or which date to Hugh's own lifetime and are thus likely to be true. Quite a lot of petitions about Hugh mention his 'great lordship', and not only he, but members of his retinue and his close circle such as his brother-in-law Ralph Camoys and his steward John Botiller were complained about. Under the protection of his 'great lordship', his men often felt they could do whatever they liked – and indeed they could, as no-one stopped them.

William Dawtrey of Yorkshire presented a petition *c.* 1323. He was an adherent of the king's executed cousin Thomas of Lancaster, and 'because the said William was in [Lancaster's] company, the people of the king and the people of Sir Hugh Despenser the son, by order of the said Sir Hugh, arrested the said William and took him to Ripon, and imprisoned him there.' Revealingly, not only did Hugh command the king's men as well as his own – Hugh himself wrote in March 1321 that 'we will send some of the king's men and our own' to his castles in Glamorgan if necessary – Dawtrey stated that he had made a fine for his release 'with the king and with Sir Hugh.' [68] Claiming that men had been adherents of Thomas of Lancaster and taking their lands was a common Despenser tactic which Hugh the Elder also used, for example, to seize two manors from Nicholas Plescy. [69]

Sir John Botetourt wrote to Hugh the Younger between March 1322 and March 1323, addressing him as 'the very honourable and wise lord, Sir Hugh Despenser the son' and asking for his help in a dispute with the exchequer over his Buckinghamshire manor of Iselhampstead, now called Chenies. According to a later petition, Hugh stated that Botetourt had been an adherent of Thomas of Lancaster and one of the men who forced him into exile, and 'by his royal power' forced Botetourt to sign Chenies over to him. On Saturday, 26 March 1323, Hugh sent John Botetourt a letter ordering him to attend a personal meeting with him and the king at Langley, Hertfordshire 'this Monday morning and not before' (which was Easter Monday, 28 March) to discuss how he could put right some violation Botetourt had allegedly committed and was continuing to commit against Hugh. Chenies lies only five miles from Langley, so Hugh was deliberately giving Botetourt plenty of time to worry what the king and his chamberlain might do to him.

Hugh declared that Chenies must be handed over to him as part of Botetourt's restitution for the wrong he had done him, and because Edward wished Hugh to have the manor. He added 'the king can hang and draw you' because Botetourt had received his son John the younger – pardoned for adherence to Bartholomew Badlesmere on 16 February 1323 – and followed up this not entirely subtle threat with 'May God keep you,' a conventional ending to a letter, but almost absurdly out of place in the context. Another insight into Hugh's character is revealed by his statement 'we requested that we might make known to you when it would be time to talk to the king,' i.e. he wished to be the one to send the letter ordering Botetourt to come to Edward and himself in two days. He seems to have revelled in his sinister reputation and taken satisfaction in scaring people he believed had injured him. That he asked Edward if he might do this, and that Edward agreed, also reveals something about their relationship.

John Botetourt might be forgiven if he quaked in his boots when he went to meet Hugh and Edward, and coincidentally or not, this was exactly the time when Hugh seems to have imprisoned John Inge and his council. Late March 1323 was the first time Hugh and Edward had come south since the campaign against the Contrariants a year before (and they returned to the north of England in late April), so perhaps Hugh was taking his first real opportunity to avenge himself on those he deemed his enemies or felt had let him down. John

Botetourt died on 25 November 1324 – presumably of natural causes as he and his wife were born in the 1260s – and Hugh wrote to the keepers of Edward's great seal on 1 December, asking them to do what they could to expedite his widow Maud's affairs. With Hugh's usual sarcasm, this letter called the late John 'our dear friend,' and he called Maud 'our beloved lady' (*nostre bien amee dame*), though probably meant this more sincerely. The first letter demonstrates again that Hugh was not shy about threatening people with terrible punishment and that the king did his bidding in all matters, and the second, much more surprisingly, that he was capable of kind consideration towards the widow of his victim. Chenies was in his possession at the time of his downfall, and a week after his execution Queen Isabella made Maud its keeper. [70]

Hugh's wife Eleanor and their third son Gilbert also benefited from one of his schemes. In July 1322 Edward had granted the manors of Melton Mowbray and Crick, forfeited by John, Lord Mowbray, to Eleanor, to pass to Gilbert after her death, and in November 1325 Eleanor was addressed as 'lady of Melton Mowbray'. [71] A John Deyville owned 20 pounds of rent in Melton and Crick for life as a gift of John Mowbray, and at Nottingham on 26 December 1324, released those rents to Eleanor and Gilbert. [72] Deyville stated later that he had been imprisoned at the Tower of London by Hugh until he agreed to do this, and indeed he is mentioned as a prisoner there on 27 June 1324. [73] Alice Danvers complained between 1322 and 1326 about a William Horewode 'of the household of the king and Sir Hugh Despenser the son,' a telling phrase which demonstrates Edward and Hugh's extraordinary closeness (and almost makes them sound like a married couple). Horewode came to her manor of Werham with Richard Okelond and 100 armed men, threw Alice out of her home, and stole her goods. He later returned bearing Hugh's letters which prevented Alice's return to her home, and Hugh gave his father's long-term adherent Ingelram Berenger her manor. A Hugh Hanford made the same complaint about Hugh, Horewode, Okelond and Berenger regarding his manor of Stratfield Turgis, Hampshire, also in or before 1326. [74]

Frisot Montclar and his brother Totte were the keepers of the former Knights Templar manor of Temple Guiting in Gloucestershire, appointed to this position by Thomas, earl of Lancaster in or before 1316. (The brothers were wine merchants from Lucca in Italy and moved to England in 1294 or earlier.) [75] On 13 April 1322 three weeks after Lancaster's execution, the king confirmed Frisot and Totte as keepers of Temple Guiting for life at a rent of 50 pounds a year, and that November received an instalment of 25 pounds from Frisot. [76] Hugh seized the manor from Frisot and Totte two years after Lancaster's execution 'by his great power and lordship,' and took all their goods from Guiting to a value of more than £100. They had to wait until the reign of

Edward's son to seek restitution, though did not get it. [77] Hugh and the king were in Gloucestershire in January 1324 and were certainly close to Temple Guiting, and this would more or less fit the timing of the Montclar brothers' complaint that Hugh took it two years after Lancaster's execution. The manor was officially granted to Hugh by the prior of the Hospital of St John in Jerusalem on 28 June 1324, no doubt with some coercion, some months after he had unofficially occupied it. [78] Various entries in the chancery rolls call Frisot Montclar the 'king's valet' or 'king's merchant', and he had been Edward's receiver in the Agenais, in Gascony. Edward had been staying at Guiting on 21 February 1322 shortly before Hugh officially came back from exile, when he gave Frisot 'permission to attend to his own affairs' rather than take part in the campaign against the Contrariants. [79] Frisot seems to have been in royal favour, but this did not protect him and his brother from Hugh. Possibly also when Edward and Hugh were in Gloucestershire and Worcestershire in early 1324, Hugh imprisoned a man called Henry Cowley in Gloucester for taking venison from his chase at Malvern, later removed him to prison in Hereford, and forced him to acknowledge a debt of 100 marks to secure his release. [80]

Another petition was presented by Thomas Bishopstone, and is supported by the record of an order from the king to his sergeant Simon Croyser to arrest Bishopstone on 1 June 1324. [81] Bishopstone stated later that one Roger Lumbard (evidently from northern Italy) told Hugh maliciously that Bishopstone was an enemy of the king and an adherent of Adam Orleton, bishop of Hereford, with whom Edward and Hugh were feuding. Lumbard claimed to Hugh that Bishopstone was sending Orleton's letters overseas and smuggling his allies 'and other people whom our lord the king deems his enemies' abroad too, and had even made a passage along a cliff by the sea to enable them to flee more easily. Hugh therefore had Simon Croyser arrest Thomas Bishopstone and search his houses in the East Sussex village of Bishopstone (between Eastbourne and Brighton), and the unfortunate man and his friends had to pay £100 to improve his standing with Hugh and to be allowed to return to the area. [82] Thomas Bishopstone was given no chance to defend himself against the charge of adhering to the bishop of Hereford, and the accusation of Hugh's informant Roger Lumbard sufficed to condemn him. The sum of £100, or in modern terms several hundred thousand pounds, seems to have been a common amount for Hugh to demand from his victims. This petition confirms that Hugh could use royal officials to his own ends; the command to Croyser to arrest Thomas Bishopstone was issued in the king's own name. It also reveals that Hugh employed informants, and this is surely how he knew at Easter 1323 that John Botetourt had been receiving his son, a Contrariant. Hugh and Edward were at the village of Bishopstone on 31 August 1324 which is hardly likely to be a coincidence, especially as Edward never went there at any other time in his reign. [83] Again, the king was not merely turning a blind eye to Hugh's blackmail of his own subjects, but facilitating and even taking part in it.

Simon Croyser was involved in another of Hugh's schemes, according to several inquisitions and petitions. Although he also benefited financially, Croyser claimed in 1327 that he had not dared to resist Hugh in the matter which in fairness is hardly implausible. Margaret Sutton was one of the two sisters and co-heirs of Sir John Somery, who died in August 1322. Hugh and his father, with the help of Croyser and, supposedly, Sir Oliver Ingham, arrested Margaret's husband John Sutton on Monday, 12 February 1325. They imprisoned him in chains at Westminster for three weeks until 'through fear of death' and 'through the hardships and duress of the prison and at Hugh's persecution' he assigned eight of his and Margaret's manors to Hugh, including Dudley in Staffordshire. Hugh's steward John Botiller took the fealty of the Suttons' tenants on Hugh's behalf. After his imprisonment, Sutton was made to appear before Ingham, accused of adhering to Thomas, earl of Lancaster and Humphrey Bohun, earl of Hereford, in 1321/22. [84] Hugh was at Westminster on the dates specified by John Sutton, but Oliver Ingham was in Gascony. [85] Sutton also changed his story somewhat, stating on another occasion that Hugh had imprisoned him at Westminster on Tuesday, 6 March 1324 and that he wrote letters patent in favour of Hugh on 21 March that year. [86] John Sutton's release of the eight manors to Hugh was witnessed at Westminster on 12 October 1325. Hugh may have been at Caerphilly in South Wales 150 miles away only three days before, so whether he was personally present is unclear; usually it would seem unlikely that he could have made it in time, but he did ride large distances remarkably quickly in 1325/26. [87] Coincidentally, another John Sutton was forced to recognise a debt of £2,000 to Hugh on 20 February 1325, at the same time as he was holding John Sutton husband of Margaret née Somery captive at Westminster. [88] It seems odd that Sutton would mix up the date of his imprisonment by more than a year, and his handing over the manors to Hugh took place at least eight months after he was imprisoned, but there is so much evidence supporting his claims that it is impossible to doubt that overall the story is genuine, if not perhaps in all the details. Sir John Somery had been a loyal royal knight who took part in Edward's campaign against the Contrariants, but this did not protect his sister and brother-in-law from Hugh after his death. Then again, Hugh did not go after Somery's other sister and co-heir Joan Botetourt (daughter-in-law of John and Maud Botetourt, above), though as a widow she would have made a much easier and softer target. It may be that the victims of Hugh's extortions were people he thought, whether accurately or not, had wronged him in some way, and that he felt their handing over several manors to him was their 'payment' for their offence.

The deaths of Hugh and his father and Edward II's deposition in 1326/27 brought a veritable flood of petitions complaining about the behaviour of the two Despensers. It is difficult to be sure if all the petitions are entirely true or if sometimes there was an element of jumping on the anti-Despenser bandwagon, but there is no doubt whatsoever that the overall picture of Hugh's period of dominance in the 1320s was one of illegal and quasi-legal land grabs, coercion, extortion, oppression, false imprisonment, threats and blackmail. His greed for land and money was unrelenting and endless, and the king did not simply tolerate it, he actively aided his beloved chamberlain. Hugh did not only desire wealth, but power, and in 1324/25 he reached the zenith of his authority.

Chapter 12

Directing the War

If you were ever wise and prudent, think now and use your ingenuity in every possible way you can how you can better hurt and torment the French this winter.

Numerous letters relating to the War of Saint-Sardos between Edward II of England and Charles IV of France in 1324/25 are extant, and make it apparent that Hugh Despenser the Younger, rather than Edward, was the man directing English policy. He wrote to Sir Oliver Ingham in April 1325:

> 'We beseech you not to take it amiss that we do not write to you often, as we know you would like, but we are so busy with our lord the king's affairs, both those affecting his said land [of Gascony] as well as the others which affect him, that we are not able to do it…though nevertheless we will not refrain from putting into action regularly what you advise us for the good of our lord the king, however we can.' [1]

Hugh had never been appointed to take over control of Edward's government, but did so anyway. He admitted to his friend Arnaud Caillau that 'we know little of this business,' meaning the Gascon situation, but neither that nor his lack of official authority to lead the war stopped him. [2] Not only did he write far more letters to Gascony than the king, men on the ground in the duchy wrote far more letters to Hugh than to Edward, asking for his aid and advice and giving him information. At the beginning of September 1324, for example, the former seneschal of Gascony Richard Grey wrote to tell Hugh that Edmund of Woodstock, earl of Kent and the king's lieutenant in Gascony, was being besieged at La Réole by Charles de Valois; he did not tell Edward this important news about his own half-brother. [3] Hugh's kinsman Ralph, Lord Basset of Drayton, twice seneschal of Gascony, told him on 6 December 1323 that he was writing with news he did not dare tell the king. [4] (Hugh seems to have been genuinely fond of Basset, calling him 'fair cousin' and 'beloved cousin,' and talking of 'the honour of you and all of us who are of your lineage.') [5] Basset wrote a letter of credence in early 1325 in which he talked of 'the will of the king and Sir Hugh' and 'on behalf of the king and Sir Hugh.' He wrote in another letter to Hugh in person: 'sire, if it pleases our lord the king and you, I would gladly come to our said lord and you in England…I am most ready to return at the command of the king and yours.' [6]

The Gascon lord Arnaud Caillau sent Hugh copies of his letters to the king, as did others such as Amaury Craon, yet another seneschal of Gascony, and Raymond Durand, seneschal of Les Landes. [7] John Sturmy, admiral of the eastern fleet in England, told Hugh on 13 September 1324 to send him whatever instructions 'please our lord the king and you.' [8] Hugh's knight Sir John Felton told him 'I beg you that you may please send me your wishes on all matters, and my lord's,' putting Hugh's commands even before the king's. [9] Guilhem-Ramon Caumont told Hugh in May 1325 that he had left his own father because the latter had taken the French side and he himself wished to live and die in the service of Edward II, and 'I have no other father after God except him [Edward] and you.' Caumont wrote that he knew Hugh would see he had also sent a letter to the king, and added 'do not be upset for anything, sire, because I have not written to you as abundantly as to him.' [10] (That Caumont thought Hugh might be jealous of the king is perhaps rather revealing.) Girard Oron, Edward's envoy to the county of Savoy, also told Hugh he knew Hugh would see Oron's letters to the king, and asked him to hasten Edward's response. [11]

Hugh wrote in October 1324 to the 'very dear lord and our very faithful friend' Henri, Lord Sully, butler of France, who had been with him and Edward in Yorkshire two years previously and was briefly captured by Robert Bruce. This letter began with Hugh expressing his astonishment that Sully had sent letters to England, but had not sent any to Edward or to Hugh himself. Hugh pointed out that he knew about Sully's letters even though he personally had not received them, a hint that little of what happened in England escaped him, and made it clear that he expected letters on the subject of foreign policy to be sent to both the king and himself in future. He added that if Sully wished for better relations between Edward II and Charles IV, he should involve Hugh, as he was making every effort to improve the situation. [12] Hugh's many letters of 1324/25 indicate that his contemporaries were right to complain that he saw himself and behaved as a second king in England. In February 1325 he told Ralph Basset, the mayor of Bordeaux Robert Swynburn, Raymond Durand of Les Landes, and Arnaud Caillau that 'our lord the king and ourselves [meaning himself] are very grateful to you,' and told an unspecified correspondent that 'neither our lord the king nor ourselves believe that you or anyone around you intend anything but good.' [13]

On occasion it seems even Hugh realised that coupling himself with God's anointed might be too much, and fortunately we have the drafts of many of his letters so we can see what he originally dictated and how he amended his own words before sending them. In one letter to Sir Robert Wateville in late April 1325, he wrote 'it seems to our said lord [the king] and to us that you have acted wisely,' but told his scribe to cross out the words 'and to us.' In the same letter, Hugh first wrote 'which excuse our said lord and ourselves hold as true,' and 'our said lord the king and ourselves would like to clear you of blame,' but amended those parts as well so that they referred to Edward only. He did keep in the part where he wrote 'it is neither the king's intention nor ours to easily believe words spoken against you.' Wateville, for his part, told Hugh of 'the good lordship which I have always found in my lord the king and in you.' [14] It may even be that on occasion the king allowed Hugh to dictate correspondence in his own name, or at least to have influence over what he wrote. One letter of September 1323, supposedly sent from Edward to his exchequer officials, ordered them to 'make an effort so that we become rich.' As Edward had never written anything like that in the previous 16 years of his reign, and as it is so reminiscent of Hugh's command to John Inge in January 1321 to work diligently on his behalf so that Hugh would be rich, several historians have pointed out that Edward's statement perhaps represents Hugh Despenser's wish rather than the king's. [15]

In a letter of 28 September 1324 to Edward's half-brother Edmund, earl of Kent and the king's lieutenant in Gascony, Hugh took it upon himself to inform the earl about the 'unease of heart which the king our lord has for you,' though he removed it before sending the letter. [16] This was six days after Kent had been forced to surrender to his uncle Charles de Valois at La Réole, though news of this had not yet reached England; if it had, Hugh might not have removed his comment. He did tell Kent of 'the great suffering which the king takes to heart and the deep anxiety he has over you.' Hugh's utter certainty that he had the right to hear all news from Gascony is evident from the start of this letter, where he complained to Kent that he had heard nothing from him since 10 August. It is clear from many letters of 1324/25 between England and Gascony that their writers were frustrated about correspondence not arriving, and there were also problems with ships laden with money, provisions and men departing late or not at all. This letter from Hugh to the earl of Kent contains a humorous comment sometimes interpreted as 'even I cannot control the wind.' What Hugh actually wrote was 'And truly, sire, there is no other reason that the ships did not arrive on time with you except that a strong wind was against them which we cannot turn by our command.' [17] He wrote somewhat defensively though also arrogantly to another correspondent that he could not be held guilty of any negligence or oversight in the pursuit of the war, because he had always given and always would give all that he could to the matter, more than any other man could. He repeated this line to the archbishop of Dublin, one of Edward's envoys in France and Gascony. To another correspondent he wrote that it was not his fault if matters were not going as they should, and that no-one could organise and arrange them better than he. [18] Hugh was not a man much given to modesty or self-deprecation.

Probably in December 1324, Hugh sent a carefully-worded letter which the king almost certainly did not know about to the constable of the fortified Gascon town of Libourne, Sir John Haustede. Hugh wrote that he had heard from several people that Haustede and his son William took bribes 'very willingly and often' to pass on provisions to the king's enemies. He went on:

> 'This would not be at all honourable for you if it were so, though we, who desire your honour and good both because of the affection we have for you and because you were suckled with our said lord [the king], cannot believe that you could allow such a thing to happen. Therefore we beseech you and advise you to restrain yourself from such inappropriate misdeeds which could be damaging to you and a blemish on your honour which we do not wish at all. And we are warning you in case you have done something which you should not have, which we cannot believe, so that you have an opportunity to mend your ways, and if not, you are advised of it meanwhile.' [19]

Hugh was the last man in any position to criticise someone for taking bribes; he was very much a 'do as I say, not as I do' kind of person. He wrote to the archbishop of Dublin 'it is said truly, and many people know it, that it is easier to see a mote in the eye of another than a staff across your own eyes,' seemingly unaware (for once) of the irony. [20] His enormous influence is apparent from the obsequious way men in Gascony addressed him: 'the very noble man, my very honourable lord'; 'the very noble and wise man, his very dear and very honourable lord'; 'my very noble and powerful lord'; 'my very honoured and very dread lord'; 'the noble man and his very honourable lord, honours and all manner of reverences,' and so on. [21] Even Hugh's social superiors flattered him: John Warenne, earl of Surrey, called him 'very dear cousin' five times in one short letter of May 1325, and Edmund of Woodstock, earl of Kent, addressed him numerous times as his 'very dear and beloved nephew.' Hugh did not reciprocate with 'uncle,' but only called the earl 'very dear lord' and 'sire'. A letter Hugh wrote to Edward II in 1324 began 'Honours and reverences, very honourable lord,' a salutation less deferential than men used to address him, though he did end the letter by saying 'we would be most glad and joyful to do whatever would please you.' [22]

Tewkesbury Abbey in Gloucestershire, where many of the Despensers and Clares are buried, including Hugh, his wife Eleanor and their eldest son Huchon, and Eleanor's grandfather, father and brother, earls of Gloucester.

[Craig Robinson]

Hugh's tomb in Tewkesbury Abbey; his remains were collected from five locations and buried here more than four years after his execution. The sarcophagus of Abbot John Coles (died 1347) was placed on top of his, and the decoration was much vandalised after the Dissolution.

[Craig Robinson; all photographs inside the abbey copyright to and used with kind permission of the Vicar and Churchwardens of Tewkesbury Abbey]

The tomb and effigies of Hugh's eldest son Hugh or Huchon, lord of Glamorgan (d. 1349) and his wife Elizabeth Montacute (d. 1359) in Tewkesbury Abbey. [Craig Robinson]

Hugh's grandson Edward Despenser, lord of Glamorgan (1336–75), eldest son of his second son Edward (d. 1342); the Kneeling Knight of Tewkesbury Abbey. [Craig Robinson]

Stained-glass image of Hugh in Tewkesbury Abbey, from the 1330s/1340s, commissioned by his wife Eleanor and finished by their son Huchon. [Craig Robinson]

Stained-glass image of a lady kneeling and naked in humility in Tewkesbury Abbey, most probably Eleanor Despenser, née Clare. [Craig Robinson]

Westminster Abbey, where Hugh was knighted on 22 May 1306.

The Houses of Parliament in London, still officially named the Palace of Westminster and standing on the site of the great medieval palace which burned down in 1834. Hugh married Eleanor Clare in the royal chapel of the palace on 26 May 1306 in the presence of her grandfather Edward I.

Hugh's great stronghold of Caerphilly, South Wales which passed to him and Eleanor in 1317; it was built by her father the earl of Gloucester, and was her birthplace in 1292. Their teenage son Huchon was besieged here from November 1326 to March 1327. [David on Flickr]

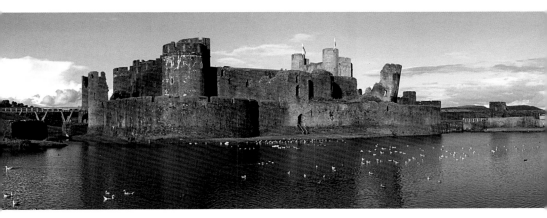

The Great Hall, Caerphilly Castle. Much of what exists today was built and modelled by Hugh in the 1320s. [Crown copyright (2017) Cadw, Welsh Government]

A carved corbel of a bearded man wearing a crown in the Great Hall of Caerphilly which dates from Hugh's rebuilding and renovation of the hall, and was surely intended to represent Edward II. The man next to him (on the left) may therefore have been intended as a depiction of Hugh himself; he has long hair and seemingly a goatee-style beard.

[Crown copyright (2017) Cadw, Welsh Government]

Manuscript illustration of Queen Isabella and her army with Hugh's execution in the background, from Receuil des Croniques d'Angleterre, vol. 1, fo. 316v, dated 1471 to 1483 and now in the British Library.

[Used with permission]

The spectacular Carreg Cennen, forfeited by the Contrariant John Giffard (whose father built it) and given to Hugh by Edward II in November 1322. [Zingyyellow on Flickr]

The marketplace, Hereford, probably either the site of Hugh's trial or his execution. [Jules Frusher]

The site of Hereford's long-vanished castle which belonged to Hugh and where he was either tried, or executed. [Jules Frusher]

Cardiff Castle which passed to Hugh and Eleanor in 1317, and where he and his father (possibly not accurately) were said to have had the Welsh lord Llywelyn Bren hanged, drawn and quartered.

Neath Castle, one of Hugh's many castles in South Wales, where his constable Sir John Iweyn was beheaded by the Marcher lords in May 1321. [Patricia Jones]

Although the many extant letters from the War of Saint-Sardos relate mostly to the progress of the war, some nice personal details crept into them: Ralph Cobham told Hugh that he had fallen from his horse and broken his foot most painfully, and Robert Wateville, plaintively, that he was a bad sailor and was dreading the return journey from Gascony to England. This was not without good reason, as in May 1325 it took two Gascons 11 days to sail from Portsmouth to Bordeaux. Money was so short in Gascony that John Felton sold his own horses to provision the castle of Saintes, and Oliver Ingham begged Hugh to help him as the two horses he had brought with him from England had died and he had no money to buy more. Fighting broke out in Bordeaux between the English and Welsh on one side and the locals on the other. [23]

Hugh told several men that he had read their correspondence out loud to Edward and the royal council, so clearly was a fluent reader. [24] In early October 1324 at Portchester in Hampshire with Edward, Hugh wrote a letter to the former seneschal of Gascony, Sir Richard Grey, telling him that Grey's illness weighed heavily on him and that he prayed to God that he would, by his grace, improve the affliction. Hugh originally added 'amen' to this sentence then told his clerk to cross it out. [25] Possibly the former seneschal was the same Richard Grey who complained in June 1312 that a large group of men had 'maliciously killed a she-bear of his,' and he was a distant cousin of Hugh. [26] At some point when he was at Portchester, possibly at this time, Hugh and his allies Robert Baldock and Robert Holden, controller of the king's wardrobe, imprisoned dozens of merchants of Winchester, Southampton and Salisbury at Portchester Castle for six or seven days until they agreed to buy tuns of wine at a massively inflated price. They were 'old wines taken at sea from the enemy' which had been stored at Portchester for many years or even decades, and therefore were 'rotten and putrid', and the merchants 'received them by force and fear against their will.' Their debt was cancelled early in Edward III's reign. One of the merchants, Henry Canavecer, claimed dramatically that because he was unable to sell the wines in England he shipped them to Flanders at great cost, and that he and his people were imprisoned when many of the tuns broke and 'scarcely escaped with their lives.' [27] Forcing men to pay considerably over the odds for bad wine would certainly be one of Hugh the Younger's more inventive crimes and methods of raising money.

Edward II unfairly treated his wife and the king of France's sister Isabella, loyal to and supportive of him for many years, as an enemy alien, and confiscated her lands on 18 September 1324. [28] She received a smaller income from the Exchequer instead which did not only hurt her financially, it seriously limited her ability to dispense patronage and to act as a great magnate in her own right. [29] This confiscation, as it was one of the factors which pushed Isabella into opposition to him, was a great mistake on Edward's part, though Isabella herself blamed Hugh and his ally Walter Stapeldon, bishop of Exeter and treasurer of England, rather than Edward. Although it is often stated that Edward failed to exempt the queen's French servants from the general arrest of French people in England, he did in fact exempt eight. [30] The War of Saint-Sardos did not go too well for England, though Gascony's chief towns Bordeaux and Bayonne remained in English hands and quite a few Gascon noblemen stayed loyal to Edward. Early panicked predictions that the entire duchy would fall to the French certainly did not come true. Hugh thought (wrongly) in early October 1324 that nothing was left except Bayonne, but boasted that the English would recover 'all that is ours and much more besides,' while complaining about the 'false representation and sudden plotting' and the 'treachery' of the French. [31] In early 1325, Edward decided to send Queen Isabella to her homeland to negotiate a peace settlement with her brother Charles IV, and she left England on 9 March 1325 with a large retinue and plenty of money (though later accused Hugh, unfairly, of sending her overseas 'meanly and against the dignity of her highness and her status'). It has often been assumed that Isabella was desperate to leave England to plot against Edward with Roger Mortimer, though evidence of 1325/26 shows that she wanted to rid herself of the hated Hugh, not her husband, with whom she badly wished to reconcile since Hugh had edged her out of Edward's life. [32] Isabella had given her husband a gift on 1 January 1325 as was customary at his court on that date, though sadly the royal clerks did not record what it was. [33]

Edward later claimed with reference to Hugh that before Isabella left England, 'towards no-one was she more agreeable, myself excepted.' [34] Either Edward was lying, or he was deceiving himself, or the queen and her husband's loathed favourite or lover had taken to addressing each other with a kind of poisonous sweetness, at least in front of Edward. The *Vita* wrote that Isabella was 'delighted to leave the company of some whom she did not like,' a reference to Hugh and perhaps also to his father and their allies, and added

> 'small wonder if she does not like Hugh, through whom her uncle [Thomas, earl of Lancaster] perished, by whom she was deprived of her servants and all her rents; consequently she will not (so many think) return until Hugh Despenser is wholly removed from the king's side.' [35]

This is a useful comment for revealing how things really stood, as the *Vita* ends abruptly in late 1325 and was not written with hindsight. The queen would not return for more than 18 months, and then at the head of an invasion force and in alliance with Edward and Hugh's enemies, and determined to destroy Hugh.

In March 1325 Hugh paid over 50 pounds for cloth for the knights in his retinue, who included former followers of the earl of Lancaster such as Gilbert Talbot, his son Richard who was probably not yet 20 and who that year became the husband of the imprisoned Elizabeth Comyn, and Thomas Wyther. These men had pragmatically switched sides after the battle of Boroughbridge. Another of Hugh's knights was his kinsman Walter Beauchamp, marshal of the king's household. [36] Hugh and Edward spent the first half of March 1325 at the Tower of London, and Hugh's wife Eleanor must also have been there, as she conceived a child born on or just before 14 December 1325. None of them went to Dover to see Isabella off on 9 March. Edward and Hugh spent a few days that month at Henley-on-Thames, and on 22 March the king's chamber account records a rather intriguing payment of half a mark there to a woman called Katherine of Langley, 'who talked privately with the king and Sir Hugh.' [37] April saw king and chamberlain at Beaulieu Abbey in Hampshire, where Edward himself went fishing with a local fisherman called Jack Bere and eight others, and ordered an oystermonger to travel the 90 miles from London with oysters for 'the king and Sir Hugh.' A very curious entry in Edward's account, while he and Hugh were at Eling just outside Southampton on their way to Beaulieu, talks of the village as the place 'where the king frightened Sir Hugh.' [38] Presumably this means a practical joke or prank of some kind as the word can also be translated as 'startled', and Edward was a very playful type of person although Hugh himself was not. On 1 June 1325 Edward officially pardoned Hugh for his piracy of 1321, and on the same day made him constable of the city and castle of Bristol for life. [39] At Bisham in Berkshire on 10 June, Edward paid 100 shillings to repair the church in the Buckinghamshire village of Hambleden which had belonged to Bartholomew Badlesmere and which Edward gave to Hugh on 12 February 1323. The king granted Hugh the right to hold a fair in Hambleden on the feast day of St Bartholomew (24 August) and the two following days which seems like an example of rather malicious humour on Edward's part. Bisham itself had belonged to Edward's cousin Thomas, earl of Lancaster, and on 24 March 1322 just two days after Lancaster's execution, Edward also granted it to Hugh. [40]

Hugh's last letter to Edward's half-brother Edmund of Woodstock, earl of Kent, was sent on 21 June 1325 when he and the king were at the palace of Eltham. [41] He spent half the letter saying that he hoped the earl was well and that it would ease his heart to hear good news of his health, in such extensive and exaggerated fashion that it comes across as sarcastic or even perhaps as a kind of subtle threat, given that his previous letters to Kent had demonstrated little concern for his well-being. Hugh told the earl that if he wished for anything which he could do for him, Kent only had to ask and Hugh would gladly do it to the best of his ability. It is hard to imagine that the king's own half-brother felt happy about having to go cap in hand to the royal favourite if he wanted something, though in February Kent had admitted to Hugh that the latter was in a better position to ask Edward for a favour he wished for one of his clerks than he himself was. [42] Hugh once told Kent openly that the latter's messengers 'came to my lord the king and to us' and remained with them both for six weeks. This letter also stated that 'the king and ourselves were as distressed and displeased as we possibly could be' about the failure of the ships to depart for Gascony because of the lack of wind; Hugh seems to have been rubbing his closeness to Kent's brother and his power in the earl's face. [43] Kent would later be one of the judges who condemned Hugh to death and clearly loathed him, yet in his letters to him was always scrupulously polite, even ingratiating ('very dear nephew, please send us faithfully regular news of your health, and your commands').

It is apparent from the remarks of various chroniclers and other evidence that even the great English magnates were scared of Hugh, of going against his wishes and of telling him things he did not want to hear. One of the very few men who dared to speak the truth to him was his loyal household knight John Felton. After the surrender of the earl of Kent to his uncle Charles de Valois at La Réole in September 1324, Felton wrote to Hugh:

'Know, sire, that those around Sir Edmund have put all the blame on you because of the lack of funds and people [sent from England] and I told them the blame was theirs. And, sire, do not show this letter to very many people, because there are many who are plotting as much evil against you as they can, and particularly those who by your advice are in his [Kent's] company.' [44]

A few weeks later, Felton repeated this warning and told Hugh of the 'wicked faction' around the earl of Kent who were accusing Hugh of all manner of evils. [45] John Travers, constable of Bordeaux, was another who was wary of the intentions of Kent and his retinue towards the powerful chamberlain. He told Hugh:

'Sire, may it please you to recall, you commanded me when I left you in London, on the faith and the oath which I owe you, that I would let you know whenever I might hear something detrimental to your well-being, and the behaviour of certain people towards you in the parts where I am...' [46]

Travers therefore sent his messenger William Dalling to England to inform Hugh orally of many delicate matters and to show him things which Travers did not dare to commit to writing; he hinted in the letter that the messengers sent by the earl of Kent would not tell the whole truth about events in Gascony. Hugh replied a few weeks later calling the messenger Dalling his 'beloved' and saying that 'our said lord the king and ourselves are extremely grateful to him' and to Travers as well. Hugh advised Travers to ignore empty flattery, presumably a dig at the earl of Kent and those around him, and added 'as a result of your good conduct the king and ourselves may discuss continuing our good will towards you,' a sentence as haughty and self-important as any Hugh ever wrote. [47] Hugh's awareness that Kent's associates were 'plotting evil' against him with the earl's knowledge surely confirms that his gushing over Kent's health in a letter some months later was not sincere. The earl of Kent did not return to England, but in December 1325 married Roger Mortimer's first cousin Margaret Wake and remained in France with his sister-in-law the queen, returning with the invasion force in September 1326. The king is known to have sent only one letter to his half-brother while Kent was in Gascony, and it was not amicable: Kent accused the Gascon lord Arnaud Caillau of treason, and Edward ordered him to desist. Hugh told Caillau with barely concealed satisfaction that the king was 'rebuking' his brother on Caillau's behalf. [48] Arnaud Caillau, a relative of Piers Gaveston, was high in the favour of the king and Hugh, who called him 'very dear friend' and 'our good friend,' and in 1326 was one of only four recipients of a 'secret message' from the king of Aragon, with Edward II, Hugh, and Ralph Basset. [49]

The death of Hugh's half-sister Maud in May 1322 may have loosened any ties Hugh felt he had to Maud's widower Henry of Lancaster, the king's first cousin, the queen's uncle and the heir of his executed brother Thomas, earl of Lancaster. Henry annoyed the king and by extension Hugh in 1324/25 with his sympathy for Adam Orleton, bishop of Hereford (a man Edward despised), his adoption of his late brother's arms, and his setting up a cross outside Leicester in honour of Thomas's memory. Edward accused his cousin of treason and summoned him to appear before parliament in June 1325, though in the end the charges were not heard, perhaps because Henry 'was of better blood than the others' who attended. [50] It would have been sensible for the king and Hugh to court Henry as an ally, yet they did not, and suffered the consequences when he joined his niece the queen against them in October 1326. Edward spent much time between 1324 and 1326 at Kenilworth Castle in Warwickshire, part of Thomas of Lancaster's inheritance which he kept for himself.

In early July 1325, the king sent 84 mares and foals to Hugh's castles of Chepstow and Cardiff as a gift, perhaps to replace his 60 mares stolen by the Contrariants four years before, and bought two gallons of honey for the pregnant Eleanor Despenser to make a sweet called *sucre de plate*. [51] For all the king's enjoyment of Hugh's company, he still, unconventional as ever, liked spending time with his lowborn subjects. He had a friend or acquaintance called Colle Herron, a Thames fisherman who spent seven days in the king's company in August 1325, and who also had spent time with him on another occasion years before. [52] There were plenty of occasions in the 1320s when Edward chatted to and spent time with fishermen and women, carpenters, blacksmiths, shipwrights and other people considerably down the social scale, invited them to visit him, and even went fishing with them. It is impossible to imagine Hugh Despenser doing the same thing. Hugh was with Edward at the Tower of London on 18 July 1325, when the king took the manor of Clopton, Suffolk into his own hands. [53] It was held by a woman called Alice, widow of William Legh, who complained after Hugh's downfall that he had persuaded Edward to take her manor because of his 'ill-will' towards her. Clopton was restored to her on 7 September 1328, in the next reign. [54] Edward's official reason for taking Clopton from Alice Legh was the feeble excuse that she 'gave the king to understand that she should prosecute some business for the king's advantage wherefrom great benefit should arise to the king which agreement she has in no wise observed, wherefore the king is unwilling that she should reap advantage from her deceit in this behalf.' [55] This is one of those occasions where it is difficult to be sure if the complaint against Hugh is true, though for sure he was someone who easily felt 'ill-will' towards others.

Queen Isabella negotiated a treaty with her brother over several months, and Edward ratified it on 13 June 1325; its terms were fairly catastrophic for him, though this was not the queen's fault. Isabella seems to have been enjoying her long visit to her homeland, and dined with numerous relatives and other nobles and went on pilgrimage. She surely found Hugh Despenser's dominance of her husband and his government suffocating and was glad to escape, and Hugh does seem to have gone out of his way to limit her influence over the king and even to come between them as a couple as much as he could. The vexing issue of homage for Gascony and Ponthieu remained. Edward, as duke of Aquitaine and count of Ponthieu, owed homage to his overlord the king of France for the territories. The ceremony of homage simply had to take place, in France, or Charles IV would have the right to confiscate the lands and Edward and his descendants would lose them permanently. Clearly this was not an option, but travelling to France was fraught with danger for the king. He might be kidnapped or killed by the Contrariants hiding on the continent. Mass rebellion might break out in England in his absence. He could not take Hugh Despenser with him, as it was said he and his father would be tortured if he went to France:

the *Vita* says that if the Despensers 'are found within the kingdom of France [they] will assuredly not lack bad quarters,' a reference to a punishment (*mala mansio*) where the victim was stretched out and tied to a board. [56] Equally, he could not leave him behind, as this would be putting him in danger without the king's protection: the *Vita* also says that the two Despensers, grossly unpopular throughout England at all levels of society, 'realised that in the absence of the king they would not know where to live safely.' [57] Adam Murimuth, royal clerk and chronicler, agrees that the whole country hated the Despensers and that therefore they did not wish Edward to go abroad and leave them behind. [58] Edward and Hugh had created a climate where they did not and could not feel safe: they had alienated many people by their vindictiveness towards the Contrariants and their families, and by their greed, despotism and theft of others' lands. There would be many men only too willing to kill Hugh Despenser if they got the chance. Edward was in a dilemma, and his only other option was to make his son duke of Aquitaine and count of Ponthieu send him in his place. This also had drawbacks, as Edward would lose the income from his French lands, and his son might be at risk too. Although Charles IV was the boy's uncle and his mother was at the French court, France was an enemy country, and the heir to the throne was only 12.

The matter was discussed at the parliament which began at Westminster on 25 June 1325, and Hugh the Younger said to the magnates advising the king to go in person to France: 'Now we shall see who will advise the king to cross over to his enemies; he is a manifest traitor whoever he may be.' [59] Edward of Windsor would be appointed nominal regent of the kingdom in his father's absence, but as he was still a child Hugh Despenser the Elder would really be in charge, says the *Vita*, because he was 'shrewder than all and more experienced' (the earl of Winchester was now 64). Unfortunately, 'he was hated by everyone and even the king's son.' [60] The king hovered in Kent for a few weeks in August and early September 1325, trying to decide what to do and changing his mind almost daily: making arrangements to go himself and appointing his son as regent, then deciding to send his son, claiming to be ill, then once again deciding that he would go. He stayed with his friend William, abbot of Langdon for a few days, and on 30 August was at Langdon Abbey with Hugh, Hugh the Elder, their ally Edmund Fitzalan, earl of Arundel (whose son was married to Hugh's eldest daughter), the chancellor Robert Baldock, the royal justice Robert Mohaut, and unnamed others. They ate seafood in the abbot's garden. [61] Two weeks previously, Hugh had travelled along the Thames to meet Edward at Faversham, in a barge whose captain was called Hick atte Wose. [62]

Hugh Despenser the Younger was to change the course of English history in early September 1325, when he begged Edward not to leave him alone in England.

Accordingly Edward made the fateful decision to send his son to swear homage to Charles IV which ultimately would bring both Hugh and himself down when Queen Isabella kept the boy with her in France and betrothed him to a daughter of the count of Hainault in order to pay for ships and mercenaries to invade England. On the other hand, whatever choice Edward made in September 1325 is likely to have been the 'wrong' one and to have brought about the downfall of the Despensers and even himself; they had become so hated by 1325 that their regime was precarious, and the king had painted himself into a corner where every option available to him was equally unattractive and risky. [63] The *Anonimalle* chronicle says that Hugh 'made a great sorrow, and lamented piteously to the king that if he passed beyond sea, [Hugh] would be put to death in his absence.' [64] Even then, Edward hesitated: he made Edward of Windsor count of Ponthieu on 2 September, but waited eight days before making him duke of Aquitaine, and continued issuing safe-conducts for his own retinue to accompany him abroad, including his cousin Henry of Lancaster, in the days between. [65] Edward of Windsor sailed for France on 12 September, and swore homage to his uncle Charles IV a few days later.

Numerous men in Gascony during the War of Saint-Sardos in 1324/25 had told Hugh that Edward needed to go there in person. Hugh often replied that the king would, and Edward genuinely seems to have wished to lead an army to the duchy until as late as May 1325. [66] One very interesting letter from Hugh to Ralph Basset in early October 1324 reveals that Edward intended to go to Gascony taking Robert Bruce with him, if matters between the two that November went well. The draft of this letter shows that Hugh originally referred to Bruce as 'the king of Scotland', then remembered that the English government never, under any circumstance, acknowledged Bruce as such, and removed those words. [67] Edward himself told his half-brother the earl of Kent on 23 February 1325 (in his very abrupt letter mostly rebuking Kent for his actions against Arnaud Caillau) that 'our arrival in those parts will be soon, with God's help.' [68] On 10 July 1325, Edward finally revoked his order to his army to assemble at Portsmouth on 2 August. [69] Given what happened in September 1325, one wonders whether Hugh would have done what he could to prevent Edward leaving England. Perhaps he did, whatever he said to his correspondents, as Edward did not go to Gascony and indeed never set foot in his duchy.

Some modern historians have speculated that Isabella had schemed and plotted for her son to join her in France in cahoots with Roger Mortimer and others, even Charles IV, so that she would have a weapon to use against her husband. There are no grounds whatsoever except imagination and centuries of hindsight to think that this was the case, or that there was some huge conspiracy across Europe to deprive the king of England of his throne. It is entirely possible that Isabella was hoping for her husband to come to France so that she had access to him without the constant irritation of Hugh's presence, and could persuade him to restore her lands, to allow her the political influence she had always enjoyed, and to treat her once again as his loving and supportive wife and queen, as he always had. One historian has suggested that Isabella's awareness that Hugh was behind the king's decision not to cross the sea may have been 'the ultimate sign to Isabella that Despenser had supplanted her in a way that Gaveston never had' and may have been a major factor in her decision to rebel. [70] Indeed, the realisation that Hugh wielded so much power that he could even persuade the king of England not to meet the king of France may well have shocked the queen, however much she had grown used to his dominance over Edward and his government.

Hugh was at Tonbridge in Kent – where a decade previously he had seized the castle – with his wife Eleanor on 21 September, rejoined the king at Maresfield in Sussex two days later, and was at Westminster without Edward on 3 October. He may have made a flying visit to his stronghold of Caerphilly 150 miles away around 9 October. [71] Despite Hugh's protestations to the king that he would be killed if Edward left him behind when he went abroad, he seemingly felt perfectly confident to travel around England and Wales without him. He, his wife Eleanor and Edward were all at the royal palace of Sheen west of London around 16 October (Hugh may also have been at Westminster on the 12th when John Sutton signed over eight manors to him after being imprisoned in chains a few months earlier). Eleanor was about seven months pregnant, and to keep her comfortable, Edward bought firewood for her chamber. Another gift from the king had been waiting at Sheen for Eleanor to arrive: 47 caged goldfinches, in addition to some caged larks he had bought for her in June. [72] Hugh left his wife and her uncle at Sheen and set off for Wales (where exactly not stated) where he arrived sometime before 8 November. Edward also left Sheen and sailed along the Thames to Cippenham, where on 31 October he received a visit from Katherine Holditch, wife of Hugh's chamberlain Clement, who wished to seek his help on some unspecified 'great business.' [73] Hugh in Wales and Edward in or near London exchanged letters on at least three occasions in the first half of November 1325. [74] One of Edward's letters probably informed Hugh of the dramatic news from the French court.

Chapter 13

The Queen's Hatred

Things are not at all progressing as they should, for which we know well you are not in any way to blame, but those who know the least about it always prefer to speak evil of those who are close to a lord rather than good, as some people do to us, even though it is not our fault.

Queen Isabella, under the protection of her brother the king of France, felt confident enough to make her hatred of Hugh public, and to issue an ultimatum to her husband. In front of Charles IV and messengers sent by Edward, Isabella stated:

'I feel that marriage is a joining together of man and woman, maintaining the undivided habit of life, and that someone has come between my husband and myself trying to break this bond; I protest that I will not return until this intruder is removed, but, discarding my marriage garment, shall assume the robes of widowhood and mourning until I am avenged of this Pharisee.' [1]

Isabella loathed Hugh so much she could not bring herself to utter his name. Not only did she dress and portray herself as a widow in mourning for her husband who had been taken from her by a third party, she informed the French court that she was frightened of Hugh, and threatened – in a letter or speech which does not survive – to destroy him with the help of Charles IV and other Frenchmen. The author of the *Vita* recorded a letter sent to Isabella by all the English bishops in December 1325 which quoted her lost missive:

'But as for what you [Isabella] have written, that what your brother the king of France and your other friends of France intend to do on your behalf, will turn out not to the prejudice of the lord king [Edward] or anyone else, but to the destruction of Hugh alone…' [2]

In November 1325, a valet of the king's chamber called Jack Pyk told Edward – presumably passing on a rumour he had heard – that Hugh had been killed. Edward sent three servants 'hastily' to Wales to see what was happening.

They returned to the king at Isleworth on 20 November and told him that 'thanks to God,' Hugh was alive and unharmed. Edward gave the men 10 marks each 'for their good news,' a large sum (the equivalent of several years' wages for them) which represents his enormous relief. On 19 November the day before the men returned, the king had sent a runner called Syme to Wales with letters for Hugh; he must have been deeply anxious. [3] This also gives some indication of the anguish Edward must have felt almost exactly a year later when Hugh really was killed, and not by a quiet assassin, but in the most painful and public manner possible. The king heard of Isabella's speech about Hugh on or just before 14 November 1325 when he cut off her funding. It seems highly likely that he heard of her threat to destroy Hugh at the same time, and perhaps he thought she had had Hugh assassinated. Although she had not and there is no evidence that she ever tried to, this may only have hardened the king's determination to keep Hugh with him, regardless of what Isabella said or did or threatened and even if it ended their marriage for good. Edward's complete refusal to send Hugh away, in the face of his wife's threats, left Isabella with no choice but to stay in France and behave as a widow in mourning for her lost husband and the sad death of a happy marriage destroyed by a third party. Her public ultimatum had failed, and her husband had chosen his lover (assuming Hugh was) over her, also publicly.

Isabella made it clear in October/November 1325 that she sought Hugh's destruction, and it took her a year to achieve it. Although she could hardly have publicly announced that she wanted to bring down her husband as well, her behaviour in 1325/26 tends to indicate that she genuinely wished for a reconciliation with Edward and wanted Hugh out of her life and her husband's; not only that, but dead. At some point in late 1325 or early 1326, she formed an alliance with the Contrariants who had fled from England and were now living openly at the French court, including Roger Mortimer. Although Isabella and Mortimer's association is often written in modern literature as a great and passionate love affair, there is no evidence that it was anything of the sort, and is far more likely to have been – at least at this early stage – an alliance between people who wanted nothing more than the destruction and death of Hugh Despenser the Younger, and who could use each other to achieve it. Isabella would never be able to resume her position as Edward's wife and queen or to hold her lands while Hugh was around; Mortimer would never be able to get his lands, family and income back and would remain a penniless and powerless exile for the rest of his life.

Neither had the ability to bring Hugh down alone, but together, with the military ability of Mortimer and his Contrariant friends and most importantly with Isabella's control of the heir to the English throne, they had a far better chance of achieving it. Without Edward of Windsor, the queen and Mortimer and the other English exiles on the continent had little chance of striking a death blow at Hugh Despenser, but custody of Edward II's heir gave Isabella a considerable advantage. The boy was unmarried, so his mother could arrange a marriage with the daughter of a wealthy nobleman and thereby would be able to pay for ships and mercenaries to invade England with the dower, and Edward of Windsor was also a powerful figurehead. Few Englishmen would be willing to support the detested royal favourite against their queen and their future king. Isabella used her 13-year-old son as a weapon to try to force her husband to do what she wanted, by refusing to let the boy return to his father and his home. Not even the loss of his son, however, persuaded the king to send Hugh away from him. One could argue that Edward chose Hugh Despenser not only over his wife, but over his own child.

Hugh's reaction to all this is unrecorded. He left Wales to attend the parliament which was due to begin in London on 18 November, though must have arrived late, and was back at Westminster on or before 28 November. Edward wrote to the queen and their son in France on 1 December 1325, ordering them home. This would be his last ever letter to his wife, whom he addressed rather abruptly as *Dame* or 'Lady'. He told Isabella of the 'great sickness of heart' he was suffering because of her long absence from him, but if those words touched Isabella, what came next can only have hurt her: Edward demonstrated that Hugh remained his chief concern and main priority. He expressed his astonishment that Isabella would not return to him because of her fear of Hugh, because she had always behaved so amicably towards him and 'demonstrated very faithful affection' for him in the king's presence, and sent 'very special letters to him of recent date which he has shown to us' (any letters Isabella sent to Hugh, if Edward was being truthful on this point, have not survived). Edward's letter went on:

> 'And indeed, Lady, we know for truth, and you know it too, that [Hugh] has always encouraged all the honour for you with us that he could; no evil or disgrace was ever done to you since you came into our company by the incitement or encouragement of anyone.'

The king also wrote to Isabella's brother Charles IV and 16 French noblemen and prelates:

> 'It is not fitting that she should fear Hugh, or any other man living in our kingdom; because by God, if Hugh, or any other man living under our authority, wished her evil, and we came to be aware of it, we would chastise

him in such a manner that others would learn from it; and this is, and has been, and always will be our entire will, and we have sufficient power to do this, by God's mercy. And, very dear and beloved brother[-in-law], know for certain that we have never at any time been able to perceive in private or in public, in word, or in deed, or in countenance, that [Hugh] did not conduct himself in all ways towards our consort as he should towards his very dear lady.'

Edward went on to tell the French king about Isabella's friendly behaviour towards Hugh and the letters she sent to him, and that he could not believe she was now saying otherwise and that someone else must be filling her head with this nonsense. He added that he knew for certain 'after our person, [Hugh] is the person of our kingdom who wishes her the most honour, and he has always demonstrated this, and we testify this to you in good truth.' [4] It is difficult to be sure whether Edward was lying to his wife and her brother, or whether he was deceiving himself and genuinely did believe that Isabella herself was lying about her fear of Hugh. Perhaps his deep love for the other man blinded him to reality; perhaps he did not want to see what was really happening. Isabella was adamant that she had good reason to fear Hugh; Edward was equally adamant that she did not. Neither would shift from their position.

The day after he wrote these letters, the king went from Westminster to Sheen to visit his niece Eleanor Despenser, and returned to Westminster the same night. He took only eight attendants, all of them valets of his chamber who were given 'boots for the water', and it appears that the king rowed himself along the Thames, with the attendants following behind in another boat. [5] Edward gave Eleanor a generous gift of 100 marks 'by the king's own hands,' and the following day she sent a servant with a gift of a set of clothes for him. Eleanor must have been close to term at the time of the visit, as she gave birth on or just before 14 December 1325, at Sheen. On that date, Edward made an offering of 30 shillings to the Virgin Mary in gratitude that 'God had granted [Eleanor] a prompt delivery of her child' (it was at least the tenth time she had given birth). [6] This was most probably the Despensers' youngest child Elizabeth, though the royal account gives neither the name nor sex of the infant. Although it was usual for Edward to pay messengers for bringing him news of children born to his sisters and nieces, the offering demonstrating his relief at a 'prompt delivery' to one of them appears to be unique. Edward's visiting Eleanor a few days before she gave birth also implies a degree of solicitousness, and perhaps somewhat adds fuel to the fire of their rumoured liaison. Hugh is not mentioned in Edward's account at this time, but was at Westminster on 28 and 30 November and 3 December 1325, and may also have been at Sheen with his wife when the king came to visit her. He withdrew £1,000 from his bankers on 16 December, days after his child was born, and on 8 and 30 November paid out a total of 60 pounds for Eleanor's expenses. [7] Some months before, he had withdrawn 40 marks for her expenses. With both her husband and her uncle giving her frequent and generous amounts of money – Edward had sent her yet another gift of 100 marks on 10 April 1325 – Eleanor must have lived very well. [8]

Edward was at his Westminster cottage of 'Burgundy' on 3 December, a place where he often liked to spend time in preference to his much larger and more luxurious residences, and was present when several of his servants bought carthorses there. He took a keen interest in the purchase of carthorses, and in February 1325 himself examined several being offered to him and refused all of them, though compensated the dealer with 10 shillings for his time. A few weeks later Edward ordered his servants not to buy two of the 10 carthorses which were being offered by another horse dealer, also at Burgundy. [9] Probably Hugh was with the king at his cottage, and on 2 December 1325 his household knight Sir William Lovell acknowledged a debt of 40 pounds to him. Lovell later claimed that he had been 'compelled by force' to do so 'for the purpose of remaining as one of the knights of Hugh's retinue for two years.' [10] In the following days, four of Hugh's squires were given a gift of fur by the king at the Tower of London, and Edward paid 36 pounds for 6,000 stockfish to be sent to Hugh's castles in Wales.

Hugh's son Huchon received 24 shillings' worth of *camoca* (heavy and expensive silk) and lawn cloth for making an *aketon* (a padded or quilted defensive jerkin) from his great-uncle, and his weapons were repaired by an armourer of London; the young man, now 16 or 17, was old enough to own military equipment. Edward also bought considerably more cloth for *aketons* presumably for himself and Hugh, including some of checked vermilion velvet with gold stripes and some of vermilion, yellow and white silk. In January 1325, he had paid the wife of one of his chamber staff to make shirts to wear under *aketons* for himself and Hugh. [11] Huchon Despenser was obviously sometimes at court with his father and great-uncle, and his father must have hired someone to oversee his military training. Whoever it was did a good job: Huchon was a famously excellent soldier in the 1330s and 1340s. Before the boy's departure from England in September 1325, Huchon also sometimes spent time with his mother's first cousin Edward of Windsor, the king's son and heir, who was about four years his junior. Edward II sent letters under the secret seal to his son and Huchon at Shoreham, Sussex on 18 July 1324. [12]

No official record exists of the London/Westminster parliament of November/December 1325, but Queen Isabella's refusal to return to England or to allow her 13-year-old son to do so must have dominated proceedings.

Edward II made a speech, recorded by the *Vita*, in which he proved himself as keen as ever to defend Hugh:

> '[Isabella] says that Hugh Despenser is her adversary and hostile to her. It is surprising that she has conceived this dislike of Hugh, for when she departed, towards no-one was she more agreeable, myself excepted. For this reason Hugh is much cast down; but he is nevertheless prepared to show his innocence in any way whatsoever.' [13]

This speech echoes what Edward said in his correspondence to the French court and to Isabella and their son, and he ordered all the bishops of England also to write a letter to her asking her to come home and to repeat his defence of Hugh to her yet again, no doubt to Isabella's supreme irritation. The bishops' letter told Isabella 'because you delay your return out of hatred for Hugh Despenser, everyone predicts that much evil will follow,' which is obviously Edward's own statement rather than the bishops' and also obviously untrue ('everyone' was predicting nothing of the sort). The letter also claimed that 'Hugh Despenser has solemnly demonstrated his innocence before all, and that he has never harmed the queen, but done everything in his power to help her.' The Rochester chronicle says that during Parliament, in the chapel of the Tower of London, Hugh told the attendees that anyone who failed to counsel the king properly on the matter was a fool or a traitor. Neither he nor Edward received any advice, however, because everyone was too afraid to speak the truth to them. [14]

In late 1325 and early 1326, Hugh was still pursuing the adherents of Roger Damory, almost four years after Damory's death, on the grounds of 'certain trespasses' they had committed against him – most probably attacking his lands during the Despenser War. On 31 December 1325, many dozens of men and women of the Suffolk town of Sudbury including the mayor and two bailiffs acknowledged a joint debt of 1,000 marks or £666 to Hugh, cancelled in Edward III's reign because it had been made 'under duress'. [15] Hugh and Edward II were in Haughley 20 miles away from Sudbury on this date, and Sudbury is less than five miles from Hugh's manor of Lamarsh and under 10 from his manor of Kersey. Some of these people had been named as Damory's adherents in August 1321 when the king was forced to grant a pardon to the Marcher lords and their followers for their terrible destruction of Hugh's and his father's lands. [16] Edward withdrew the sentence of outlawry on four of the Sudbury men on 3 January 1326 as 'the king wills for certain reasons that no further proceedings shall be taken against' them, presumably because three days earlier they had satisfied Hugh by acknowledging the huge debt to him. [17] Hugh also ordered four of his men including Sir Robert Wateville to 'have the body of Robert Chedworth brought before him at a certain day,' and made the four acknowledge that they owed him £200 as his security that they would do so. [18] Chedworth was a knight of Essex who in December 1316 had acted as the attorney of Hugh's sister-in-law Elizabeth Burgh (who married Roger Damory a few months later and who held the manor of Sudbury), and who sometime before August 1323 broke into the Deddington and Caversham houses of William Aylmer, Hugh the Elder's steward. [19] He had also been an adherent of Damory and was pardoned as a Contrariant in July 1322. [20] In October 1326 after the queen's invasion, Elizabeth Burgh paid Robert Chedworth for taking her letters to the queen and 'reporting rumours from the king's court.' [21] Never a man with much capacity for forgiveness, Hugh also accused a William Grey from Glamorgan of having been an adherent of Damory and imprisoned him until he acknowledged a debt of £100 to him; Grey had paid 45 pounds of it by the time of Hugh's downfall. [22]

Hugh probably stayed with the king and with his family in London for much of December 1325. The festive season of 1325/26, Edward's last as a free man and Hugh's last ever, was spent in and around Bury St Edmunds in Suffolk, and they visited Hugh's Essex manor of Lamarsh on the way there. Eleanor Despenser stayed at Sheen for Christmas, and presumably her newborn infant was also there with her wet-nurse and other servants, and sent her uncle letters and a gift of a dappled palfrey horse with saddle on 1 January. [23] It was the custom at Edward's court to exchange gifts on that date, and Eleanor may have sent her husband one too, but we have no record of it. In January 1326, Edward went to visit his half-brother Thomas, earl of Norfolk in East Anglia, with Hugh in tow. The king tried to reconcile Norfolk, and made the earl's sister-in-law Joan Jermy the *mestresse* or governess of his daughters Eleanor and Joan, replacing Hugh's sister Isabella Hastings. He made other efforts as well, all in vain: the earl immediately joined his sister-in-law the queen and brother the earl of Kent when their invasion force arrived a few months later. Hugh was with the king at Haughley in Suffolk on 1 January when his wife's gift to Edward of a palfrey arrived, and then left for the Norfolk village of Winfarthing 20 miles away with six hobelars, i.e. armed men on horseback. The six were brothers called Thomas, John and Henry Palington; Roger atte Watre, who 18 months later would be one of a group of men who attacked Berkeley Castle and temporarily freed a deposed Edward from captivity; Robert le Ireys which means 'the Irishman'; and Henry Lambard, presumably from Lombardy. [24] Sometime before 14 June 1325, the three Palington brothers and Robert the Irishman were assaulted and robbed by two dozen men in a house in Fleet Street in London, perhaps because of their association with the detested Hugh (though it may simply have been a random attack). [25]

Winfarthing, Hugh's destination, had belonged to the late Aymer Valence, earl of Pembroke, and on 28 April 1325 was given to Hugh as part of the lands he held from his ward Laurence Hastings, Pembroke's great-nephew and co-heir. It was later held in dower by Laurence's mother Juliana. [26] Juliana had recently married Sir Thomas Blount, steward of Edward's household since 14 May 1325, who wrote letters to the king and Hugh on 17 January 1326 saying that his wife was ill and that therefore he would be late reaching Edward. [27] A few months later, after Hugh's downfall, but before Edward's deposition, Blount and Juliana petitioned Queen Isabella and her son Edward of Windsor because Hugh had delayed the handing over to them of a part of Juliana's rightful dower, including Winfarthing. [28] Even Thomas Blount, appointed steward of the king's household and thus a man trusted by Edward and Hugh, was not able to prevent the royal favourite keeping some of his wife's lands, and even Juliana's own relationship to Hugh – she was the stepdaughter of his late uncle the earl of Warwick, her late husband was his sister Isabella's stepson, and her son was his own ward and his daughter Eleanor's fiancé – did not protect her either.

Queen Isabella in France wrote a letter to Walter Reynolds, archbishop of Canterbury on 5 February 1326 in response to the letter sent to her some weeks before by the bishops, in which she set out her reasons for not returning to England and Edward. The queen referred to Edward as 'our very dear and very sweet lord and friend,' which is highly unconventional and speaks to Isabella's great affection for her husband (she had addressed him repeatedly as 'our very sweet heart' in a letter to him of March 1325), and called Hugh *nostre mauvoillant*, literally 'our evil-wisher', though it can also mean 'devil'. [29] Isabella expressed her amazement that Reynolds would think she could have anything but a 'very great and reasonable cause' for failing to return to Edward, and that she only did so to avoid danger to her person and 'for fear of the said Sir Hugh, who has the governance of our said lord [the king] and his entire kingdom.' Hugh, she wrote, wished to dishonour her as much as he could, and she knew this for certain and had proved it (she did not explain how). Isabella asserted that above all else, after God and the salvation of her soul, she wished to return to Edward's company and to live and die there, and begged Reynolds to excuse her because she could not carry out his request to return to her husband, as to do so would put herself in danger of death. She admitted that she had long hidden her hatred of Hugh and dissembled to protect herself – clearly a response to her husband's statements about her friendliness to Hugh – and ended the letter by stating that she was so distressed about the whole situation she could write no more of it. [30] It seems most likely that Archbishop Reynolds, who had long been an ally of the king, shared the letter with Edward, and therefore Hugh must have heard of it too.

It is beyond all doubt that Isabella of France feared and loathed Hugh Despenser. She had also written a letter on 8 December 1325 to his ally Walter Stapeldon, bishop of Exeter and treasurer of England, who had fled from the French court back to England some weeks earlier. Isabella was furious with Stapeldon and the tone of this letter is irate, yet considerably less personal than her letter of 5 February 1326: she did not accuse Stapeldon of wishing to dishonour or to harm her, and neither did she call him an 'evil-wisher' or say that she hated him. Her greatest accusation against the bishop was that he was more loyal to Hugh than to her and in league with him which she clearly found unforgivable. [31] Isabella's reaction to Hugh was so extreme it seems genuine. Whether she was correct in her belief that her life was in danger from him cannot be known; it seems melodramatic, but she does seem to have truly believed it. The notion one sometimes sees nowadays that Hugh raped Isabella is the invention of two writers of the twenty-first century, and there is not a shred of evidence for it. To smear someone as a rapist, a terrible crime, without any real proof beyond rhetorical questions, is not fair. For all his atrocious treatment of Elizabeth Burgh, Elizabeth Comyn and the others, Hugh was never accused of hurting them physically, and the often-repeated story of his torture of Lady Baret is at the very least grossly exaggerated and has no supporting evidence beyond the word of his enemies. On the other hand, there is no doubt that Isabella conceived a terrible hatred for and fear of Hugh, and she must have had some reason for this, unless she was lying or exaggerating to have an excuse not to return to Edward and to act against him in league with Mortimer. Yet, there is no reason to think she ever hated Edward or that she desired or was working for his downfall, and she seems truly to have mourned for the breakdown of her marriage which she blamed on Hugh. There is evidence that Isabella hoped to reconcile with Edward as late as November 1326, two months after she returned to England at the head of an army. Nor is there any reason to think that she fell passionately in love with Mortimer and that for this reason did not want to go back to her husband and so invented a fear of Hugh as an excuse; her alleged great love affair with Mortimer in 1325/26 is simply modern romanticising. It does seem that Hugh did or said something, or Isabella believed he did or said something, which frightened the queen so much she believed her life was in danger if she went near him. Hugh's almost casual threat to harm John Inge and his threat to John Botetourt that Edward would have him hanged if he did not hand over a manor to Hugh, do give an idea of how he could treat even people who did his bidding, and it is not hard to see how he could be frightening. Whether he ever really would have hurt the queen, or whether he believed himself so untouchable that the king would permit Hugh harming his own wife, we cannot know. One of the charges against Hugh at his trial accused him of sending money to the French court to have Isabella and her son Edward of Windsor murdered, though there is no other evidence for this allegation.

Edward's refusal to take his wife's fears seriously and to send Hugh Despenser away from him was to result a few months later in Hugh's appallingly slow and agonising execution and the king's forced abdication. On 8 February 1326 at Gaywood in Norfolk, Edward told all his sheriffs and his two admirals to issue a proclamation that armed men should be ready to set out 'against the aliens, strangers and enemies of the king who may attack the realm.' Clearly he was expecting an invasion from France at any moment. Edward added that

> 'the queen is adopting the counsel of the Mortimer, the king's notorious enemy and rebel, and of other rebels, and that she is making alliances with the men of those parts and other strangers…to come in force with the king's son against England, to aggrieve and destroy the king's men and his people.' [32]

At this point, Edward did not believe that Isabella and her new allies wished to destroy him personally. His proclamation is the first evidence of the queen's association with Roger Mortimer and other English Contrariants in France which Edward may have heard about from former members of the queen's household returning to England. The proclamation came just three days after Isabella wrote her letter to the archbishop of Canterbury. Perhaps Edward, on hearing that she was allying with his enemies, was too angry with his wife to believe her protestations that she wished nothing more than to return to him. He also perhaps still thought that his wife had tried to assassinate Hugh the previous November, and now she was allied with Roger Mortimer, who certainly had sent assassins after Hugh and his father sometime before mid-November 1323. [33] It is obvious from Edward's last letter to Isabella on 1 December 1325 and the way he was to refer to her later in 1326 as 'the king's wife' rather than as 'the queen' that he was bitterly angry with her. When Isabella fell to her knees in front of her husband two months after she had invaded his kingdom, Edward refused to talk to her or even look at her.

In the early months of 1326, Hugh joined and left the king numerous times. He was with Edward in East Anglia for much of January, and on 30 January the king appointed Hugh's eldest sister Alina Burnell constable of the great North Wales stronghold of Conwy Castle. [34] For a woman to be appointed constable of a castle was an extremely rare occurrence – Alina was only the second in the fourteenth century, after Isabella Vescy at Bamburgh – and probably Hugh influenced the king to choose his sister. Edward took the opportunity to spend five days at the famous pilgrim site of Walsingham in early February with Hugh, and gave the remarkably large sum of 20 marks to his chamber squire Oliver of

Bordeaux 'when the king sat beside his bed a little before midnight' the night before his proclamation about Isabella. Later in 1326 Edward gave a gift of cash to six of his servants who 'woke up at night every time the king himself awoke' which implies that they slept inside his chamber. It perhaps also implies that worry over the ongoing situation with his wife caused the king insomnia. [35] Hugh was with Edward until 7 February and was in London on 10, 11 and 12 February, where Edward wrote to him. [36] Hugh owned a house in Aldgate and also owned the New Temple, given to him, with some coercion involved, by the prior of the Hospital of St John in Jerusalem on 28 June 1324 along with five manors. He spent 22 pounds repairing the Temple in March 1326. [37] Inside it stood a chapel dedicated to St Thomas, a hall, a cemetery, a cloister, a plot of land, a stone wall and another of earth, and some houses built 'in the front part near the highway.' [38]

Eleanor Despenser, meanwhile, was probably still at the royal palace of Sheen, and the king sent her letters on 10 February. [39] Hugh had re-joined the king at Kimbolton, Cambridgeshire by 22 February, and on the 24th they were in Rothwell, Northamptonshire, 25 miles away. Hugh briefly left court between Kimbolton and Rothwell, and Edward sent his runner Montz 'secretly' with letters for him. [40] The king's chamber account also records, somewhat intriguingly, that Hugh 'made a small affray' in Rothwell. [41] His squire Thomas Bradeston was hastily sent to help sort the situation. No more details of the affray are available, but even in his late 30s Hugh had not learned to control the tendency to violence he had demonstrated at the Lincoln parliament exactly 10 years (almost to the day) before when he punched John Ros repeatedly. Perhaps he was suffering from the stress of the queen's hostility and alliance with Roger Mortimer and his other enemies, the Contrariants on the continent.

Chapter 14

The Last Summer

Evil tongues are reporting various unspecific and not very credible things, and we do not wish you in any way to take such words to heart; therefore we beseech you not to allow such things to give you melancholy, understanding that neither our lord the king nor ourselves believe anything of you or anyone around you except good.

Edward wrote to his son Edward of Windsor and his brother-in-law Charles IV on 18 March 1326, in another attempt to get the boy back. The king was still excessively concerned with defending Hugh: Queen Isabella 'feigns a reason to withdraw from us [Edward] by cause of our dear and faithful nephew[-in-law] H. Despenser, who has always served us well and loyally,' he wrote to young Edward, whom he addressed affectionately throughout the letter as *Beaufuitz* or 'fair son'. Charles IV had sent Edward II a letter (which does not survive) informing him that he had spoken to Isabella, who assured her brother that 'she greatly wishes to be with us [Edward] and in our company' and that her pretence of friendship towards Hugh was 'necessary to pass the time and escape worse.' Edward protested, in the middle of a long, rambling and emotional letter, that Isabella had no need to do this, because 'no evil was done to her at any time…since she left the king and came to the king of France, she has sent to our dear and faithful nephew H. Despenser letters of great and special friendship.' He also wrote 'we fully perceive…that she does not love us as she ought to love her lord, and that the matter which she speaks of our said nephew, for which she withdraws herself from us, is feigned and untrue.' [1]

Both Hugh and Eleanor Despenser were at Kenilworth Castle (which had belonged to the executed Thomas of Lancaster) with the king on 28 March 10 days later, and received gifts from him: a silver goblet with foot and cover for Eleanor, and for Hugh a cup, salt-cellar, goblet, two basins, two plates and three smaller salt-cellars, all silver. [2] Eleanor travelled to Kenilworth from Sheen with her cousin, the king's nine-year-old second son John of Eltham, sometime between 1 March and 8 June and stayed there with him for 18 days, perhaps at this time. [3] Hugh had been in London on 21 and 24 March and was back there on the 31st, and paid 10 pounds for saddles from a London saddler called William Pickerell. [4] Around this time, Hugh must have received a letter sent to him by Pope John XXII on 20 March 1326:

> 'His participation in the king's government is given by the queen as a reason for her being unable, without personal danger, to return to the king. The pope suggests that Hugh should retire, and should devise methods by which the queen may no longer fear to return to her husband.' [5]

If Hugh had taken this advice, he might have saved his life and spared Edward II the fate of deposition, and English history might be entirely different, but he did not. On 22 April, John XXII wrote again to Hugh to 'persuade him, instead of causing grievances to princes and prelates, to abstain from provoking enmities, and to study to promote friendships.' Some weeks later, the pope took a less irritated tone, and asked Hugh to 'continue his good offices' promoting harmony between the king and queen. John also sent a letter to Edward assuring him that neither his half-brother the earl of Kent nor Kent's messenger 'said any ill of Hugh Despenser,' and was also writing to Isabella in France urging her to reconcile with Edward. [6]

One of the king's and Hugh's most loyal allies in Gascony was Sir Simon Montbreton, of whom it was said 'he will not fear to do anything which could be to the profit and honour of our lord the king.' [7] In July 1324 Edward gave Montbreton two parts of the Hertfordshire manor of Patmore, forfeited by John Patmore. In or before June 1326 Hugh made Montbreton acting constable of Bristol Castle which Hugh held for life, and paid him 20 pounds. [8] Montbreton was given permission on 13 May 1326 to marry – as long as she consented – Isabel or Elizabeth Sully, stepmother of Aline Mowbray and widow of William Braose, who died on or shortly before 1 May 1326 two years after Hugh forced him to take legal action against Elizabeth Burgh over Gower. [9] John Patmore was imprisoned as a Contrariant, and in September 1324 Edward granted his wife Sarah five pounds annually from her husband's confiscated lands. [10] Perhaps inevitably, after Hugh's downfall Sarah Patmore accused him of conceiving 'certain rancours' against her husband and of persuading Edward to hand over two parts of Patmore's manor to Simon Montbreton. [11] It is difficult to be entirely sure with such accusations against Hugh if they are really true, or if after his death they provided an easy way to have one's petition approved by claiming to have been yet another victim of the loathed and disgraced royal favourite. Sarah duly got the manor of Patmore back from Simon Montbreton early in 1327. One historian has also pointed out that Hugh and his father were 'soft targets' after their downfall and suggests that some petitioners used their name to give their requests more credibility and as 'a clever device to elicit a favourable response.' [12] As late as 15 January 1322, however, John Patmore had accompanied several Despenser adherents such as Peter Ovedale and Philip Joce on the campaign against the Contrariants, and something must have made him switch sides; perhaps the 'certain rancours' Hugh allegedly conceived against him were true. In October 1323 Patmore was said to have 'now adhered' to the recently-escaped Roger Mortimer of Wigmore. [13]

As another example of a possibly exaggerated or false claim against Hugh, six men petitioned Edward III in 1327 because they had been imprisoned in Colchester for the murder of a couple called Ponsard and Alianore Mount Martin, and claimed that Hugh prevented their release. [14] Hugh did have a certain penchant for imprisoning people, but in this case the half-dozen men had committed a genuinely serious crime, and perhaps his name was added to their petition as a way of making the new rulers of England early in Edward III's reign more sympathetic towards them. In March 1330, one claim against Hugh was proven to be false and to be 'manifest deception of the king [Edward III].' [15] Geoffrey Bulstrode claimed that on 25 September 1324 Hugh had seized lands and tenements in Chalfont St Peter, Buckinghamshire which belonged to him. [16] Four commissioners discovered that Bulstrode had no estate in Chalfont of which he could have been deprived by Hugh (and the latter was 70 miles away in Portchester on the date in question), though Hugh did take possession of any of Bulstrode's cattle found grazing on his land. Finally, Hugh lent the abbot of Leicester £100 on 28 January 1325, to be repaid by the end of September. Many years later in 1337, the abbot begged Edward III to pardon him the debt which the king did, on the grounds that Hugh had invented the loan as a 'pretext' to extort money from him. This also seems dishonest; £100 was certainly removed from Hugh's account with the banking firm the Peruzzi and paid out by them to the abbot of Leicester. [17] Then again, Hugh also lent the abbot of Waltham Holy Cross £100 in October 1324 yet made the abbot acknowledge a debt to him of £200, so perhaps he had done something similar to the abbot of Leicester. [18]

On 19 May 1326 at Marlborough in Wiltshire, Edward II attended the wedding of Hugh's retainer Sir Robert Wateville and Hugh's teenage niece Margaret Martin née Hastings. Hugh was almost certainly also present, and had told Wateville – whom he addressed as his 'very dear friend and companion' – the previous year that he wished him to be married. He lent Wateville 100 marks on 16 June. [19] Edward had ordered Wateville's arrest on 15 April 1325 and he was accused of cowardice over his conduct in Gascony, but Hugh told Wateville soon afterwards that 'the king is much softened towards you and much taken out of his great melancholy [over Wateville's behaviour] which makes us glad.'

He added that Wateville need not fear to come to the king, as he, Hugh, would do whatever he could to help him with Edward 'in the most skilful way we can,' and that Wateville was welcome as long as he did nothing in Edward's presence which might offend him. [20] Edward was to show Wateville conspicuous favour and generosity in 1326, and clearly Hugh's pleading with him on the knight's behalf had worked well. Wateville told Hugh that he 'felt strongly confident of your good lordship' and that Hugh had helped his regain his position (he was a former Contrariant), yet would abandon him and Edward later in 1326. [21]

While at Marlborough Hugh may have seen his third daughter Eleanor, who in April 1325 was in the care of his sister Lady Hastings, the bride's mother, and perhaps still was. [22] After the Wateville-Hastings wedding, Edward and Hugh travelled together towards Saltwood in Kent, and on 22 May passed through Caversham in Berkshire, yet another manor which belonged to Hugh. [23] It was 26 May 1326, when the king and his beloved chamberlain travelled from Otford to Maidstone, that marked Hugh and Eleanor Despenser's twentieth wedding anniversary, and Hugh was now about 37 or 38. Only some months after the birth of their youngest child, Hugh may already have known that he was set to become a grandfather via their eldest daughter Isabella, now 14, and her husband the earl of Arundel's 13-year-old son Richard, painfully young though they were. Isabella and Richard were to claim in 1344 that they had been married as children against their will 'by fear of their relatives' and 'on coming to years of puberty expressly renounced' their marriage vows, but were 'compelled by fear and blows to cohabit' resulting in their only child Edmund. Who hit them to make them sleep together, assuming the story is true, is unclear, but Edmund was born in or before late 1326. [24] While at Saltwood, the king played an unspecified ball game in the park with Robert Wateville and Thomas Blount, steward of the royal household, but not with Hugh, who perhaps thought it beneath him. [25] There are also no references to Hugh playing dice or cross and pile, the medieval form of heads or tails, with the king, both of which Edward loved and played often.

Far more seriously, at Saltwood king and chamberlain met two envoys sent to England by Pope John XXII, who was attempting to reconcile the king and queen. The envoys were Guillaume Laudun, archbishop of Vienne and a Dominican friar, and Hugues Aiméry, bishop of Orange, both of whom had met Edward a few times before. The envoys asked Edward and Hugh questions in French about the complaints Isabella had made concerning Hugh. The envoys' aim and the pope's was to ensure the safe return of the queen and her son, but their trip to England proved pointless as Edward utterly refused to send Hugh away from him as Isabella demanded. Even when threatened with an invasion, even when his own wife and son refused to return to him, even when the pope himself begged him to send Hugh away, Edward would not do it. Hugh told the envoys that Isabella could return safely at any time, but that Roger Mortimer had said he would stab her if she did, so evidently people in the queen's entourage were still sending him reports of events at the French court. [26] Hugh had people everywhere: in October 1324 he told Ralph Basset he was hopeful that talks between Edward II and King Robert Bruce would progress well that November, and that he had 'several confidants in those parts [Scotland] who have spoken to us' on the matter (which he told Basset to keep secret). At the same time, he informed the admiral John Sturmy that he had a man who belonged to the faction of Mortimer and the other exiles, who told Hugh plenty of things about them that he knew, but which Hugh could not put into writing. He told Sturmy to send good spies to where the exiles were. [27] Ralph Basset also informed Hugh in December 1323 that he was spying on their movements, at Hugh's command. [28] If Hugh had been the killer and torturer he is sometimes depicted as nowadays, he could have sent assassins after Mortimer as Mortimer had done to him and his father in 1323 – he knew where the rebels were – but he did not.

Eleanor Despenser was staying at Leeds Castle 25 miles away while Hugh and Edward were at Saltwood – the king sent her a gift of 20 marks – and on 13 June they joined her there, spending a few days at the archbishop of Canterbury's manor of Sturry on the way. [29] At Sturry, Hugh spent over 90 pounds on cloth for his household staff which they received twice a year at Christmas and Pentecost (as was customary). [30] Some kind of virus or stomach disorder was going around: four of Hugh's servants including his chamberlain Clement Holditch were left behind near Saltwood, ill, and Edward bought a pomegranate for all of them at an almost unbelievably expensive one pound each. The king's valet Edmund Fisher was also seriously ill presumably with the same condition, and died on 12 June. [31] On 15 June at Leeds Castle, the king purchased four cows to provide 'milk for the mouth of the king and Sir Hugh,' an oddly wholesome drink for Hugh the 'evil genius'. [32] Later that day, Edward and Hugh rode towards Rochester, and at Boxley Down on the way encountered Hamo Hethe, bishop of Rochester. Hethe was one of the few important men of the realm kindly disposed towards them – at the parliament which deposed Edward seven months later he was one of only four men who spoke up in the king's favour – and rode with them towards Rochester.

Sitting in the chamber of the prior of Rochester, the king asked Hethe if it were true that a queen who had once disobeyed her husband had been put down out of her royalty. This is perhaps an indication that he was considering the possibility of asking the pope to annul his marriage to Isabella, though if he did there is no other evidence of it except rumours reported by two chronicles a year or two before that Hugh was exerting himself at the papal court to procure an annulment of the royal marriage. The rumours have been taken too seriously by some modern writers, and there is no evidence at all that Hugh and Edward did any such thing. Hethe replied sharply that whoever had told the king this deserved no thanks. The bishop went on to talk about a Biblical story where one royal adviser had been hanged and the other elevated, and said he would preach it in the king's presence if Edward wished it. Hugh commented that he would enjoy it, as it applied to himself, and Edward joked 'the bishop would not spare you, my lord, in his preaching.' The following day, 16 June, at noon, Bishop Hethe rode with the two men towards Gravesend, and the king told Hugh ruefully that Hethe had never asked him for anything, unlike others whom he had promoted to high office and who had proved ungrateful. Edward ordered Hugh to give Hethe whatever he wanted, and Hugh replied 'My lord, most willingly, since he has well deserved it and has always borne himself well towards you.' [33] On the 17th, Edward and probably Hugh were back at the Tower of London, and Edward paid 25 sailors of the ship *La Despenser* to bring Eleanor to them there in a barge. He also sent a ship called *La Godyer* (i.e. 'Goodyear') to Cardiff to be delivered to Hugh's officials there. [34]

At the Tower on 19 June 1326 – the fourteenth anniversary of Piers Gaveston's death, as Edward was surely painfully aware – the king made one last unsuccessful attempt to bring his son Edward of Windsor back home, and wrote to the boy, Charles IV, and the bishop of Beauvais. By now the king had finally realised that endlessly harping on his dear faithful wonderful Hugh was not working, and for once did not mention him. [35] Neither, of course, did he make any attempt to remove Hugh from court. The king passed the Nativity of St John the Baptist on 24 June, the twelfth anniversary of his defeat at Bannockburn, playing dice with Hugh's cousin Sir Giles Beauchamp, and on the 28th asked a canon to say prayers for Piers Gaveston's soul. [36] Hugh and his son Huchon were with the king at Westminster on 1 July and at Sheen the following day, and on the 9th Edward went stag hunting; perhaps Hugh and his son accompanied him. Eleanor Despenser dined privately (the word in the king's accounts also translates as 'secretly' or 'covertly') with her uncle in the park of Windsor Castle on 11 July. Their cook was called Will Balsham, and had been one of Queen Isabella's staff in France before returning to England, as many of the queen's servants did in late 1325 and early 1326. Edward and Eleanor must have dined in a remote corner of the park, as the king gave Balsham 40 shillings to buy himself a hackney horse to follow them there, the money given to him 'by the king's own hands between two silver dishes.' [37] There is no mention of anyone else attending the king or his niece during this pleasant-sounding picnic. Perhaps they sat in the shade; two chronicles comment that the summer of 1326, Hugh Despenser's last, was so terribly hot that there was a drought in England, rivers dried up and 'conflagrations' burst out spontaneously. [38] Two weeks later when he was again with Eleanor, Edward paid a man to bring them fresh water from a well, perhaps an indication of the heat. [39]

Hugh was at Westminster with the king on 22 July 1326, and received gifts from him: cloth with gold and silver thread for his chapel at the Tower of London and, poignantly, a large and surely very expensive manuscript of the doomed love story of Tristan and Isolde. [40] On this day he left court and headed for Wales, and Edward sent letters after him on the 25th. Simon Sheppey, Hugh's keeper of the wardrobe, went with him, as did some of his other officials. [41] Eight hobelars were said on 9 July to have 'followed Sir Hugh at all times wherever he went,' and presumably they accompanied him to Wales and back. [42] Eleanor Despenser kept her uncle company in her husband's absence, and on 25 and 26 July the king and his niece sailed along the Thames in Surrey where he spent 18 pence on two kinds of fish, roach and dace, for her from a fisherman in Byfleet, gave two shillings to a fisherman called John Walton who 'sang before the king every time he passed through these parts,' and handed out three shillings in alms to seven fisherwomen of Kennington in Eleanor's presence. By 30 July 1326 Hugh had reached Wales where Edward sent him more letters, though it was only a flying visit, as by 5 August he had returned to the king at Portchester in Hampshire, about 125 miles from Caerphilly. [43] Hugh spent part of 1325 and 1326 riding large distances within a strikingly short time, surely only with a small retinue, as taking a large number of servants and possessions would have slowed him down considerably. Given his fear in September 1325 that he would be murdered without the king's protection and given that there were rumours that November that he had been killed, this behaviour seems remarkably cavalier, though perhaps he felt safe with eight armed men around him all the time.

A former ally of the king and his second cousin, Henry, Lord Beaumont, whose support Edward had lost as a result of the 1323 peace settlement with Scotland, travelled to France with Edward of Windsor in September 1325. He returned to England, and was imprisoned at Warwick Castle sometime before 5 August 1326. The Sempringham annalist says he was sent under guard to Kenilworth Castle that February because he 'would not swear to the king and Sir Hugh Despenser the son, to be of their part to live and die.' [44] One of the charges against Hugh at his trial a few months later also says that he forced people to take this oath. He had Sir William Cockerell arrested and imprisoned in the Tower until he swore an oath to live and die with him, and he had to pay Hugh £100 (the usual amount). This debt was recorded on the Close Roll on 13 April 1324. [45] Presumably even Hugh was finally realising the precariousness of his regime and his lack of support and was trying to shore it up by forcing people to take oaths of loyalty. John of Brittany, earl of Richmond and a first cousin of the king, was staying in France with the queen and refusing to return, as was the king's own half-brother the earl of Kent, though in Kent's case at least this was out of hostility to Hugh, not to Edward. Another of Isabella's allies on the continent was Sir John Cromwell, former steward of the royal household, but by now utterly disillusioned with Edward. It is likely that the rebels were in touch with Edward's other half-brother the earl of Norfolk and their first cousin Henry of Lancaster. As well as with noblemen, Edward and Hugh were feuding with various bishops, and seem to have gone out of their way to make as many powerful enemies as possible. Hugh Despenser was undoubtedly an intelligent man, yet by 1326 was behaving in ways that seem unaccountably foolish. Like his successor as royal favourite, Roger Mortimer, he seems to have believed himself untouchable, even immortal, no matter what he did and no matter how few allies he had left. William Airmyn, the new bishop of Norwich, became the latest target of the king's and Hugh's wrath in 1326, and fled to join Isabella. Hugh ranted about Airmyn's betrayal of the king when he and Edward met Bishop Hamo Hethe in June 1326. [46]

By late August 1326, Queen Isabella had left the French court and travelled to the county of Hainault, ruled by Willem, whose wife Jeanne de Valois was her first cousin. Isabella betrothed her son Edward of Windsor to one of Willem and Jeanne's daughters. Hugh had known as early as October 1324 that Roger Mortimer and the other English exiles were planning an invasion of England with the assent of the count of Hainault and perhaps the king of Bohemia (a close ally of France), and would land in Suffolk or Norfolk. A man of their faction had informed him of this, and the invasion force did indeed arrive in Suffolk, yet the advance knowledge did Hugh no good whatsoever. [47] War broke out again with France, and Edward attempted an invasion of Normandy on or just after 10 September 1326 when he and Hugh were at Portchester in Hampshire, under the command of Hugh's knight Sir John Felton. It seems that the king's son Edward of Windsor was in Normandy, and presumably Edward hoped to seize the boy and bring him back to England. Felton was later pardoned 'for invading Normandy and committing depredations while the king [Edward III, i.e. Edward of Windsor] was there.' [48] Edward II sent letters to Hugh's sister Alina Burnell on 2 September 1326, at Conwy where she was constable of the castle, with urgent news: he wrote the letters under his secret seal and told the messenger to return with Alina's answer 'wherever the king may be.' [49] Perhaps Edward and Hugh believed that this part of the kingdom would support Isabella, and on 20 October a few weeks after the queen's invasion Edward replaced Alina as constable with the sheriff of Shropshire and

Staffordshire, probably because he wanted an experienced military man in such an important post. [50] The sheriff, William Ercalowe, later became the steward of Hugh's son Huchon. Alina Burnell outlived Hugh by 37 years, and whatever he had done she seemed to remember her brother with affection: she paid for two chaplains to 'celebrate divine service daily' for Hugh, her nephew Huchon and William Ercalowe. [51] On 16 September 1326, Hugh prudently withdrew £2,000 from his cash deposits with the Italian bankers the Peruzzi. This in fact left him overdrawn to the tune of £181, but as he was their most important client in England, they permitted it. [52] A barrel containing £1,000, presumably of this money, was found at Caerphilly Castle after his downfall, and another £868 of Hugh's was found in the Tower of London. [53] £10,000 belonging to Hugh and his father was left in the possession of the abbot of Malmesbury in Wiltshire, and not discovered until August 1337. [54] So astonishingly wealthy had the Despensers made themselves that this staggeringly large sum – tens of millions in modern terms – was not missed or even known about until 11 years after their downfall.

Chapter 15

The End

When one is in trouble owing to evil plotting and treachery, one must be sincere and willing and work vigorously to find a good way out, because from this, honours come.

T he invasion force of Queen Isabella, her son Edward of Windsor, the king's half-brother the earl of Kent, Roger Mortimer, other Contrariants and about 1,500 armed men, landed in Suffolk on 24 September 1326. They were immediately joined by Edward's other half-brother the earl of Norfolk. Another man with them was Sir Jean Beaumont, brother of the count of Hainault, whom Hugh had probably met when Beaumont took part in his brother's jousting tournament at Mons in 1310. The *French Chronicle of London* says 'the mariners of England were not minded to prevent their coming, by reason of the great anger they entertained against Sir Hugh Despenser.' [1] Edward, Hugh, Hugh the Elder and Eleanor Despenser were at the Tower of London, with the king's 10-year-old second son John of Eltham, when they heard the news on 28 September. London exploded into chaos and anarchy; the king and Hugh's ally Walter Stapeldon, bishop of Exeter, was caught by a mob and beheaded with a bread knife, and Hugh's secretary John Marshal was also beheaded in the middle of Cheapside. [2] Unable to hold a hostile city, and remembering how the Marchers had kept them penned in during the parliament of August 1321, Edward and the two Hugh Despensers decided to head for South Wales in the hope that they would find support in Hugh's lordship. They left London on 3 October, and Hugh and Edward never saw Eleanor, or the king's son John, again.

The queen and her allies pursued her husband and Hugh west, ransacking Despenser lands and taking money from abbeys as they went. Isabella helped herself to £800 which the chief justice and Edward's ally Hervey Staunton had stored at Bury St Edmunds; he died the following year without recovering the money. [3] The earls of Norfolk and Kent sent their men far and wide to plunder Despenser manors, grabbing whatever they could. [4] Isabella captured a manor belonging to the brother of the brother of Robert Baldock, the chancellor of England and Hugh's faithful ally, and destroyed all his goods.

[5] The queen was joined by her uncle and Edward's cousin Henry of Lancaster, plus a number of the English bishops, the archbishop of Dublin, northern lords and the remnant of the Contrariant faction. Edward's support collapsed like a house of cards. The unpopularity of Hugh Despenser and his father ensured that few men were willing to help their own king, and soon Edward became little more than a fugitive in his own kingdom. The king sent out spies to report his wife's movements to him, though it did not help, and also sent out numerous writs ordering armed men to him, but they never materialised or simply joined the queen. The king put a ransom of £1,000 on Roger Mortimer's head on 28 September, and according to the much later chronicler Thomas Walsingham, Isabella responded by putting one of £2,000 on Hugh's. [6] She sent a letter to London on 6 October, urging the mayor and citizens to help her 'destroy Sir Hugh Despenser, our enemy and the enemy of the whole realm, as you well know,' for the common good of the whole country. Isabella asked them to do this 'on the faith which you owe to our lord the king and to us.' At this point, the queen seems not to have known that Hugh and Edward had left London three days earlier, as she asked the mayor and citizens to capture Hugh and keep him under strict guard. [7] The *Anonimalle* chronicle says 'the king would not leave the company of his enemies,' and that Isabella pursued him to make him leave the Despensers and because she wanted 'to re-join her lord [husband] if she could.' [8] One wonders if English history might be different had Edward abandoned the Despensers and gone to his wife. Isabella, her son Edward of Windsor, and the earl of Kent issued a proclamation at Wallingford on 15 October, declaring Hugh Despenser the Younger to be a public enemy who had to be destroyed. The allegations against him would be repeated in greater detail at his show trial a few weeks later.

At Chepstow, South Wales on 18 October, Edward received letters from Hugh the Elder, who had remained in Bristol. [9] This would be Hugh's last ever communication from his father. Isabella and her allies arrived at Bristol that day, and on the 27th the city fell to them. Hugh the Younger himself was keeper of the city and castle for life, and on or just before 21 October surrendered his possession of Bristol into the king's own hands, probably in a fruitless attempt to protect his father. [10] Hugh the Elder, aged 65, was given a show trial and not allowed to speak in his own defence, and was immediately hanged in his armour on the gallows used for common criminals on the same day the queen and her allies took Bristol. [11] His head was sent on a spear to be displayed on the walls of Winchester, the town of which he was earl, and his body, horribly, was fed to dogs. And thus ended the life of the man who had been a loyal royal servant for many decades, whose father had died in rebellion against Edward II's grandfather as far back as 1265. Whether Isabella had wanted the elder Hugh dead or not – and one chronicle written far away in Suffolk claims, probably erroneously, that she pleaded for his life – his close association with his son and his own corruption and brutality condemned him. Hugh and Edward heard of his father's death on or before 5 November when they were at Neath. [12] Hugh the Younger's retainer and nephew-in-law Sir Robert Wateville abandoned him and Edward even though both men had shown him great favour in 1326 (the king gave him many gifts of cash and visited him when he was ill), and was with Isabella at Bristol on 26 October. [13] He probably witnessed the execution of his wife Margaret's grandfather Hugh the Elder the following day. Hugh the Elder's godson Edward of Windsor, not yet 14, also saw him die.

Also on 18 October at Chepstow, Sir Thomas Wyther, a former Lancastrian knight now in Hugh's service, swore an oath on the Host in Edward's chamber. In front of the king and Hugh, Wyther promised never to leave Hugh as long as he lived, and Edward paid him 20 marks. [14] This, more than anything else, reveals Hugh's utter desperation; the powerful chamberlain, who had once held the kingdom in his hand, was now reduced to bribing men to stay with him. This happened only three and a half weeks after Isabella's invasion force had landed in Suffolk, and if Edward and Hugh had ever been in any doubt as to the precariousness of their situation, they could not have been now. As the *Anonimalle* points out, 'everyone feared [Hugh] and hated him from the bottom of their hearts,' and in his hour of need, he found that he could rely on almost no-one. [15] Hugh and the king were also forced to pardon Roger Seyntmor, whom Hugh in 1319 had ordered John Inge to 'harm and harass,' and three others for supporting the invasion force 'on condition that they do not rise against the king again or assist the rebels.' [16] Even long-term Despenser stalwarts such as Ingelram Berenger, John Haudlo and Hugh's own brother-in-law Ralph Camoys seem to have remained on the sidelines in late 1326. Edward would not abandon Hugh even at this desperate stage, and Hugh could have fled abroad with all his money and tried to establish himself there, but to his credit he did not abandon Edward either. In 1326 during their flight, an annalist called them 'the king and his husband.'

Hugh and Edward with several others including possibly the earl of Arundel and certainly Hugh's confessor Richard Bliton tried to sail from Chepstow on 20 October, probably trying to reach Hugh's Lundy Island in the Bristol Channel, and ultimately Ireland. [17] After five days they had gone nowhere, and the king's chamber account records a payment to Bliton for praying to Saint Anne that 'she would send us a good wind'. [18] Saint Anne refused to oblige, and they landed at Cardiff and made their way to Caerphilly. Hugh's son Huchon joined them here, or perhaps had been with them the entire time since London; on 20 October he was one of three people ordered to seize the lands and goods of Henry of Lancaster, earl of Leicester, into the king's hands. Another man probably with them at some point was the loyal Gascon lord Arnaud Caillau; some weeks later the queen paid 158 men to pursue Caillau by ship along the English coast which suggests that he had been with Edward and Hugh and was now fleeing back to Gascony. [19]

King and chamberlain left Caerphilly at the beginning of November, leaving Huchon behind. As Edward's biographer Seymour Phillips has pointed out, their doing so has no obvious logic. [20] The castle could, and did, withstand a long siege, they had a huge amount of cash and treasure inside (£1,000 of Hugh's held in one large barrel and £13,000 of Edward's in 26 barrels), and there was ample food and drink. Probably by now Edward and Hugh had no plan at all and were just wandering around in despair. They left Caerphilly under the command of Sir John Felton, who swore an oath on the Gospels to keep Huchon and all the money and treasure inside safely and not to give them up to Isabella or Edward's son Edward of Windsor. [21] This oath may have been taken at Hugh's command rather than Edward's; one correspondent in Gascony told the king in early 1325 that 'when I left Portchester, Sir Hugh made me swear on the Gospels' that he would inform Edward honestly of the damage he found in the duchy. [22] Also left inside Caerphilly were many members of Edward and Hugh's households (or rather household, singular). Edward, Hugh and a few others went to Neath Abbey and stayed there until 10 November, accompanied at that point by the king's nephew Edward Bohun, aged about 14 and son of the earl of Hereford who fell at the battle of Boroughbridge. The abbot of Glastonbury in Somerset, Adam Sodbury, gave refuge in his abbey to Hugh's ally Robert Baldock, though when is unclear, as Baldock was with Edward and Hugh at their capture on 16 November. Sodbury also took possession of a quantity of Hugh's treasure, and Edward left £6,000 inside Neath Castle. [23]

The queen sent a search party to find the king and Hugh. They included Edward's cousin and Hugh's former brother-in-law Henry of Lancaster, earl of Leicester and now calling himself earl of Lancaster, Master Rhys ap Hywel who had been imprisoned in the Tower by Hugh years before, and two sons of Llywelyn Bren. [24] Capture was inevitable; it was merely a matter of time, and it finally came on Sunday, 16 November 1326. The St Paul's annalist says that Hugh and Edward were found and taken in a wood during a great storm with terrific thunder and lightning which lasted the whole day, and while this sounds like dramatic licence, the *Anonimalle* also says there was 'marvellous thunder' throughout that Sunday. [25] They seem to have been found near Llantrisant only about 10 miles from Caerphilly; perhaps they had decided to seek refuge in the castle again after their aimless wanderings to Neath. With them were only Robert Baldock the chancellor, Robert Holden the keeper of the king's wardrobe, and a handful of knights, squires and clerks. The knights were former Lancastrian adherents, one of them Sir Thomas Wyther who had sworn an oath to Edward and Hugh a month before not to leave Hugh as long as he lived. On 17 November the day after their capture, Edward and Hugh's ally Edmund Fitzalan, earl of Arundel, was beheaded in Hereford on the orders of his cousin Roger Mortimer, without a trial and also without an experienced executioner; a 'worthless wretch' took off his head with 22 strokes of an axe. Two other men of much lower rank were killed with him for no better reason than that they had annoyed Mortimer or were in the wrong place at the wrong time, also without a trial. Eleanor Despenser was imprisoned in the Tower with some of her children also on 17 November. [26]

Hugh and Edward were forcibly separated; both knew Hugh was going to his death. Henry of Lancaster took over custody of his cousin the king, and led him to Kenilworth in Warwickshire via his castle of Monmouth. Lancaster was in Hereford for Hugh's mock trial and execution, however, so it is possible that Edward was also in the town when Hugh was killed, though one hopes he did not have to witness it. [27] Robert Baldock was also arrested and treated inhumanely, and although as a cleric he could not be executed, he died in misery at Newgate prison in London a few months later. Edward, still the king albeit from this point on little more than in name only, was treated with respect. One chronicle from Flanders which gives a detailed and mostly accurate account of the events of 1326, states that after Edward was captured, Isabella went to his chamber and knelt in front of him, and begged him for God's sake to 'cool his anger' with her. He refused to talk to her or even to look at her. [28] The chronicle does not say exactly when and where this happened except that it was after Edward's capture on 16 November, though it hardly seems likely that Isabella would have asked Edward to forgive her after she had his beloved Hugh grotesquely executed. It seems that even at this late date, after the executions of the earls of Winchester and Arundel, Isabella was still hoping for some kind of reconciliation with her husband, or at the very least his forgiveness for her actions. She had maintained for a year that her quarrel was with Hugh, not Edward, and she seems to have genuinely meant it. Even at this late stage, Edward's own downfall and deposition was not inevitable, and perhaps not yet even desired or looked for by the queen and her allies. His fate was discussed at Wallingford over Christmas which he himself spent at Kenilworth 'in great depression,' and was ultimately decided by Parliament in London in January 1327. [29]

No consideration or respect was shown to Edward's chamberlain and favourite. Hugh was tied to a mean horse and led slowly to Hereford; the journey of 65 miles took eight days, to show him off to as many people as possible. People yelled abuse at him and pelted him with rubbish and manure. A sergeant-at-arms called Simon of Reading was made to go in front of Hugh, carrying his coat of arms reversed as a sign of disgrace, and Hugh's 'hood was taken from his head' and a chaplet of sharp nettles placed there. Two squires rode alongside him blowing bugle horns in his ears which must have been deafening, but might at least have drowned out some of the insults people were hurling at him. [30] The men in charge of bringing Hugh to the queen were Sir Henry Leyburne, once a retainer of Piers Gaveston, and Sir Robert Stangrave, a former sheriff of Surrey who had accompanied Hugh's father to Scotland in 1322. [31] One of the men waiting for him in Hereford was Sir Thomas Wake, previously a ward of the king who had been at court and witnessed a royal charter as recently as 20 April 1326, and who was to play a vital role in Edward's deposition in January 1327. [32]

Hugh refused to eat or even drink anything after his capture. The *Brut* chronicle says that Isabella wished him to be taken to London, presumably so that as many people as possible would see the powerful favourite humiliated and executed. Because after eight days Hugh was 'feeble' from lack of sustenance and 'almost dead,' however, it was decided that he would be executed at Hereford instead so that he would not slip quietly away and cheat his enemies of their revenge and the grand showpiece of his execution. [33] This may have been Hugh's intention, so that he would not be taken to London where his wife and some of his children were, and who might be made to witness his savage death. On arrival at Hereford, Biblical verses were scrawled or carved onto Hugh's arms, shoulders and chest, and he faced his triumphant enemies. He had not seen Roger Mortimer since the latter was imprisoned at the Tower in February 1322, and probably not since the parliament of August 1321 which exiled Hugh and his father. It was also over 20 months since he had last seen the queen, who cannot have been anything but delighted that her husband's loathed and feared favourite was now at her mercy and would die for his crimes against her. Also present were Henry of Lancaster, Edward's half-brothers the earls of Norfolk and Kent and his son Edward of Windsor, now 14. There was no real trial, only a list of accusations and a conviction read out in French by Sir William Trussell. He is difficult to identify certainly as there were several English knights with this name active in the early fourteenth century, but he was possibly the one knighted with Hugh, Edward and Mortimer in May 1306. Trussell addressed Hugh by his first name without the 'Sir' to which he was entitled as deliberate disrespect, though had called his father Hugh the Elder at his own show trial a month earlier 'Hugh, sire'. [34] How much Hugh the Younger even heard of his indictment is debateable; he was probably barely conscious from lack of water and food, and perhaps partially deafened by the blowing of bugle horns directly in his ears for days on end.

'Hugh Despenser, in the parliament of our present lord king Edward, held at Westminster in the fifteenth year of his reign [August 1321], by investigation of the prelates, earls and barons and all the community of the realm, it was found to be notorious that your father and you, Hugh, were traitors and enemies of the realm, for which cause, by the assent and command of our lord the king and all the baronage, your father and you, Hugh, were exiled from the realm never to return which was done by the assent and permission of our lord the king and all the baronage and all those who were duly summoned to parliament.

'Against which judgement and exile, your father and you, Hugh, returned to the realm, and were found at court without authorisation. And you, Hugh, in returning to the realm, feloniously robbed two dromonds to the value of £60,000 sterling, to the great dishonour of the king and the realm, and to the great peril of merchants who often visit foreign countries. After this felony committed by you, Hugh, you approached our lord the king and made him ride in arms against the peers of the realm and others of his faithful liegemen, to destroy and disinherit them contrary to Magna Carta and the Ordinances, and so riding in force and in arms, seizing royal power, you, Hugh, and your father and your adherents feloniously robbed the good men of the realm. With Andrew Harclay and other traitors, your adherents, you had the good earl of Hereford and Sir William Sully and Sir Roger Burghfield feloniously and maliciously murdered. [These men were killed at the battle of Boroughbridge on 16 March 1322, at which Hugh was not present.]

'You took the good earl of Lancaster, who was the first cousin of our lord the king and his brothers, and uncle of the very noble king of France and his sister my lady the queen of England, and had him falsely imprisoned and robbed, and in his own hall in his castle, by your royal power which you had seized from our lord the king, had him judged by a false record contrary to law and reason and Magna Carta and also without a defence, and you had him martyred and murdered by hard and piteous death. And this wickedness and tyranny done to such an exalted person could not sate you of spilling the blood of Christians, and also on this same day, to further torment my said lord, you had his barons and knights before his vanquished eyes condemned to death by drawing and hanging. By this false record contrary to law and reason, you shamefully had them hanged without mercy: Sir Warin Lisle, Sir William Tuchet, Sir Thomas Mauduit, Sir Henry Bradbourne, Sir William Cheney, Sir William FitzWilliam the younger. At York, my lord [Roger] Clifford, my lord [John] Mowbray, Sir Jocelyn Deyville. At Canterbury, the lord [Bartholomew] Badlesmere and

Sir Bartholomew Ashburnham. At London, Sir Henry Tyes. At Windsor, Sir Francis Aldenham. At Gloucester, the lord [John] Giffard and Sir Roger Elmbridge. At Bristol, Sir Henry Wilington and Sir Henry Montfort. At Winchelsea, Sir Thomas Culpepper. [This is a complete list of the lords and knights executed in 1322 except Stephen Baret and William Fleming.]

'Many other magnates you had sent to hard prison, to murder them without cause for covetousness of their lands, such as the lord [Roger] Mortimer and Mortimer the uncle, and the lord [Maurice] Berkeley and Sir Hugh Audley the father and son, and the children of [the earl of] Hereford who were the nephews of our lord the king. And great ladies, wives of these lords, and their children, you kept in prison and orphaned. And after the deaths of their barons, you pursued widowed ladies such as my lady Baret, and as a tyrant you had her beaten by your mercenaries and shamefully had her arms and legs broken against the order of chivalry and contrary to law and reason, by which the good lady is forever more driven mad and lost.

'And many other such people who should have been ladies of great honour, you made follow the court on foot in great poverty, without pity and without mercy, and every day they were held in such great ignominy that God by His mercy sent our good and gracious lady and her son [Queen Isabella and Edward of Windsor] and the good men who have come in their company to the land, by which the realm is delivered.

'Hugh, after this destruction of our noble liege lord [Lancaster] and of other men of the realm done falsely, shamefully and treacherously, you, Hugh, and your father and Robert Baldock, who between you treacherously embraced royal power, had our lord the king and his people led to Scotland to the enemies, where you, by your treacherous conduct, lost more than 20,000 of his [Edward II's] people who died piteously by your error, to the great dishonour and damage of our lord the king and of all his people, without achieving anything.

'After returning, you, Hugh, your father, and Robert Baldock, falsely and treacherously counselled our lord the king to leave my lady the queen in peril of her person in the priory of Tynemouth in Northumberland, in the borderlands. You had our lord the king led in flight to Blackhow Moor, where his enemies of Scotland, by your treacherous conduct, surprised him, to the great dishonour and damage of the king and his people, as was well evident by the fires and the dead bodies. And in such great misfortune and peril of her person, my lady [Isabella] who was your liege lady, by your treacherous deed might have been lost, to the perpetual dishonour and damage of the king and his realm, if God had not sent her deliverance by sea, thereby rescuing her from danger to her life and saving her honour, in such grief of heart and body that no good lady of her status and nobility should have at any time.

'Hugh, neither this treason nor cruelty could suffice for you, but by the royal power which you had seized from our lord the king, you destroyed the privileges of Holy Church. The prelates such as Hereford, Lincoln, Ely, Norwich, you feloniously robbed of their goods inside Holy Church, and outside, you carried off their horses and their plate and baggage, and made them go on foot. And their lands and possessions you seized by force, against law and reason. It did not only suffice for you to make war on the ministers of Holy Church, but also you plundered it, as a false Christian, renegade and traitor against God Himself. And because you knew that God made miracles by my good lord [Lancaster] whom you murdered so cruelly against the law without cause, you, Hugh, as a false Christian, sent armed men into Holy Church and had the doors of monasteries shut down and closed so that no-one was bold enough to enter the Church and worship God or his saints, for which merit and in defiance of you, God made divine gifts and miracles.

'After this wickedness, you falsely and treacherously counselled our lord the king, to the disinheritance of his crown and his heirs, to give to your father, who was false and a traitor, the earldom of Winchester, and the earldom of Carlisle to Andrew Harclay who was a notorious traitor and criminal, and to you, Hugh, the land of *Canteruaure* [Cantref Mawr?] and other lands which belong to the Crown. And also, Hugh, you, your father and Robert Baldock had my lady the queen ousted from her lands which were given and assigned to her by our lord the king, and set her on her journey [to France in March 1325] meanly, against the dignity of her highness and of her status. As a false and disloyal traitor, you daily encouraged and procured discord between our lord the king and herself, by your complete royal power. And, Hugh, when my lady the queen and her son, by the command and assent of our lord the king, crossed the sea to save the land of Gascony which was about to be lost, by your treacherous counsel you sent over the sea a large sum of money to certain evil men, your adherents, to destroy my lady and her son, who was the rightful heir of the kingdom, and to prevent their return to this country which would have been to their damage and destruction, if you had succeeded in doing this.

'Hugh, your father and Robert Baldock and the other false traitors, your adherents, travelled around the kingdom by land and by sea, assuming royal power, making magnates and lesser people, by constraint, promise and assure you that they would maintain you in your false quarrels against all people, regardless of the fact that such confederations were false and treacherous and against the bond and estate of the king and his crown. By your royal power you had them put in arduous prison, such as Sir Henry Beaumont, who did not want to swear that they would assent to your wickedness. And when you, Hugh, and the other false traitors, your adherents, knew that my lady and her son were returning to this land, you made our lord the king, by your treacherous counsel, remove himself from them, and led him out of the kingdom in great danger to his person. And to the great dishonour of himself and of his people, you feloniously took the treasure of the realm and the great seal with you.

'Hugh, as a traitor you are found, and as such are judged by all the good people of the realm, great and lesser, rich and poor. By common assent you are found as a thief and a criminal, and for this you will be hanged. And because you are found a traitor, you will be drawn and quartered, and [the pieces of your body] sent throughout the realm. And because you were exiled by our lord the king and by common assent, and returned to the court without authorisation, you will be beheaded. And because you were always disloyal and procured discord between our lord the king and our very honourable lady the queen, and between other people of the realm, you will be disembowelled, and then they will be burnt.

Withdraw, you traitor, tyrant, renegade; go to take your own justice, traitor, evil man, and convict!' [35]

Some of the charges were reasonable, some contained enough of a kernel of truth to seem vaguely plausible and many others were laughably absurd, and they provide a handy reminder that propaganda is not a modern invention. Hugh and his father were blamed for everything that had gone wrong in the previous few years; the queen and her allies did not yet dare blame Edward himself, at least in public, and so the king was presented as Hugh's victim and almost as a child with no agency of his own. The charges reveal a great deal about Isabella's attitude towards Hugh and what she blamed him for: leaving her in danger at Tynemouth in 1322, persuading her husband to confiscate her lands, and sending her to France with little money. The phrase 'in such grief of heart and body' indicates that the queen still found the memory of Tynemouth painful. Isabella did not accuse Hugh of persuading Edward to remove her children from her which as previously noted is an invention of the late twentieth century. Nor is there any hint of sexual impropriety, also a modern invention. There are several references to the execution of the earl of Lancaster in March 1322, for which Hugh and his father alone were blamed. One of the men sitting in judgement on Hugh was the earl of Kent, who had been another man who sentenced Lancaster to death; the hypocrisy of this was ignored. The charge relating to the mysterious 'Lady Baret', presumably the widow of the Contrariant Stephen Baret executed in 1322 (though the list of men executed read out by Trussell did not even mention him), is generally assumed by modern writers to be absolutely true and accurate, yet there is nothing whatsoever to confirm the story. It is impossible to believe that all fourteenth-century chroniclers would have missed the gross abuse and torture of a noblewoman into insanity, or that Lady Baret or her family would not have petitioned for restitution in Edward III's reign when it was safe to do so and the other victims of the Despensers did. This charge against Hugh at his show trial is the only mention of the tale, and other than one reference in 1324 to Baret's widow Joan Gynes or Mandeville, there is no evidence that a 'Lady Baret' even existed.

There had, of course, never been the slightest doubt that Hugh would be sentenced to death, and a gallows had already been built for him, a staggering 50 feet high. He was roped to four horses which dragged him through the streets to the gallows, and there he suffered his drawn-out and atrocious death of slow strangulation, castration, disembowelment and beheading in front of a jeering mob and the queen, Roger Mortimer, the earl of Kent and his other enemies. The St Paul's annalist wrote that Hugh sustained his torments 'humbly and patiently.' [36] The most graphic account of Hugh's death is found in the work of Jean Froissart written a few decades later which adds the detail that Hugh was castrated because he was a heretic and a sodomite 'even with the king.' Froissart is a hugely unreliable source for Edward II's reign and was not even born until about 1337, but he knew Hugh's grandson Edward, Lord Despenser (born 1336) very well, so may have heard family stories. He also based his account of Hugh's execution on the work of Jean le Bel, a chronicler who was an eyewitness to it. Simon of Reading was executed with Hugh, hanged on the same gallows beneath him, but not given the full traitor's death. His execution is puzzling; he was a sergeant-at-arms in the royal household and not, as far as is known, a Despenser official or involved in any of Hugh's extortions. Various chroniclers say he was hanged because he 'insulted the queen,' but this was not a capital offence in England in 1326, and he was given no trial to prove the allegation. Perhaps Reading's real crime was that in April 1323 he had been granted lands in Worcestershire forfeited by John Wyard, a faithful adherent of Roger Mortimer for many years. [37]

Hugh's head was taken to London and carried along Cheapside to the sound of trumpets, and on 4 December 1326 was impaled on London Bridge; one hopes his children in the Tower did not have to see it. [38] The four quarters of his body were sent to Carlisle, York, Dover and Bristol, in the north-west, north, south-east and south-west, more or less the four corners of the kingdom. Four days after his death, Isabella took possession of Hugh's jewels and 30-plus gold cups and pitchers (just one of which was worth more than most people earned in a year) which he kept in the Tower. [39] The queen had also helped herself to the money and possessions of the earl of Arundel, including £524 in cash, days after his botched beheading. [40] Not content with destroying Hugh completely, Isabella took revenge on his family. Huchon was besieged for months at Caerphilly and threatened with execution, and on 1 January 1327 came the cruellest order: Hugh's middle three daughters Joan, Eleanor and Margaret Despenser were forcibly veiled as nuns, in three separate convents far apart. [41] Isabella the eldest daughter was safe as she was married and pregnant or had recently given birth, and Elizabeth the fifth daughter was safe as she was only a year old, but the other three became the targets of the queen's wrath. Joan the eldest of the three was no more than about 10 or 12 years old, and Margaret only 3. Margaret was taken to Watton Priory in Yorkshire which was about 30 miles from where she was then living with Sir Thomas Houk, Eleanor to Sempringham Priory in Lincolnshire, and Joan to Shaftesbury Abbey in Dorset.

It is difficult to discern any motive on Isabella's part except vindictiveness. Edward had sent three of Roger Mortimer's eight daughters to convents in 1324, but they were not forced to take binding lifelong vows as nuns and were later released, and they were much older. Even Isabella's previous affection for Hugh's widow Eleanor did not save Eleanor's daughters. The later chronicler Henry Knighton wrote that Eleanor Despenser behaved and was treated by Edward as though she were queen while Isabella was abroad in 1325/26. [42] If Isabella thought that Eleanor had usurped her position as queen, this can only have angered her. One historian has suggested that the continental chronicler who stated that Eleanor had a sexual relationship with her uncle the king might have heard it from someone in Isabella's entourage in 1326. [43] Knighton's rather cryptic comment also perhaps implies that that Edward and Eleanor were intimate (or perhaps it does not). If the queen knew or suspected that Eleanor had slept with her husband, this must also have made her feel angry and betrayed and perhaps revolted because it was incest, and Eleanor was imprisoned at the Tower until 25 February 1328 with some of her children and servants. [44]

The Despenser adherent Sir John Felton held out at Caerphilly Castle with Huchon Despenser for months. On 4 October 1324, Hugh the Younger had told Felton how much he appreciated his diligence, loyalty and good conduct, and that he felt 'much great joy' when he heard good news of Felton, as if he were his own cousin. On another occasion Hugh told him that the king 'has greatly given you his heart' because he was so pleased with Felton's service. Felton responded that he would strive to serve Edward and Hugh as loyally and well as he could, and he kept both his word and the oath he swore to them on the Gospels: he saved the life of Hugh's eldest son. [45] Queen Isabella offered several pardons 'of the forfeiture of their life and limbs' to all the men inside Caerphilly, deliberately excluding Huchon by name, but they refused to give him up. [46] The besieging force included 25 knights, 21 squires and 400 footmen, while of the approximately 135 men inside the castle, the only knights were John Felton and Thomas Lovell. [47] Among the garrison were a large number of Edward's chamber staff who had worked under Hugh, including Giles of Spain, Peter Plummer, Henry Hustret, Walter Cowherd, Simon Hod, John Pope and a few others; five of the hobelars said earlier that year to have followed Hugh wherever he went; Hugh's blacksmith Will of Denbigh and Edward's blacksmith John Cole; and Edward's master carpenter William Hurley, who worked on the famous Octagon Tower of Ely Cathedral as well as on the great hall of Caerphilly. [48] Most of the men inside Caerphilly had no military training, yet bravely held out for months against the besieging force, and some of them were later involved in plots to free Edward II from captivity after his deposition, and even after his reported death. Finally on 20 March 1327 the garrison surrendered when the queen gave up and agreed to spare Huchon's life, though he was kept in prison until July 1331, until December 1328 in the custody of Roger Mortimer. Huchon was then moved to Bristol Castle where his jailer was Sir Thomas Gurney, sentenced to death in absentia two years later for the murder of Huchon's great-uncle Edward II. [49] Had John Felton and the others not defended Huchon so staunchly, he would certainly have been executed, despite being only about 17 and not guilty of anything except being Hugh the Younger's eldest son. In early 1329, Huchon's mother Eleanor married (perhaps not voluntarily) William Zouche, lord of Ashby in Leicestershire, who had led the siege of Caerphilly.

Edward II was forced in January 1327 to abdicate his throne to his 14-year-old son, who became Edward III, and was kept under guard at Kenilworth and then at Berkeley Castle. Hugh Despenser the Younger had done what no-one had done in England before: he brought down a king. The dowager queen Isabella and Roger Mortimer ruled England during the young king's minority and acted in avaricious and enormously unpopular ways indistinguishable from those of their predecessors, until Edward III overthrew their regime on 19 October 1330. He had Mortimer hanged at Tyburn on 29 November, four years and five days after Hugh's execution, also on charges of usurping royal power. On 15 December 1330, the young king gave permission for Hugh's remains in London, Carlisle, York, Bristol and Dover to be collected and buried. [50] Whatever was left of Hugh after four years' exposure to the elements was interred at Tewkesbury Abbey in Gloucestershire, the mausoleum of the Clares and Despensers, and is still there today. Rather peculiarly, the sarcophagus of Abbot John Coles (died 1347) was placed on top of Hugh's and remains there, and the richly decorated carving on his tomb was much vandalised during the Reformation. Edward II lies just 10 miles away from Hugh in Gloucester Cathedral. Eleanor Despenser and Huchon were also buried at Tewkesbury Abbey when they died in 1337 and 1349, and so were some of Hugh and Eleanor's descendants: their grandson Edward Despenser, lord of Glamorgan (the famous 'Kneeling Knight' of Tewkesbury), great-grandson Thomas Despenser, who was briefly earl of Gloucester in the late 1390s, and their great-great-granddaughter Isabella Beauchamp née Despenser, countess of Warwick and the grandmother of Richard III's queen Anne Neville.

Contemporary chroniclers were unanimous in their dislike and disapproval of Hugh; no-one had a good word to say about him. His greed and despotism ensured that hardly anyone lifted a finger to help him in late 1326, even to help their king. Hugh was not, contrary to popular modern belief, a murderous, torturing psychopath and rapist, yet he abused his position and took advantage of anyone he could, including vulnerable men and women. He could even turn against friends who had served him loyally for years, committed blackmail and false imprisonment, demonstrated almost pathological greed, and was a pirate and an extortionist. Whatever he did or said to Queen Isabella caused her to loathe and fear him to the extent that she did what no queen of England had ever done before (or since) and invaded her husband's kingdom with an army, and – whether she had intended to do so or not – forced the deposition of a king for the first time in English history.

Hugh's enemies did many of the same things they accused Hugh of doing, such as imprisoning men or releasing them without authority, executing men without authority or without allowing them a defence, returning to England without authority, seizing lands which were not theirs. Thomas of Lancaster, although promoted as a saint in and after 1322, was a grasping and despised landlord; John Mowbray had men beheaded without trial in May 1321, and robbed a church; Queen Isabella granted herself the largest income anyone in England except kings received throughout the entire Middle Ages (£13,333 a year which dwarfed even Hugh's), and bankrupted her son's kingdom in under four years; Roger Mortimer, sometimes touted as the great hero who saved England from the tyranny of Hugh Despenser, gave himself a grandiose earldom and disinherited people including his own first cousin Mortimer of Chirk's son, and kept for himself Alice Lacy's great lordship of Denbigh, taken from her by Hugh Despenser the Elder. Mortimer killed his cousin the earl of Arundel and others in 1326 without a trial and had Edward II's half-brother the earl of Kent judicially murdered in 1330, and was hanged by Edward III for usurping royal power. In and after 1327, the people of England realised that they had merely replaced the regime of the king and his ruthless greedy favourite with that of the queen and her ruthless greedy favourite, hardly an improvement. Hugh did what most of his peers would have done if they could: as one historian has pointed out, 'all magnates, to a greater or lesser extent, had the potential to operate grasping, extortionate regimes' and to manipulate the legal process in their favour. [51] Hugh Despenser the Younger's sins were writ large; as the king's favourite, he had a greater stage to play on than his rivals did, and a far greater scope to do whatever he wished without interference. His crimes and misdeeds destroyed a king, his own family, and himself.

Appendix 1

Hugh's Children

Hugh (Huchon), lord of Glamorgan (before July 1309–8 February 1349)

The first Despenser child and Edward I's eldest great-grandchild. In Edward II's accounts Hugh was always called Huchon or Huchoun which must have been his family nickname, and the *Anonimalle* chronicle calls him Hughelyn or 'little Hugh'. [1] He was released from Bristol Castle on 5 July 1331 and acquitted before Parliament on 30 September, having been in captivity for almost five years since his father left him at Caerphilly at the end of October 1326. [2] Huchon came into his mother Eleanor's large inheritance on her death and thereafter was lord of Glamorgan. In her IPM of July 1337 he was said to be '28 and more' or '29 and more', placing his date of birth before July 1309 and perhaps in 1308 (Eleanor turned 15 in October 1307 so was probably too young to give birth before 1308). He was old enough in December 1325 to own weapons which were being repaired and to have an *aketon* made for him. [3] Huchon Despenser married Elizabeth, daughter of William Montacute, earl of Salisbury, before 27 April 1341. [4] He fought in the early years of the Hundred Years War and died on 8 February 1349, aged 40 or almost, perhaps of the Black Death then ravaging England; his and Elizabeth Montacute's magnificent tomb and effigies can still be seen at Tewkesbury Abbey in Gloucestershire. Huchon had no children and his heir was his nephew Edward (1336–75), eldest son of Hugh the Younger's second son Edward, and also the heir of Hugh the Younger's sister Alina Burnell (d. 1363). [5]

Edward (c. 1310/13–30 September 1342)

Edward, the second Despenser son, first appears on record on 23 November 1315, and perhaps was born as early as 1310 and certainly by 3 October 1313, as he inherited lands on 3 October 1334 and must have been at least 21 then. [6] Edward II gave 20 marks on 21 October 1310 to a messenger for news he had brought to the king 'respecting the Lady Eleanor Despenser' which probably relates to the birth of a child, perhaps Edward. [7] Edward married his second cousin Anne Ferrers, daughter of William, Lord Ferrers and granddaughter of Anne Despenser, older sister or half-sister of Hugh Despenser the Elder. Edward and Anne had four sons; Edward the eldest, his uncle Huchon's heir as lord of Glamorgan, was born in 1336 and was a great knight much admired by the chronicler Jean Froissart. Their middle sons were Hugh and Thomas, and Henry the fourth, born in 1341 or 1342, became bishop of Norwich and lived until 1406. Edward the elder was killed at the battle of Morlaix in September 1342, aged about 30 or 32. [8] His grandson Thomas Despenser (1373–1400), the younger Edward's only surviving son, was made earl of Gloucester by Richard II in 1397, and married Edward III's granddaughter Constance of York.

Gilbert (before 9 July 1322–22 April 1382)

The third son, Gilbert Despenser first appears on record on 9 July 1322, when his great-uncle Edward II granted his mother Eleanor five confiscated manors to pass ultimately to Gilbert out of 'affection' for him. [9] He may have been born in the mid or late 1310s. Gilbert had lands in Gloucestershire, Hampshire and Surrey, and held the Wiltshire manor of Broadtown, part of the Basset inheritance which passed to Hugh Despenser the Elder in 1281, as a gift of his brother Huchon. [10] Gilbert was a knight by December 1344, and by July 1349 was wealthy enough that Sir John Ryvere acknowledged that he owed him £1,500. He was imprisoned in the Tower of London in December 1344 'by reason of certain excesses,' and was released on the mainprise of his brother Huchon and his cousin William Bohun, earl of Northampton, Edward II's nephew. [11]

   Sir Gilbert Despenser was a household knight of Edward III and of Edward's grandson and successor Richard II, and was granted 40 marks a year by Richard (then aged 12) on 10 December 1379, a confirmation of a grant made by Edward III on 12 February 1368. [12] He married a woman called Ella Calverleye and had a son called John, who was born around early May 1361. Ella was the sister of John Calverleye, and John Despenser inherited his uncle's manor in Norfolk, but died shortly before 6 October 1375, aged 14. John Despenser's heir was his aunt Annora Coroner, Ella and John Calverleye's sister. [13] Gilbert Despenser died on 22 April 1382, in his 60s. As his son John died before him, his heir was his elder brother Edward's grandson Thomas Despenser, then eight years old and a ward of the king. [14]

John (before 22 November 1324–shortly before 10 June 1366)

The youngest surviving son of Hugh and Eleanor, John Despenser first appears on record when Edward II bought a saddle for him on 22 November 1324. [15] As he was old enough to be able to ride he must have been at least a toddler then, and may have been born in the late 1310s. He was given rents in the Lincolnshire manor of Carlton by his eldest brother Huchon in September 1351, and granted 20 pounds a year by his kinsman Edward III in November 1363. [16] According to the chronicle of John of Reading, John Despenser was murdered around the feast of St Barnabas (11 June) in 1366, and his body thrown on a rubbish heap. His killers were hanged. [17] Although the chronicler's account cannot be confirmed, the date he gives is correct: on 10 June 1366, the escheator was ordered to take John's lands and goods in Hampshire into the king's hands as he had recently died. [18] There is no IPM for John, and it is not clear if he married and left children, or if he was knighted; he is rather obscure.

Unnamed son (died 1320/21)

An entry in Edward II's wardrobe account indicates that Hugh and Eleanor had a son who died at the end of 1320 or beginning of 1321; the king bought a piece of gold and silk tissue on about 13 January 1321 'for the son of Hugh Despenser the son.' Other similar entries make it apparent that the cloth was intended to lie on the boy's coffin or tomb, and he may have been stillborn or died shortly after birth and never had a name. Edward always sent two pieces of cloth for adults and for the teenage son of William Montacute when he died in 1317 which also indicates that the Despenser boy was a small child. [19]

Isabella, countess of Arundel (c. 1312–after 1356)

Hugh and Eleanor's eldest daughter, named after Hugh's mother Isabella Beauchamp. Isabella Despenser married Richard Fitzalan, son and heir of Edmund, earl of Arundel, at the royal manor of Havering-atte-Bower, Essex on 9 February 1321. She was then eight and he seven, which places her date of birth in 1312 or the beginning of 1313, and she was probably the third Despenser child behind Huchon and Edward. [20] Isabella and Richard had one son, Edmund, born in 1326 when his parents were at the start of their teens: he was said by the pope to be 18 in December 1344 and 20 in early 1347. [21] Edmund was Hugh the Younger's eldest grandchild. Isabella and Richard's unhappy marriage was annulled in December 1344, and he granted her six manors in Essex for her sustenance. [22]

Edmund was made illegitimate by the annulment and did not become earl of Arundel – the title and lands passed to his much younger half-brother Richard, born *c*. 1346 – but by July 1347 was married to the earl of Salisbury's daughter Sybil Montacute. [23] Her sister Elizabeth married his uncle Huchon Despenser, and another sister, Philippa, married Roger Mortimer's namesake grandson and heir, born in 1328. Edmund and Sybil had three daughters. Isabella Despenser is hard to trace after the annulment. She was still alive in 1356, when she was involved in a lawsuit against the prior of the Hospital of St John in Jerusalem in England, and apparently was dead by November 1369, when three of the manors given to her by Arundel seem to have been back in his hands. [24]

Joan, or Johane in contemporary spelling (c. mid-1310s–15 November 1384)

The second daughter, named after her maternal grandmother Joan of Acre. On 1 June 1323, a papal dispensation was granted for Joan's betrothal to John FitzGerald, eldest son and heir of Thomas, earl of Kildare. [25] John, who was born in 1314 and was probably about the same age as his fiancée, died later that year. Joan became a nun at Shaftesbury Abbey probably in 1327 at the same time as her younger sisters were forcibly veiled by Queen Isabella, though unlike theirs, Joan's order to be veiled is missing, and it is not impossible that she entered the Church voluntarily. Her eldest brother Huchon ordered 10 marks from the income of Broadtown to be granted to Joan yearly for her upkeep, and also 10 marks from his manor of Fairford. Joan died on 15 November 1384, close to 70 years old. [26] Confusingly, however, an entry on the Close Roll of 15 February 1351 states that Joan was then dead, and ordered the sheriff of Lincolnshire to continue to pay 20 pounds a year to her sister Eleanor for the rest of her life. [27] It seems likely that the sisters' names were confused, and that the sister who had died was Eleanor.

Eleanor, or Alianore in contemporary spelling (c. late 1310s or early 1320s– shortly before 15 February 1351?)

The third daughter, Eleanor was looked after by her father's sister Isabella Hastings and Isabella's damsel Margaret Costantyn, probably with her cousins, Edward II's daughters Eleanor of Woodstock (b. 1318) and Joan of the Tower (b. 1321). Edward gave Margaret Costantyn a gift of 50 shillings in April 1325 for taking good care of the girl. [28] She was betrothed by 27 July 1325 to her father's ward Laurence Hastings, born in 1321 and the future earl of Pembroke, but on 1 January 1327 Queen Isabella, ignoring this, ordered Eleanor to be veiled at Sempringham Priory in Lincolnshire. [29] She was no more than 10 years old and may only have been five or six. Eleanor and her younger sister Margaret Despenser were 'to be admitted and veiled without delay, to remain forever under the order and regular habit of the house.' An entry on the Close Roll of 15 February 1351, as noted above, ordered the sheriff of Lincolnshire to continue to pay 20 pounds a year to Eleanor, 'notwithstanding that Joan her sister is dead, as on 26 June in the eleventh year of the reign [1337] the king [Edward III] granted to Eleanor and Joan, Hugh's daughters, nuns of the house of Sempringham, £20 to be received yearly for their lives…in aid of their maintenance and clothing.' [30] As Joan was still alive into the 1380s, it seems likely that their names were confused here, and that Eleanor Despenser had died not long before 15 February 1351.

Margaret (c. 2 August 1323–1337)

The fourth daughter, born at Cowick, Yorkshire on or just before 2 August 1323. On 1 January 1327 Queen Isabella ordered Margaret to be sent to Watton Priory and veiled as a nun, although she was only three years old. [31] Two months later, Thomas Houk or Hook (a knight of Yorkshire) petitioned the new king Edward III saying that he had kept Margaret in his household for more than three years with a nurse and a great retinue. [32] Thomas Houk's manor, Hook, is a village in Yorkshire about eight miles from Margaret's birthplace, and Watton Priory was about 30 miles from Hook and from Cowick. She was living with Sir Thomas presumably in Hook in 1326/27 which suggests that she was taken directly from his home to be veiled at a nearby priory. She may never have known her family and never have left a small area of Yorkshire. Margaret Despenser died in 1337, barely into her teens, when her aunt Elizabeth Burgh sent wax images and a painting of the four evangelists for her sepulchre. [33]

Elizabeth, Lady Berkeley (14 December 1325?–13 July 1389)

The fifth daughter and youngest Despenser child, most probably the infant born to Eleanor at the royal palace of Sheen west of London on or a little before 14 December 1325. [34] As she was only a year old, Elizabeth escaped Queen Isabella's order to veil her older sisters at the beginning of 1327, and in 1338 married Maurice Berkeley, son and heir of Thomas, Lord Berkeley of Gloucestershire. Maurice was a grandson of Roger Mortimer via his mother Margaret, Mortimer's eldest daughter, and was some years Elizabeth's junior, born c. 1330. Their eldest son Thomas, Lord Berkeley junior was born on 5 January 1353, and they had three younger sons and apparently three daughters. Maurice Berkeley succeeded his father as Lord Berkeley in October 1361, and died in June 1368. Elizabeth called herself Lady Elizabeth Berkeley, lady of Portbury, a manor near Bristol where she spent much of her life. She married a second husband, Sir Maurice Wyth of Somerset, and outlived him too. Elizabeth died on 13 July 1389 at age 63, the last surviving of Hugh's children (three of whom lived into the 1380s, and perhaps four if Nicholas Litlington, the abbot of Westminster who died in 1386, was his illegitimate son). [35] Her eldest son Lord Berkeley died on the same date in 1417. Elizabeth Berkeley née Despenser was her father's daughter: her second husband Maurice Wyth's will of July 1383 ended 'It is my final wish that my said wife hold herself contented with all bequeathed to her.' [36]

Appendix 2

Hugh's Itinerary

An asterisk denotes where Hugh's location coincided with Edward II's.

1306

22 May: Westminster* (knighted; *Menestrellorum*, 185; *Langtoft*, vol. 2, 368-9)

26 May: Westminster* (wedding; E 101/369/11, fo. 96v; *Langtoft*, 368-9)

1307

27 October: Westminster Abbey?* (Edward I's funeral)

1 November: Berkhamsted?* (Gaveston's wedding)

2 December: Wallingford? (Gaveston's tournament)

1308

25 February: Westminster?* (Coronation)

1309

c. March/April: Dunstable (Tomkinson, 'Retinues at Dunstable', 76, 78; Maddicott, *Lancaster*, 95-102)

5 August: Stamford* (*CChR 1300–26*, 130)

1310

c. early January – *c.* July: overseas, jousting (*CCR 1307–13*, 198; *CCW*, 308; *CIM*, 20; *CFR 1307–19*, 54; 'Le Tournoi de Mons de 1310')

1311

Before November: out of court (*AL*, 200)

1312

22 February: Wambrook, Dorset? (SC 8/259/12929)

8 September: Westminster?* (*CPR 1307–13*, 492)

1313

3 February: Westminster* (*CPR 1307–13*, 527-8)

7 April: Sheen* (*CPR 1307–13*, 561)

3 May: Westminster* (*CPR 1307–13*, 571)

9 October: Westminster* (*CPR 1307–13,* 20)

5 November: Westminster* (*CCR 1313–8*, 22)

1314

12 June: Berwick-on-Tweed* (*CDS*, 69)

23, 24 June: Bannockburn, then Dunbar Castle* (*Lanercost*, 208)

c. 9 – 28 September: York*, parliament (Hugh was summoned for the first time; *PROME*; *Parliamentary Writs*)

1315

3 January: Langley* (Phillips, *Edward II*, 242)

c. 20 January – 9 March: Westminster*, parliament

20 February: Westminster* (*CPR 1307–13*, 265)

c. 20 – 23 May: Tonbridge Castle (*CPR 1307–13*, 306-7; *CFR 1307–19*, 248; *CIPM 1307–17*, 351-2)

23 May: Hadleigh, Essex* (*CFR 1307–19*, 248)

25 June: Before Chancery (*CIPM 1307–17*, 352)

16 October: Impington* (*CIPM 1307–17*, 353)

23 November: Westminster?* (*CPR 1307–13*, 402)

1316

c. 27 January – 22 February: Lincoln*, parliament

14 May: Westminster* (C 53/102, no. 12; the first time Hugh witnessed one of Edward's charters)

18 July: Westminster* (C 53/103, no. 58)

30 August: London (CAD A.8019)

18 October: Crayke* (Phillips, *Edward II*, 306)

8 November: Newburgh Priory* (*CFR 1307–19*, 310; C 53/103, no. 45)

17, 20 December: Clipstone* (*CCR 1313–8*, 443)

25, 27 December: Nottingham* (C 53/103, nos. 39, 43)

1317

3 January: Clipstone* (C 53/103, no. 38)

20 January: Daventry* (C 53/103, no. 37)

27 February: Clarendon* (*CCW*, 464)

8 April: Clarendon* (*CCR 1313–8*, 459)

11 April: Andover* (C 53/103, nos. 16, 18, 32)

17, 20 April: Westminster* (*CPR 1307–13*, 632, 640)

17, 22, 24 May: Westminster* (*CChR 1300–26*, 340; *CPR 1307–13*, 666; C 53/103, no. 29)

1, 16 June: Westminster* (*CCR 1313–8*, 477; C 53/103, no. 8)

11 July: Leicester* (C 53/104, nos. 86-8)

2 August: Nottingham* (C 53/104, no. 75)

4 November: Westminster* (*CCW*, 479)

8 November: Windsor?* (SC 8/18/868B)

1318

30 January or shortly before: Westminster* (*CPR 1317–21*, 103)

26 February: Sheen* (*CPR 1317–21*, 109)

20 March: Westminster* (*CCR 1313–8*, 607)

20 May: York, according to E 40/4878

22 May: Westminster*, according to *CCR 1313–8*, 612. It is impossible that Hugh could have travelled from York to London so quickly, so the place or date given in E 40/4878 may be in error.

2, 9, 10 June: Westminster* (C 49/4/26; *CCR 1313–8*, 619; C 53/104, no. 6)

4, 8, 18, 19 July: Northampton* (C 53/105, nos. 91, 92; Phillips, *Valence*, 167-8)

27 July: Woodstock* (*CPR 1317–21*, 275)

9 August: Leake* (*CCR 1313–8*, 113)

c. 20 October – 9 December: York*, parliament

20, 21, 24, 30 November: York* (*CFR 1307–19*, 380, 381; *CChR 1300–26*, 396, 398; *CPR 1317–21*, 255; C 53/105, no. 46)

1, 6, 8, 10 December: York* (C 53/105, nos. 33, 39-42; Tout, *Place*, 244; *CPR 1317–21*, 259)

28 December: Beverley* (SC 8/18868A)

1319

1, 3 January: Beverley* (*CFR 1307–19*, 388; *CPR 1317–21*, 262)

10, 14, 18 January: York* (*CPR 1317–21*, 265, 266, 308)

1, 4, 12, 23, 26 February: York* (*CPR 1317–21*, 271; C 53/105, nos. 26-31)

15, 16, 22, 24, 26, 27, 28 March: York* (*CPR 1317–21*, 362, 365; C 53/105, nos. 17, 20-25)

4, 8 April: York* (*CCW*, 585; *CPR 1317–21*, 325)

8, 10, 12 April: Kirkham* (C 53/105, nos. 18, 19; SC 1/36/68; *CCR 1318–23*, 132-3)

15, 18, 23 April: York* (C 53/105, nos. 15, 16, 18A)

c. 6 – 25 May: York*, parliament

16, 28 May: York* (C 53/105, nos. 6, 11, 12; *CPR 1317–21*, 340)

3, 4, 8, 15 June: York* (C 53/105, nos. 2-5)

4, 9, 19 July: York* (C 53/106, nos. 1, 34, 35)

28 July: Durham* (*CFR 1319–27*, 2)

5 August: Newcastle-on-Tyne* (C 53/106, no. 32)

12, 21 August: Gosforth* (C 53/106, nos. 30, 31)

c. 7-17 September: Berwick-on-Tweed* (*Cartae*, 1063-5; C 53/106, no. 29)

21, 22, 25, 26 September: Newcastle* (*Cartae*, 1063-5; C 53/106, nos. 26-28)

8, 9, 12, 22 October: York* (C 53/106, nos. 21-25)

6 November: York* (C 53/106, nos. 19, 20)

1 December: York* (*CPR 1317–21*, 414; *Foedera 1307–27*, 409-10; *CDS*, 129)

Sometime before 6 December: Cheshunt (*CPR 1317–21*, 467-8, 473)

Before 10 April 1320, sometime in 1319/20: Colchester (SC 8/56/2761; *CPR 1317–21*, 440-1)

1320

After 7 January: Newcastle (*CPR 1317–21*, 414, 552; *Foedera 1307–27*, 409-10; *CDS*, 129)

10, 12, 23, 24 January: York* (C 53/106, nos. 17, 18; *CCR 1318–23*, 219; *CPR 1317–21*, 416)

7, 22 February: Westminster?* (*CFR 1307–19*, 15, 18; *CCR 1318–23*, 336)

5, 6 March: Canterbury* (C 53/106, no. 11; Eleanor was also there: *Recueil de lettres anglo-françaises*, 113-4)

10 April: Westminster* (*CPR 1317–21*, 440-1)

18 April: Lambeth* (C 53/106, no. 9)

27 April: Westminster* (C 53/106, no. 5; DL 25/2011/1679)

9 May: Caversham? (SC 1/36/126 is a letter from Hugh dated at Caversham on 9 May in an unstated year; Edward was 22 miles away at Fulmer)

10 May: Fulmer* (C 53/106, no. 4)

13 May: Windsor* (C 53/106, no. 3)

28 May Odiham* (C 53/106, no. 2)

4 June: Westminster* (*CCR 1318–23*, 237)

5 June: London* (*CCR 1318–23*, 238)

9 June: Westminster* (C 53/106, no. 1)

19 June – 22 July: France* (*CPR 1317–21*, 449)

22 August: Easthampstead?* (*CFR 1307–19*, 32)

24-27 August: Odiham?* (*Itinerary of Edward II*, 201; Hugh was constable of Odiham Castle)

9, 13 September: Clarendon* (C 53/107, no. 33; *CFR 1307–19*, 34)

1 October: Sheen?* (*CFR 1307–19*, 33)

c. 6 – 25 October: Westminster*, parliament

7, 17, 20, 21, 24, 28 October: Westminster/London* (C 53/107, nos. 24, 29, 31, 32; *Corr. Wales*, 184; SC 1/37/6; *CCR 1318–23*, 267, 333; *CPR 1324–7*, 510; *CPR 1338–40*, 328)

4, 5, 6, 10, 17, 18, 20, 21, 23 November: Westminster* (C 53/107, nos. 13-19, 22, 23, 27; *CPR 1317–21*, 531, 534, 545; *CCR 1318–23*, 342, 344)

28 November: Sheen* (*CCR 1318–23*, 344)

1 December: Tolworth?* (*CPR 1317–21*, 530)

4 December: Westminster (*CCR 1318–23*, 359)

15 December: London (*CCR 1318–23*, 359)

29 December: Marlborough* (C 53/107, no. 16)

c. second half of 1320, before November 1321: Paris (Deposits, 346 note 9)

1321

7 January: Chilton Foliat* (*CCW*, 517)

18 January: London* (SC 1/49/143; *Corr. Wales*, 219-20)

9, 10 February: Havering-atte-Bower* (Daughter Isabella's wedding)

16 February: Westminster* (SC 1/49/144; *Corr. Wales*, 220-1)

18 February: Marlow or West Wycombe (E 40/188)

24 February: Westminster* (C 53/107, no. 11)

1 March: Westminster* (C 53/107, no. 12)

6 March: Fulmer* (SC 1/58/10; *Corr. Wales*, 259-60)

9 March: Before Chancery (*CCR 1318–23*, 368-9)

12 March: Henley-on-Thames* (*CCW*, 519)

21 March: Cirencester* (*Cartae*, 1074-6)

28 March: Gloucester* (C 53/107, no. 10)

1, 10, 13, 16 April: Gloucester* (*CPR 1317–21*, 575; *CCR 1318–23*, 292, 366; C 53/107, no. 9)

10, 17, 18, 20, 22, 23, 24, 30 May: Westminster* (C 53/107, nos. 3-8; *CPR 1317–21*, 591; *CCR 1318–23*, 375)

2 June: Westminster* (*CPR 1317–21*, 596)

9, 11, 12 June: Sturry* (*CCR 1318–23*, 312, 382; *CPR 1317–21*, 597)

14 June: Minster-in-Thanet* (C 53/107, no. 2)

7 July: Westminster* (C 53/107, no. 1)

c. 15 July – 22 August: Westminster*, parliament

Around 1 August: Sailing on the Thames between Gravesend and Westminster (*AP*, 296-7)

27 August – 3 September: On way to Kent with king?*

c. 4/11 September: Thanet?* (*Itinerary of Edward II*, 216)

Beginning autumn 1321, for some months: Under the protection of the men of the Cinque Ports and on the English Channel as a pirate

c. 12/20 September: Harwich?* (*Murimuth*, 33; *Itinerary*, 216)

22/23 September: Hadleigh, Suffolk?* (*Itinerary*, 216)

30 September/1 October: Southampton? (SC 8/17/833)

Late 1321/Early 1322: Meeting the king and the barons of Winchelsea on the sea?* (*CCR 1318–23*, 524)

1322

25 February: Weston Subedge?* (*CCR 1318–23*, 425)

3 March: Lichfield* (Phillips, *Valence*, 223)

7 March: Cauldwell* (SC 8/15/701)

10 or 11 March: Burton* (*Gesta*, 75)

22, 24 March: Pontefract* (*Anon*, 106; 'Judgement', 264; *CChR 1300–26*, 441)

16, 25 April: Pontefract/Rothwell* (C 53/108, no. 15; *CCW*, 529: SC 1/37/113; *CPR 1321–4*, 101)

c. 2 – 19 May: York* (parliament)

16 May: York* (C 53/108, no. 8)

1 June: Rothwell* (E 40/98)

8, 16 June: Haddlesey* (*CChR 1300–26*, 444)

19, 21 June: Bishopthorpe* (C 53/108, no. 7; *CPR 1321–4*, 169)

23, 28 June: York* (*CPR 1321–4*, 141; C 53/108, no. 5)

1, 3, 10, 14, 20, 21 July: York* (*CCR 1318–23*, 469, 576; *CPR 1321–4*, 140, 189, 203; *CFR 1319–27*, 143; C 53/108, nos. 4, 25)

3 August: Newcastle-on-Tyne* (*CPR 1321–4*, 201)

6 August: Stannington near Newcastle* (E 40/4857)

Middle to end of August: Scotland* (*CPR 1321–4*, 189)

4 October: Barnard Castle* (*CFR 1319–27*, 180)

14 October: Byland* (*Gesta*, 79)

15 October: Bridlington* (*Gesta*, 79)

23 October: Cawood* (*CPR 1321–4*, 211)

31 October: York* (*CPR 1321–4*, 210; *CCR 1318–23*, 602)

6 November: Conisbrough* (*CChR 1300–26*, 450)

12 November: Tutbury* (E 101/379/7, mem. 2)

20 November: Thorne near Doncaster* (Davies, 'First Journal', 676-7)

(Parliament was held at York 14 – 29 November; Edward and Hugh arrived a week late and travelled by water from Cawood)

21, 24 November: York* (E 101/379/7, mem. 2)

4, 6 December: York* (*CCR 1318–23*, 617; E 40/4887)

19 December: Haddlesey* ('First Journal', 678)

1323

2, 6, 7 January: Cowick* (E 101/379/7, mem. 3; 'First Journal', 678)

20 January: Stow Park* (E 40/4883)

2, 3 February: Newark* (E 40/4886; E 40/5467; E 40/1432; *CPR 1321–4*, 245)

12, 15, 18 February: Pontefract* (CAD A.78; SC 1/36/67; *CPR 1321–4*, 246)

1, 5, 10 March: Knaresborough* (C 53/109, no. 9; E 101/379/7, mem. 8; *CCW*, 537; *CPR 1321–4*, 262)

26, 28 March: Langley* (SC 1/37/5)

16-19 April: London/Westminster* (*CCR 1318–23*, 637)

1, 3 May: York* (*CPR 1321–4*, 279; C 53/109, no. 5)

17, 22 May: Rothwell* (*CCR 1318–23*, 650; C 53/109, no. 1)

30 May: Bishopthorpe* (*CCR 1318–23*, 737; Davies, *Opposition*, 584)

4, 5 June: Bishopthorpe* (C 53/109, no. 6; *CPR 1321–4*, 294, 296)

1, 3, 7 July: York* (C 53/109, no. 3; *CCR 1318–23*, 722-3)

19 July: Faxfleet* (C 53/110, no. 34)

15, 20 July: Burstwick* (*CPR 1321–4*, 326-7; CAD A.13532)

30 July: Cowick* (*CPR 1321–4*, 372)

2 August: Cowick* (E 101/379/17, mem. 2; Eleanor Despenser gave birth on or just before this date at Cowick)

17 August: Ingleby Greenhow* (E 40/4880)

20 August: Pickering* (*CCR 1323–7*, 134)

27, 28 August: Ingleby Greenhow* (*CPR 1321–4*, 341, 378)

25 September: Haverah Park?* (*CPR 1321–4*, 343; CAD A.4842)

6 October: Ightenhill* (C 53/110, no. 29)

18, 19 October: Upholland* (C 53/110, nos. 26, 33)

4 November: Vale Royal* (*CIM*, 169)

c. 22 November: Nottingham* (*CCW*, 546)

13 December: Ravensdale* (E 101/379/17, mem. 2)

30 December: Kenilworth* (*CFR 1319–27*, 251)

1324

2 January: Kenilworth* (E 101/379/17, mem. 3)

c. 9 – 14 January: Hanley* (the king was a guest of Hugh at his own castle)

6 February: Berkeley?* (Eleanor was there: SC 1/46/4)

c. 23 February – 18 March: Westminster*, parliament

4, 10, 12, 15, 16, 19, 25, 28 March: Westminster* (*CPR 1321–4*, 400, 444-5, 457; *CFR 1319–27*, 262; *CChR 1300–26*, 461; *CCR 1323–7*, 67; *Cardiff Records*, vol. 1, 15-16; E 40/937)

1, 6 April: Westminster* (C 53/110, no. 12; *CCW*, 552)

9 April: Fulmer* (*CPR 1321–4*, 406; *CCR 1323–7*, 87)

13 April: Langley* (*CCR 1323–7*, 175)

10 May: Westminster* (C 53/110, no. 8)

18 May: London?* (SC 1/36/12 is a letter from Hugh written at his house in Aldgate on 18 May, but the year is not given; it may belong to 1325. Edward was in London on this date in 1324, but not in 1325)

20, 22 May: Westminster* (*CPR 1321–4*, 416; C 53/110, no. 6)

May (exact date unclear): Hugh sent Edward a short letter, so apparently they were apart (SC 1/37/108)

28 June: Tonbridge* (*CCR 1323–7*, 126; *CChR 1300–26*, 467)

1 July: London or on way there (E 101/380/4, fo. 11v)

5, 6 August: Guildford/Pirbright* (*CChR 1300–26*, 469; C 53/111, no. 20)

10 August: Easthampstead* (*WSS*, 64)

23 August: Tonbridge?* (*CCR 1323–7*, 309)

31 August: Bishopstone* (*CCR 1323–7*, 217)

24, 28 September: Portchester* (*WSS*, 64; SC 1/54/6)

4, 5 October: Portchester* (*WSS*, 79; SC 1/54/10; SC 1/54/24)

7 October: Mapledurham* (*WSS*, 80; SC 1/54/25)

c. 20 October – 10 November: London/Westminster* (parliament)

22 October: London* (C 53/111, no. 18)

31 October: Westminster (Deposits, 360–1; Edward was at Mortlake seven miles away)

1, 8, 15, 22 November: Westminster/Tower of London* (Deposits, 360–1; *CPR 1324–7*, 46; *CCR 1323–7*, 327; E 101/380/4, fo. 20v)

24 November: Cheshunt* (*WSS*, 107; SC 1/54/23)

27 November: Eltisley* (C 53/111, no. 17)

1 December: Stamford* (SC 1/36/125)

9 December: Worksop (*WSS*, 112; SC 1/54/26; Edward was in Nottingham)

26, 28, 30 December: Nottingham* (*CCR 1323–7*, 335; C 53/111, nos. 12, 14; Eleanor was also there)

1325

10 January: Ravensdale* (E 101/380/4, fo. 22v)

26 January: Langley* (C 53/111, no. 11)

6 February: Westminster* (*WSS*, 138)

23 February: Tower of London* (*WSS*, 143–6)

7, 9 March: Tower and La Rosere (Edward's house opposite the Tower)* (E 101/380/4, fo. 27r; *CPR 1324–7*, 106)

17 March: Tower/Westminster* (E 101/380/4, fo. 28v)

22 March: Henley-on-Thames* (E 101/380/4, fo. 29v)

1, 2 April: Marwell* (E 101/380/4, fo. 30r; C 53/111, no. 9)

3 April: Eling near Southampton* (E 101/380/4, fo. 30v)

22 April: Beaulieu Abbey* (E 101/380/4, fo. 31v)

4 May: Winchester* (*WSS*, 207; SC 1/54/24)

14 May: Portchester* (C 53/111, no. 7)

24 May: Henley* (SAL MS 122, 1)

1 June: Chertsey* (*CPR 1324–7*, 130; *CFR 1319–27*, 348)

6 June: Lesnes Abbey? (SC 1/36/127; year not certain)

10, 11 June: Bisham* (SAL MS 122, 5)

16, 21 June: Eltham* (*CPR 1324–7*, 133; *WSS*, 237; SC 1/54/17)

c. 25 June: Westminster* (opening of parliament)

1 July: Westminster* (C 53/111, nos. 1 and 3)

18 July: Tower* (*CFR 1319–27*, 354, 356; SC 8/238/22895)

c. 14/18 August: Travelled by barge from Pontefract on the Thames to Faversham to join the king (SAL MS 122, 24)

21 August: Sturry* (SAL MS 122, 21)

30 August: Dover* (SAL MS 122, 22)

Early September: Dover* (*Anon*, 120; *Murimuth*, 44)

23 September: Maresfield* (C 53/112, no. 25)

28 September: Tonbridge (SAL MS 122, 27; Eleanor was also there)

3 October: Westminster (SC 1/49/149)

9 October: Caerphilly? (SAL MS 122, 28)

12 October: Westminster?* (*CCR 1323–7*, 510)

16 October: Sheen* (SC 1/49/146, 146A; SAL MS 122, 29; Eleanor was also there)

8, 9, 13 November: Wales (SAL MS 122, 34, 37–8)

19, 20 November: Wales, or returning from there (SAL MS 122, 38)

(Parliament began at the Tower on 18 November; Hugh missed the start)

28, 30 November: Westminster* (CAD C.5924; SC 1/49/147)

3 December: Westminster* (SC 1/49/148; Deposits, 352 note 1)

5, 9 December: Tower* (*CPR 1324–7*, 199; SAL MS 122, 41)

12, 14 December: Probably in and around London with his family and the king; his youngest child was born at Sheen on or just before 14 December* (SAL MS 122, 40-42, 73)

21 December: Lamarsh* (*CPR 1324–7*, 204)

26, 27, 29 December: Bury St Edmunds* (*CPR 1324–7*, 206; *CCR 1323–7*, 532; E 40/938; C 53/112, nos. 20, 23)

30, 31 December: Haughley* (*CPR 1324–7*, 200; *CCR 1323–7*, 537-8)

1326

1 January: Haughley* (SAL MS 122, 46; C 53/112, no. 22)

2 January: Winfarthing (SAL MS 122, 46)

8 January: Loxne* (C 53/112, no. 22)

14 January: South Elmham* (SAL MS 122, 48)

20, 21 January: Norwich* (SAL MS 122, 49; C 53/112, nos. 1, 7, 18A, 19)

30, 31 January: Burgh* (SAL MS 122, 50)

3 February: Walsingham* (C 53/112, no. 17)

7 February: Gaywood* (C 53/112, no. 18)

10, 11, 12 February: London (SAL MS 122, 52, 73. Eleanor was probably with the king in Weeting: *CFR 1319–27*, 375)

18, 20 February: Barnwell* (C 53/112, nos. 10, 12, 15, 16)

22 February: Kimbolton* (SC 1/49/151)

23 February: Out of court (SAL MS 122, 53)

24 February: Rothwell* (SAL MS 122, 53)

28 February: Leicester* (C 53/112, no. 13)

1 March: Leicester* (SAL MS 122, 66)

10 March: Merevale* (C 53/112, no. 11)

12 March: Tamworth* (C 53/112, no. 9)

21, 24 March: London (SAL MS 122, 56-7)

28 March: Kenilworth* (SAL MS 122, 91; Eleanor was also there)

31 March: London (SAL MS 122, 58)

1 April: London (Deposits, 362)

22, 26 April: Kenilworth* (*CCR 1323–7*, 558; SAL MS 122, 61)

3 May: Barnsley (Gloucestershire)* (C 53/112, no. 2)

18/19 May: Marlborough* (Wedding of his niece and his retainer. Eleanor was also there: *CFR 1319–27*, 389)

22 May: Caversham/Bisham* (SAL MS 122, 64)

25 May: Otford* (SAL MS 122, 64)

27 May: Maidstone* (SAL MS 122, 64)

30 May – 6 June: Saltwood* (SAL MS 122, 65-6; Haines, *John Stratford*, 167-8)

15 June: Leeds Castle/Rochester* (SAL MS 122, 66; Haines, 'Historia Roffensis', 605)

16 June: Rochester/Gravesend* ('Historia Roffensis', 606)

19 June: Tower?* (*CPR 1324–7*, 278)

1 July: Westminster* (SAL MS 122, 68-9)

2 July: Sheen* (SAL MS 122, 69)

8 July: Henley-on-Thames* (SAL MS 122, 75)

18, 22 July: Westminster* (C 53/113, no. 6; SAL MS 122, 92)

25 July: Wales or on way there (SAL MS 122, 78. Eleanor was with the king)

30 July: Wales (SAL MS 122, 79)

5 August: Portchester* (SAL MS 122, 79)

6 August: Waltham* (SAL MS 122, 80)

13, 17 August: Clarendon* (C 53/113, nos. 3, 4)

2, 10, 16 September: Portchester* (SAL MS 122, 82; C 53/113, no. 2; Deposits, 362)

3 October: Tower* (C 53/113, no. 1; SAL MS 122, 88)

10 October: Chepstow* (*CPR 1324–7*, 333)

20 – 24 October: On sea at Chepstow/Cardiff* (SAL MS 122, 90)

(27 October: Execution of his father in Bristol)

31 October: Caerphilly* (SAL MS 122, 90; his son Huchon was left here)

16 November: Near Llantrisant* (captured)

16–23/24 November: On way to Hereford

24 November: Hereford (execution)

4 December: His head placed on London Bridge (*Anon*, 131)

Abbreviations

AL:	*Annales Londonienses*
Anon:	*Anonimalle Chronicle*
AP:	*Annales Paulini*
BIHR:	Bulletin of the Institute of Historical Research
Brut:	The Brut or the Chronicles of England
C:	Chancery (National Archives)
CAD:	Catalogue of Ancient Deeds
Cartae:	*Cartae et Alia Munimenta…Glamorgancia*, vol. 3
CCR:	Calendar of Close Rolls
CChR:	Calendar of Charter Rolls
CCW:	Calendar of Chancery Warrants 1244–1326
CDS:	Calendar of Documents Relating to Scotland 1307–1357
CFR:	Calendar of Fine Rolls
CIM:	Calendar of Inquisitions Miscellaneous 1308–1348
CIPM:	Calendar of Inquisitions Post Mortem
CMR:	Calendar of Memoranda Rolls Michaelmas 1326–Michaelmas 1327
Corr. Wales:	Calendar of Ancient Correspondence Concerning Wales
CPL:	Calendar of Entries in the Papal Registers: Letters
CPR:	Calendar of Patent Rolls
Deposits:	Fryde, 'Deposits of Hugh…with Italian Bankers'
DL:	Duchy of Lancaster (National Archives)
E:	Exchequer (National Archives)
EHR:	English Historical Review
FCE:	Fourteenth Century England
Gesta:	*Gesta Edwardi de Carnarvon*
IPM:	Inquisition Post Mortem
'Judgement':	Holmes, 'Judgement on…Despenser'
Knights:	Knights of Edward I, ed. Moor
ODNB:	Oxford Dictionary of National Biography
PROME:	Parliament Rolls of Medieval England
RENP:	Reign of Edward II: New Perspectives, eds. Dodd and Musson
SAL MS:	Society of Antiquaries of London, manuscript
SC:	Special Collections (National Archives)
Vita:	*Vita Edwardi Secundi*, ed. Denholm-Young
WSS:	The War of Saint-Sardos, ed. Chaplais

Endnotes

Introduction

1) *The Brut or the Chronicles of England*, part 1, ed. F. W. D. Brie (1906), 239-40.
2) See http://news.bbc.co.uk/2/hi/uk/4561624.stm, accessed 14 March 2017.
3) J. S. Hamilton, 'Charter Witness Lists for the Reign of Edward II', in ed. N. Saul, *FCE I* (2000), 5.

Chapter 1

1) *Calendar of Patent Rolls 1232–47* (1906), 222.
2) *CPR 1232–47*, 210.
3) *Calendar of Inquisitions Post Mortem 1272–91*, vol. 2 (1906), 71, 228; *Calendar of the Fine Rolls 1272–1307*, vol. 1 (1911), 152. Eight months after his birth, shortly before 11 November 1261, the boy's maternal great-grandfather Matthew Lovaine died: C. Moor, *Knights of Edward I*, vol. 3 (1930), 64-5.
4) *Vita Edwardi Secundi Monachi Cuiusdam Malmesberiensis*, ed. N. Denholm-Young 109.
5) *CPR 1258–66*, 459-60.
6) *CIPM 1216–72*, 272-3.
7) Her 1281 IPM names 13 manors in seven counties: *CIPM 1272–91*, 227-9.
8) *CFR 1272–1307*, 146, 149; *A Descriptive Catalogue of Ancient Deeds*, ed. H. C. Maxwell (1890–1915), A.537; M. Morris, *The Bigod Earls of Norfolk* (2005), 221.
9) *CFR 1272–1307*, 146; *CIPM 1272–91*, 227-9.
10) *Calendar of Close Rolls 1279–88* (1902), 88, 148; *CFR 1272–1307*, 149, 152; *CIPM 1272–91*, 71-2, 228.
11) *CPR 1272–81*, 439.
12) *CIPM 1272–91*, 227-9; Morris, *Bigod Earls*, 105.
13) *CPR 1301–7*, 88, 91.
14) T.B. Pugh, 'The Marcher Lords of Glamorgan and Morgannwg, 1317–1485', in T. B. Pugh (ed.), *Glamorgan County History, III: The Middle Ages* (1971), 603; *CFR 1319–27*, 69; *CCR 1318–23*, 543-4.

15) Morris, *Bigod Earls*, 125.

16) *CCR 1288–96*, 134.

17) *CCR 1279–88*, 179, 184.

18) *CCR 1279–88*, 148.

19) *CIPM 1272–91*, 71-2. The manors were Beaumanor and Arnesby. John died in 1275.

20) Beauchamp was between 26 and 30 in January 1268: *CIPM 1216–72*, 212-14.

21) *CIPM 1291–1300*, 377, for Maud's dower. See also *The Complete Peerage of England, Scotland, Ireland, Great Britain and the United Kingdom*, ed. V. Gibbs and H. A. Doubleday, vol. 5 (1926), 580-82.

22) *CIPM 1291–1300*, 375-7; *CIPM 1300–7*, 9-10; *Knights*, vol. 1, 70. William Beauchamp's will mentions other sons: see Oxford Dictionary of National Biography, 'William Beauchamp'.

23) ODNB, 'William Beauchamp'.

24) *CFR 1272–1307*, 388; *CPR 1292–1301*, 356.

25) N. Harris Nicolas, *Testamenta Vetusta: Being Illustrations from Wills*, vol. 1 (1826), 52.

26) *CIPM 1272–91*, 288-90.

27) *CFR 1272–1307*, 117; *CIPM 1272–91*, 182. The English counties were Wiltshire, Hampshire, Gloucestershire, Berkshire and Northamptonshire.

28) *CCR 1279–88*, 217, 220, 250-51, 252.

29) Douglas Richardson in www.soc.genealogy.medieval, accessed 7 May 2017; The National Archives, SC 1/10/109; E 159/60, mem. 14d.

30) *CCR 1279–88*, 462.

31) *CPR 1281–92*, 248, 267-8.

32) *CIPM 1361–5*, 371-3.

33) Hugh the Elder granted two manors to Philip on 24 June 1294. Philip and Margaret Goushill were married by 29 June 1308: *Calendar of Chancery Warrants, vol. 1, 1244–1326* (1927), 275.

Chapter 2

1) M. Prestwich, *Edward I* (1988), 145; *Knights*, vol. 1, 74-5.

2) The National Archives, C 241/15/5.

3) *CPR 1307–13*, 62, 74, 78; *CPR 1317–21*, 121.

4) *Calendar of Early Mayor's Court Rolls: 1298-1307*, ed. A. H. Thomas (1924), 23.

5) *Vita*, 44; M. Lawrence, 'Rise of a Royal Favourite: The Early Career of Hugh Despenser the Elder', *RENP*, 207, 214.

6) E 40/3185; E 42/63; *CCR 1346–9*, 40, 223-4.
7) N. Fryde, *The Tyranny and Fall of Edward II 1321–1326* (1979), 228-32.
8) *CPR 1292–1301*, 72-3, 75-6, 170, 181, 211, 224, 306, etc; Lawrence, 'Early Career', 210.
9) *CPR 1307–13*, 255; *Calendar of the Charter Rolls 1257–1300*, vol. 2 (1906), 463.
10) Prestwich, *Edward I*, 387, 391.
11) ODNB, 'William Beauchamp'.
12) *Complete Peerage*, vol. 12, 369-70.
13) *CCR 1296–1302*, 75.
14) S. Phillips, *Edward II* (2010), 45 note 76.
15) *CPR 1292–1301*, 233; E 30/27.
16) *CFR 1272–1307*, 339, 382.
17) M. Prestwich, *Documents Illustrating the Crisis of 1297–98 in England* (1980), 10, 15, 22, 39-41.
18) Prestwich, *Crisis*, 6.
19) H. Johnstone, *Edward of Carnarvon 1284–1307* (1946), 35-7; *CCR 1296–1302*, 130.
20) *CCR 1296–1302*, 137, 140, 144, 248, 388; *Knights*, vol. 2, 43-4.
21) ODNB, 'William Beauchamp'.
22) *CPR 1292–1301*, 351.
23) ODNB.
24) *CIPM 1300–7*, 9-10; *CPR 1292–1301*, 357.
25) *CFR 1272–1307*, 454; *CIPM 1300–07*, 62-3.
26) *Knights*, vol. 1, 75; *CFR 1272–1307*, 469.
27) *CFR 1272–1307*, 232; also *CIPM 1272–91*, 377.
28) *CPR 1281–92*, 464; *CPR 1292–1301*, 239.
29) CAD A.6278.
30) *CCR 1296–1302*, 339, 558.
31) *CIPM 1307–17*, 390-94.
32) *CPR 1291–1302*, 179; CAD A.6278.
33) *The Roll of Arms of the Princes, Barons and Knights Who Attended King Edward I to the Siege of Caerlaverock*, ed. T. Wright (1864), 204.
34) *The Chronicle of Pierre de Langtoft*, vol. 2, ed. T. Wright (1868), 204.
35) *CPR 1292–1301*, 535-7, 561; *CPR 1301–7*, 30.
36) ODNB, 'Guy Beauchamp'.
37) E 39/99/61.
38) ODNB, 'Guy Beauchamp'; Johnstone, *Edward of Carnarvon*, 92; *Calendar of Documents Relating to Scotland, vol. 3, 1307–1357* (1887), 392-4.

39) Confusingly, Hugh had two brothers-in-law called Gilbert Clare. The more important of the two was heir to the earldom of Gloucester, the older brother of Hugh's wife Eleanor, only son of Gilbert 'the Red' and born in 1291. The other Gilbert Clare was lord of Thomond in Ireland, born in 1281 and Earl Gilbert's first cousin, who married Hugh's sister Isabella *c*. 1306. Gilbert Clare of Thomond was the elder son of Thomas Clare (*c*. 1245–87), younger brother of Gilbert 'the Red'. It was this second Gilbert born in 1281 who was Edward of Caernarfon's companion before he became king.

40) H. Johnstone, *Letters of Edward, Prince of Wales 1304–1305* (1931), 19-20, 97, 107-8, 118-9, 122, 123, 133-4, 137-8; J. S. Hamilton, 'Letters of Edward of Caernarfon Reconsidered', *RENP*, 20.

Chapter 3

1) *CPR 1301–7*, 382, 386, 387, 388, 395.
2) Like Hugh, Joan was a great-grandchild of Isabel Bigod, daughter of Hugh Bigod and Maud Marshal, earl and countess of Norfolk.
3) I. Mortimer, *The Greatest Traitor: The Life of Sir Roger Mortimer* (2003), 319-24.
4) *Vita*, 109.
5) *CPR 1301–7*, 244.
6) Johnstone, *Edward of Carnarvon*, 108.
7) C. Bullock-Davies, *Menestrellorum Multitudo: Minstrels at a Royal Feast* (1978), 185-7.
8) Johnstone, *Carnarvon*, 107.
9) Pierre de Langtoft, vol. 2, 368.
10) *CCR 1307–13*, 5; *CPR 1301–7*, 443, 526-7, 536.
11) E 101/369/11, fo. 96v.
12) *CDS 1272–1307*, 477.
13) Johnstone, *Carnarvon*, 108-9; Bullock-Davies, *Multitudo*, xxx.
14) *Langtoft*, vol. 2, 368-9.
15) Gilbert was born between 23 April and 11 May 1291. *CIPM 1291–1300*, 234-51; *CIPM 1300–07*, 311-31.
16) *CChR 1327–41*, 212.
17) *CPR 1301–7*, 308 (30 December 1304).
18) It is impossible for Nicholas Litlington to have been the son of Edward III and his mistress Alice Perrers, as numerous genealogy websites state. Nicholas was the same age as Edward III himself (the king was born in November 1312)   and about 35 years older than his supposed mother

Alice. See http://www.ladydespensersscribery.com/tag/litlington-missal/, http://www.susanhigginbotham.com/blog/posts/westminsters-despenser-abbot-nicholas-de-litlyngton/ and http://www.oxforddnb.com/view/article/16775 (all accessed 17 February 2017); C. Given-Wilson and A. Curteis, *The Royal Bastards of Medieval England* (1984), 136.

19) *CPR 1301–7*, 443 (14 June 1306).
20) *CCR 1307–13*, 198; *Calendar of Inquisitions Miscellaneous (Chancery)*, *vol. 2, 1308-48* (1916), 20.
21) SC 8/33/1646; see also SC 8/41/2044, SC 8/156/7789.
22) *CCR 1318–23*, 402; *CPR 1327–30*, 278; *CChR 1327–41*, 2.
23) *CCR 1323–7*, 288; J.C. Davies, *The Baronial Opposition to Edward II: Its Character and Policy* (1918), 91; Fryde, *Tyranny*, 31.
24) *CFR 1272–1307*, 538.
25) Fryde, *Tyranny*, 31; TNA C 133/121/11; *CCR 1302–7*, 405; *CIPM 1272–91*, 288.
26) *CIM*, 245-6; SC 8/160/7986; SC 8/165/8217.
27) *CPR 1301–7*, 536.
28) *CPR 1301–7*, 427, 441, 447.
29) *Calendar of Entries in the Papal Registers Relating to Great Britain and Ireland: Papal Letters*, vol. 1, 1198 –1304, ed. W. Bliss (1893), 570.
30) *CIPM 1307–17*, 101-2.
31) *CFR 1272–1307*, 543-4; *CCR 1302–7*, 481-2.
32) *CFR 1272–1307*, 546; *CIPM 1300–7*, 290-310.
33) Lawrence, 'Early Career', 210 and note 30.
34) *Foedera, Conventiones, Literae, vol. 2.1, 1272–1327*, ed. T. Rymer (1818), 1012.
35) Not the earl of Pembroke's sister Isabella Valence, first wife of Isabella Despenser's husband John Hastings, as stated by Frances Underhill, *For Her Good Estate* (1999), 7. This Isabella died in 1305.
36) *CIPM 1300–7*, 311-31.
37) *CPR 1292–1301*, 592, 606; *CPR 1301–7*, 257.
38) *CCR 1302–7*, 533.
39) *Brut*, 202-3.

Chapter 4

1) *Vita*, 40.
2) *CFR 1307–19*, 1, 18.
3) *Scalacronica: The Reigns of Edward I, Edward II and Edward III*, ed. H. Maxwell (1907), 48.

4) *Vita*, 2.
5) *CIPM 1307–17*, 13. Gilbert was born in Limerick on 3 February 1281: *CIPM 1300–7*, 34-5.
6) T. F. Tout, *The Place of the Reign of Edward II in English History* (2nd edn., 1936), 349; *CPR 1317–21*, 53; *Foedera 1307–27*, 95.
7) *Vita*, 15; *Annales Paulini 1307–1340*, in ed. W. Stubbs, *Chronicles of the Reigns of Edward I and Edward II*, vol. 2 (1883), 259.
8) *CFR 1307–19*, 14.
9) *The Household Book of Queen Isabella of England*, eds. F. D. Blackley and G. Hermansen (1971); Davies, *Baronial Opposition*, 91 note 3; F. D. Blackley, 'Isabella and the Bishop of Exeter', in T. A. Sandqvist and M. R. Powicke (eds), *Studies in Medieval History Presented to Bertie Wilkinson* (1969), 226 note 30.
10) *Foedera 1307–27*, 36.
11) C 53/94–C 53/113.
12) *Vita*, 4.
13) Cited in French in J. R. Maddicott, *Thomas of Lancaster 1307–1322: A Study in the Reign of Edward II* (1970), 335.
14) Lawrence, 'Early Career', 215-6.
15) Davies, *Opposition*, 91 note 3.
16) *CFR 1307–19*, 17, 18; *CPR 1307–13*, 51, 68.
17) *CPR 1307–13*, 74, 78.
18) *CPR 1307–13*, 7, 32.
19) *CPR 1307–13*, 1, 21.
20) *CPR 1307–13*, 50.
21) *CPR 1307–13*, 71, 74, 78-9; P. Chaplais, *Piers Gaveston: Edward II's Adoptive Brother* (1994), 47, J. S. Hamilton, *Piers Gaveston, Earl of Cornwall 1307–1312* (1988), 147; *The Chronicle of Lanercost 1272–1346*, ed. H. Maxwell (1913), 187.
22) *CCR 1307–13*, 225-6.
23) *CChR 1300–26*, 130.
24) Maddicott, *Lancaster*, 95-102.
25) A. Tomkinson, 'Retinues at the Tournament of Dunstable, 1309', *EHR*, 74 (1959), 76, 78.
26) *CCR 1307–13*, 158-9.
27) *CCR 1307–13*, 237.
28) *CCW*, 308; *CFR 1307–19*, 54.
29) *CCR 1307–13*, 198; *CIM*, 20.
30) A. de Behault de Dornon, *Le Tournoi de Mons de 1310* (1909).
31) *Issues of the Exchequer*, ed. F. Devon (1837), 124.

32) Davies, *Opposition*, 91 note 3.

33) http://home.scarlet.be/heraldus/TournoiMons.htm (accessed 4 May 2017).

34) Hamilton, 'Charter Witness Lists', 8, 11.

35) For example, *CPR 1307–13*, 574, 610, 632.

Chapter 5

1) In February 1327, Lamarsh was worth £31 a year, North Weald Bassett £40, Kersey £27, Layham £35, Wix £10, Oxcroft £10, and Bushey £41. *CChR 1327–41*, 2, 4; *CIM*, 262.

2) J. R. S. Phillips, *Aymer de Valence, Earl of Pembroke 1307–1324: Baronial Politics in the Reign of Edward II* (1972), 17; Pugh, 'Marcher Lords', 167.

3) Mortimer, *Greatest Traitor*, 19-22.

4) *CCR 1313–8*, 222.

5) *CCR 1313–8*, 443, 450.

6) Fryde, *Tyranny*, 31, 241 note 16.

7) Davies, *Opposition*, 91 note 7.

8) *Vita*, 19-20.

9) Phillips, *Edward*, 176.

10) *Annales Londonienses 1195–1330*, in Stubbs, *Chronicles*, vol. 1, 200.

11) SC 1/49/112.

12) *Household Book of Queen Isabella*, 127-9.

13) *Household Book*, 19.

14) *Household Book*, 208; Chaplais, *Gaveston*, 75.

15) *CPR 1307–13*, 395, 398; *Household Book*, 209.

16) Hugh the Elder did not witness any of the king's charters from 27 December 1311 until 17 July 1312: C 53/98, C 53/99.

17) SC 8/259/12929; *CCR 1318–23*, 150-1.

18) *CPR 1307–13*, 203; *CCR 1307–13*, 190, 323; *CFR 1307–19*, 50. Elizabeth married Percy's son John.

19) *CPR 1307–13*, 492.

20) *CPR 1307–13*, 528, 561, 571.

21) *CCR 1313–8*, 22.

22) SC 1/37/37. Grendon was a tenant of Hugh's sister Alina in 1317, and by January 1322 was a royal knight: *CCR 1313–8*, 487-8; *CPR 1321–4*, 51, 69.

23) *CIPM 1307–17*, 230-36; *CFR 1307–19*, 164, 165; *CCR 1307–13*, 525.

24) *CPR 1307–13*, 582.

25) CAD A.10237.

26) *CIPM 1327–36*, 208-9.

27) *CFR 1307–19*, 187.
28) Phillips, *Edward*, 218; *CPR 1307–13*, 44.
29) *CPR 1307–13*, 309, 407-8; *CFR 1307–19*, 230. Despenser was justice again by 5 June 1320: *CCR 1318–23*, 240.
30) *CIPM 1307–17*, 266-7; C 134/34/5; *CFR 1307–19*, 179.
31) *CIPM 1327–36*, 208-9; *CFR 1327–37*, 161.
32) *CPR 1307–13*, 20; *CFR 1307–19*, 242, 278; *CCR 1313–8*, 145.
33) Bullock-Davies, *Menestrellorum*, 186; *CIPM 1307–17*, 263-6; *CFR 1307–19*, 180.
34) *CFR 1307–19*, 181, 203, 223, 278.

Chapter 6

1) *CDS*, 69.
2) *Vita*, 53.
3) *The Anonimalle Chronicle 1307 to 1334*, eds. W. R. Childs and J. Taylor (1991), 89.
4) *Lanercost*, 208, 229.
5) *CDS*, 41.
6) *CFR 1307–19*, 201; *CIPM 1307–17*, 325; *CCR 1313–8*, 131-8; Pugh, 'Marcher Lords', 167. The earl's IPM: *CIPM 1307–17*, 325-54.
7) *CFR 1307–19*, 201.
8) *CFR 1307–19*, 202.
9) Phillips, *Edward*, 242 note 28.
10) Davies, *Opposition*, 221, citing E 101/378/6.
11) *CIPM 1307–17*, 352-3.
12) *CIPM 1307–17*, 397-413; *Testamenta Vetusta*, vol. 1, 80.
13) *CIPM 1307–17*, 352; *CCR 1313–8*, 301.
14) Phillips, *Edward*, 242.
15) *CPR 1307–13*, 306-7; *CFR 1307–19*, 248; *CIPM 1307–17*, 351-2.
16) *CIPM 1307–17*, 390-4; *CFR 1307–19*, 268, 271; *CCR 1313–8*, 208.
17) *CFR 1307–19*, 167, 198.
18) Fryde, *Tyranny*, 33.
19) *CCR 1313–8*, 131-9, for Maud's dower.
20) *CPR 1307–13*, 667; *CCR 1313–8*, 491.
21) *Flores Historiarum*, ed. H. R. Luard, vol. 3 (1890), 173; *CIPM 1307–17*, 353.
22) *The Parliament Rolls of Medieval England*, ed. C. Given-Wilson et al (2005), January 1316.

Chapter 7

1) *CCR 1307–13*, 246; *Collectanea Topographica et Genealogica*, eds. F. Madden, B. Bandinel and J. G. Nichols, vol. 4 (1837), 64.
2) *Knights*, vol. 1, 10; vol. 4, 87-8; *CPR 1292–1301*, 516.
3) *Inquisitions and Assessments relating to Feudal Aids 1284–1431*, vol. 1 (1899), 81.
4) *Calendar of Documents Relating to Ireland 1302–7*, ed. H. S. Sweetman (1886), numbers 566, 599.
5) *CPR 1307–13*, 622, 666.
6) *Vita*, 123; see http://www.british-history.ac.uk/vch/bucks/vol4/pp237-242, accessed 11 April 2017.
7) *CPR 1307–13*, 402; *CPR 1321–4*, 324; *CCR 1318–23*, 358-9; *CCR 1333–7*, 272-3.
8) *CIPM 1327–36*, 392-3; *CFR 1327–37*, 380, 421.
9) Underhill, *Good Estate*, 15; quotations from *PROME*, January 1316.
10) *PROME*, January 1316.
11) *CCR 1313–8*, 114-5.
12) M. Vale, *The Princely Court* (2001), 109.
13) C 53/102, no. 12; C 53/103, no. 58.
14) Phillips, *Valence*, 149, 312-14.
15) *CPR 1307–13*, 577.
16) *CCW*, 464.
17) *CPR 1307–13*, 666; T. Stapleton, 'A Brief Summary of the Wardrobe Accounts of the Tenth, Eleventh and Fourteenth Years of King Edward the Second', *Archaeologia*, 26 (1836), 337-8.
18) *CPR 1307–13*, 535; Stapleton, 'Brief Summary', 337, 339.
19) *CCW*, 470.
20) *PROME*; *CPR 1307–13*, 660-1, 666.
21) *CFR 1307–19*, 350-1; *CCR 1313–8*, 583; *Cartae et Alia Munimenta quae ad Domimium de Glamorgancia Pertinent*, vol. 3 (1910), 1048-56; C 47/9/24; Pugh, 'Marcher Lords', 603 note 1.
22) *CPR 1317–21*, 125.
23) *Foedera 1307–27*, 331; *CCR 1313–8*, 468.
24) *CPR 1307–13*, 631, 640.
25) *CPR 1317–21*, 5-6, 10; CAD A.1432 and 1433. Joan was a daughter of Gilbert 'the Red' from his first marriage. Her daughter-in-law Mary Monthermer was the eldest child of Joan of Acre (Gilbert the Red's widow) and her second husband Ralph Monthermer.

26) *CPR 1317–21*, 56, 248, 255-6; *CCR 1313–8*, 534-5. The name Dinefwr is sometimes written 'Dynevor' in English.
27) E 40/4878; *CPR 1317–21*, 255-6; *CFR 1307–19*, 375.
28) J.C. Davies, 'The Despenser War in Glamorgan', *Transactions of the Royal Historical Society*, 9 (1915), 25; C 47/9/24; *Cartae,* 1048-56.
29) *CPR 1317–21*, 60.
30) *CCR 1313–8*, 531-2; *CPR 1317–21*, 60, 103, 120-1; C 47/10/43/22.
31) *CPR 1317–21*, 208, 257, 415, 456.
32) *CCR 1318–23*, 408.
33) *PROME*; Maddicott, *Lancaster*, 240.
34) *CCR 1318–23*, 96; Pugh, 'Marcher Lords', 170; *Calendar of Ancient Correspondence Concerning Wales*, ed. J. G. Edwards (1935), 184.
35) *Statutes of the Realm, vol. 1: 1100–1377* (1810), 181; *CCR 1318–23*, 492.
36) *PROME.*
37) *CPL 1305–41*, 444.
38) *CCR 1318–23*, 112-3.
39) *Vita*, 93.
40) *Adae Murimuth Continuatio Chronicarum*, ed. E. M. Thompson (1889), 33; *Anon*, 92-3; *Brut*, 212.
41) SC 8/15/701.
42) *Anon*, 92-3.
43) Davies, *Opposition*, 336-7.
44) *Anon*, 92-3.
45) Cited in R. M. Haines, *Edward II: His Life, His Reign, and Its Aftermath, 1284–1330* (2003), 124.

Chapter 8

1) *CCR 1313–8*, 274-5, 283, 419.
2) *Statutes of the Realm*, vol. 1, 183; *CCR 1318–23*, 493; *PROME.*
3) *Vita*, 66-8.
4) *Gesta Edwardi de Carnarvon Auctore Canonico Bridlingtoniensi*, in ed. W. Stubbs, *Chronicles of the Reigns of Edward I and Edward II*, vol. 2 (1883), 66-9.
5) *Flores Historiarum*, 343.
6) *CCR 1327–30*, 121 (Hugh disinheriting Bren's sons). The charge relating to Lady Baret will be discussed in chapters 10 and 15.
7) M. McKisack, *The Fourteenth Century 1307–1399* (1959), 87; Haines, *Edward II*, 185.
8) *Statutes of the Realm*, 183; *CCR 1318–23*, 493.

9) *CFR 1307–19*, 380, 388, 394; *CPR 1317–21*, 582.

10) CAD 1.8019.

11) Tout, *Place of the Reign*, 244-81 (in French).

12) Tesdale: *PROME*, January 1327; Holditch: Society of Antiquaries of London MS 122, 57, 58, 65, 66.

13) *CCR 1318–23*, 109-10; Phillips, *Valence*, 174.

14) Phillips, *Valence*, 176.

15) *Anon*, 92-3; *Chronicon Galfridi de Baker de Swynebroke*, ed. E. M. Thompson (1889), 10.

16) Cited in Phillips, *Edward*, 98. Jonathan Sumption made the peculiar comment in *The Guardian* on 5 April 2003 that Edward and Hugh's relationship was 'certainly not sexual, and on a personal level may not even have been particularly close.' We cannot possibly say that their relationship was 'certainly not sexual' any more than we can say it certainly was.

17) *Scalacronica*, 70.

18) SAL MS 122, 57.

19) *Lanercost*, 208, 229; *Flores Historiarum*, 195.

20) *Vita*, 108, 115.

21) C. Sponsler, 'The King's Boyfriend: Froissart's Political Theater of 1326', in G. Burger and S. F. Kruger (eds), *Queering the Middle Ages* (2001), 147.

22) *Galfridi de Baker de Swynebroke*, 6.

23) *CPR 1317–21*, 262, 271.

24) *CCR 1313–8*, 123.

25) *Vita*, 93.

26) *CCR 1318–23*, 132.

27) *CCR 1318–23*, 133; SC 1/36/68.

28) C 53/105, no. 31; C 53/106, no. 34; *CCR 1318–23*, 138.

29) *CFR 1319–27*, 2-3; *CPR 1317–21*, 464; *Cartae*, 1066-74.

30) *Vita*, 104. It is not entirely clear whether Edward made the threat to Lancaster's face or after his cousin had left the port.

31) *Cartae*, 1063-5. The letter ends with the conventional 'May God keep you' and 'Written at Newcastle-on-Tyne this 21st day of September,' but in it Hugh refers to a letter from Inge which he received on 22 September, so the date cannot be correct.

32) Maddicott, *Lancaster*, 249.

33) *Lancaster*, 249-50.

34) SC 8/57/2809.

35) *CCR 1323–7*, 622. Adam presumably came from Sodbury in Gloucestershire, part of Eleanor Despenser's inheritance: *CIPM 1336–46*, 79.

36) *CPR 1281–92*, 156; *CChR 1300–26*, 31, 99, 100, 106; *Knights*, vol. 4, 189-90.

37) *Statutes of the Realm*, vol. 1, 182; *CCR 1318–23*, 493.

38) *CPR 1317–21*, 414; *Foedera 1307–27*, 409-10.

39) *CPR 1317–21*, 467-8, 473.

40) *CPR 1317–21*, 358-9; *CCR 1318–23*, 147.

41) SC 8/56/2760, 61 and 62; SC 8/162/8098.

42) *CPR 1317–21*, 440-1, 510.

43) SC 8/56/2761; *a ma requeste me bailla le dyt John de Lacheleye pur estre son gardayn.*

44) *CCR 1313–8*, 447.

45) *CPR 1321–4*, 132, 181; *CChR 1300–26*, 444.

46) SC 8/56/2759. He was pardoned in 1327, *CPR 1327–30*, 116.

47) *CCR 1318–23*, 494.

Chapter 9

1) *CFR 1319–27*, 15, 18; *Vita*, 117-8.

2) *CFR 1319–27*, 16.

3) *CIM*, 245-6; SC 8/160/7986; SC 8/165/8217.

4) *CCR 1318–23*, 260, 285-6, 326; *CPR 1317–21*, 505, 596.

5) *CFR 1319 –27*, 32. Lewer was reappointed keeper of Odiham on 21 June 1321: *CPR 1317–21*, 595.

6) *CFR 1319–27*, 33; *CPR 1317–21*, 514.

7) *CPR 1317–21*, 511, 518.

8) F. J. Tanqueray, ed., *Recueil de lettres anglo-françaises 1265–1399* (1916), 113-4.

9) *CPR 1317–21*, 426, 449.

10) *CFR 1319–27*, 69-71; Essex, Suffolk, Cambridgeshire, Gloucestershire, Worcestershire, Oxfordshire, Berkshire, Buckinghamshire, Surrey and Hampshire.

11) *Flores Historiarum*, 342.

12) *CCR 1318–23*, 494; *Lanercost*, 230; *Vita*, 115.

13) See B. Wells-Furby, 'The Gower Prelude to the Marcher Rising of 1321: A Question of Evidence', *Welsh History Review*, 27 (2014), 4-27.

14) *Vita*, 108-9; also *AP*, 292-3.

15) *CCR 1318–23*, 268.

16) *CPR 1317–21*, 547-8; *CFR 1319–27*, 40-41.

17) *CPR 1317–21*, 547-8; *CCR 1318–23*, 283, 285; S. Waugh, 'The Profits of Violence: The Minor Gentry in the Rebellion of 1322 in Gloucestershire and Herefordshire', *Speculum*, 52 (1977), 29.

18) *CFR 1319–27*, 40-41, 43.

19) *CCR 1318–23*, 285.
20) Stapleton, 'Brief Summary', 340.
21) J. S. Hamilton, 'Some Notes on 'Royal' Medicine in the Reign of Edward II', *FCE II*, 37.
22) SC 1/49/143; *Corr. Wales*, 219-20. The famous line about being rich is *pernez tiele garde entour noz busoignes qe nous puissoms estre riches et ateindre a nostre entente de quele vous auez bone conaissaunce.*
23) *Corr. Wales*, 180-1.
24) *CPL 1342–62*, 164.
25) Stapleton, 'Brief Summary', 338.
26) SC 8/204/10201.
27) SC 1/58/10; *Corr. Wales*, 259-60.
28) *Cartae*, 1074-6; Stevenson, 'Letter', 760-1.
29) Lundy was granted to Hugh and Eleanor on 16 June 1322: *CChR 1300–26*, 444. Hugh had already sent instructions to Inge about it on 16 February 1321: SC 1/49/144.
30) *Knights*, vol. 4, 270; *CFR 1319–27*, 51-2.
31) W. H. Stevenson, 'A Letter of the Younger Despenser on the Eve of the Barons' Rebellion, 21 March 1321', *EHR*, 12 (1897), 759; *CFR 1319–27*, 52-3.
32) *Cartae*, 1076-7.
33) Cited in French in Maddicott, *Lancaster*, 266 note 2.
34) *CCR 1318–23*, 366.
35) *CCR 1318–23*, 367, 371; *Vita*, 110.
36) *CCR 1318–23*, 541-3.
37) *Brut*, 213.
38) *CPR 1321–4*, 167-8, 249; *CCR 1318–23*, 541; *CIPM 1317–27*, 216-7; *Flores Historiarum*, 345; *AP*, 293.
39) *CPR 1317–21*, 596; *CCR 1318–23*, 407, 508, 54.
40) *Vita*, 110-11.
41) SC 8/165/8242.
42) Waugh, 'Profits of Violence', 848; *CCR 1318–23*, 542.
43) *CCR 1318–23*, 542; *CPR 1321–4*, 294.
44) Stapleton, 'Brief Summary', 335; Davies, 'Despenser War', 58.
45) *Lanercost*, 229.
46) *CPR 1317–21*, 584-5; *CCR 1318–23*, 312.
47) *CPR 1317–21*, 591, 596-7.
48) SC 8/7/301; SC 8/106/5268.
49) SC 8/6/298; Davies, 'Despenser War', 58.
50) SC 8/163/8017.

51) SC 8/160/7975; *CIPM 1317–27*, 215-7.

52) *AP*, 296-7.

53) *Statutes of the Realm*, vol. 1, 181-4; *CCR 1318–23*, 492-4; *PROME*; *CPR 1321–4*, 153.

54) *CCR 1318–23*, 542-3.

55) *Vita*, 114-5.

56) *PROME*, July 1321.

57) *Brut*, 214; *Anon*, 100.

58) Cited in Phillips, *Valence*, 206.

59) E. B. Fryde, 'The Deposits of Hugh Despenser the Younger with Italian Bankers', *Economic History Review*, 2nd series, 3 (1951), 346 note 9.

60) *CCR 1318–23*, 400, 402; *CFR 1319–27*, 70.

61) *Murimuth*, 33.

62) *CCR 1318–23*, 402, 408.

63) *Vita*, 115-6.

64) *Brut*, 214; *Anon*, 100; *AP*, 300; *Flores Historiarum*, 198; *Scalacronica*, 70; J. A. Holmes, 'The Judgement on the Younger Despenser, 1326', *EHR*, 70 (1955), 264.

65) *CCR 1318–23*, 507.

66) SC 8/17/833; SC 8/40/1970; SC 8/7/327. The port of Winchelsea was notorious for piracy in the thirteenth and early fourteenth centuries. See T. K. Heebøll-Holm, *Ports, Piracy and Maritime War* (2013), 45-6.

67) *CPR 1321–4*, 107, 160, 385; SC 8/99/4912 and 3.

68) *CCR 1318–23*, 524.

69) *CPL 1305–41*, 449.

70) *CPR 1334–8*, 328-9; *CCR 1333–7*, 686-7.

71) *CPR 1321–4*, 77, 79.

72) *CPR 1324–7*, 130.

Chapter 10

1) *CPR 1321–4*, 45, 47; *CCR 1318–23*, 541.

2) *CPR 1321–4*, 47-8, 51, 70.

3) Hugh's petition: *CCR 1318–23*, 542-3.

4) *CCR 1318–23*, 425; Phillips, *Valence*, 223.

5) Underhill, *Good Estate*, 29-30.

6) *Gesta*, 75; thank you to Ivan Fowler for the translation.

7) M. Keen, *Nobles, Knights and Men-at-Arms in the Middle Ages* (1996), 156-7, 164-5; id., *The Laws of War in the Middle Ages* (2015), 106.

8) *CPR 1321–4*, 93.

9) *Anon*, 106.

10) *CPR 1321–4*, 73; *CCR 1318–23*, 296; *CFR 1319–27*, 100.

11) *CPR 1321–4*, 148; *CCR 1323–7*, 673.

12) *CPR 1321–4*, 92, 149, *CCR 1318–23*, 683; see also *CPR 1321–4*, 20, 77; SC 8/7/301; *CIM*, 131.

13) *CIM*, 200-1. Stephen Baret's heir was his brother David, so he cannot have had children: *CCR 1327–30*, 25.

14) *CCR 1318–23*, 604, 627; *CCR 1323–7*, 46, 48, 120, 236.

15) *CCR 1318–23*, 427, 666.

16) *CPR 1321–4*, 77; *CCR 1323–7*, 106.

17) *CCR 1318–23*, 564, 574-6; *CPR 1321–4*, 141, 179-80; *CPR 1324–7*, 102-3, 256; CAD A.4842, A.4857; E 40/198; *CChR 1300–26*, 448.

18) The National Archives, DL 42/11, fo. 66v.

19) *CPR 1321–4*, 341-2; CAD A.4880; Deposits, 348, 360.

20) *CCR 1323–7*, 327; Deposits, 348, 351, 360.

21) *Statutes of the Realm*, vol. 1, 189-90; *CCR 1318–23*, 541-6.

22) *CChR 1300–26*, 443-4.

23) *CPR 1321–4*, 115.

24) *CChR 1300–26*, 441-53, 461, 463 etc; *CFR 1319–27*, 143, 179.

25) P. Dryburgh, 'The Career of Roger Mortimer, First Earl of March', Univ. of Bristol PhD thesis (2002), 102 note 283, citing BL MS Stowe 553, fo. 25r.

26) *CCR 1318–23*, 440.

27) *CPR 1327–30*, 31.

28) Isabella's: SC 1/37/45; Eleanor's: SC 1/37/4.

29) G. A. Holmes, 'A Protest Against the Despensers, 1326', *Speculum*, 30 (1955), 210; Underhill, *Good Estate*, 31-2.

30) *CCR 1318–23*, 578, 651; *CCR 1323–7*, 65.

31) E 101/332/27, mem. 5.

32) *CPR 1321–4*, 176, 183, 191; *CChR 1300–26*, 448-9; *Cartae*, 1100-1; *CPR 1327–30*, 32.

33) *CPR 1321–4*, 183, 191.

34) Holmes, 'Protest', 211; *CCR 1318–23*, 624.

35) *CCR 1323–7*, 174; SC 8/36/1763; Pugh, 'Marcher Lords', 171-2; *CPR 1321–4*, 434.

36) SC 8/173/8631.

37) *CCR 1318–23*, 659; *CFR 1327–37*, 221; *CPR 1321–4*, 426, 433.

38) *Cartae*, 1101-4.

39) Holmes, 'Protest', 210-11; *Cartae*, 1063, 1074, 1101.

40) *The War of Saint-Sardos (1323–1325): Gascon Correspondence and Diplomatic Documents*, ed. P. Chaplais (1954), 72.

41) *CCR 1318–23*, 597.
42) *Vita*, 127-8.
43) *CPR 1321–4*, 222, 245-6; E 40/4886.
44) Pugh, 'Marcher Lords', 172.
45) *CPR 1330–4*, 404; SC 8/176/8753; E 40/4887.
46) *CCR 1318–23*, 723-4.
47) *CPR 1321–4*, 310, 381. One exception is that on 22 June 1323 Inge was named as one of three mainpernors, *CFR 1319–27*, 215. Another was Roger Seyntmor, whom Hugh had ordered Inge to 'harm and harass' in 1319, and the third was Matthew Clivedon, whose arrest Edward ordered on 2 August 1322 (*CCR 1318–23*, 586) in the company of well-known Contrariants such as John Maltravers and William Trussell.
48) *CPR 1327–30*, 32 (9 March 1327).
49) *CPR 1338–40*, 183.
50) SC 8/59/2947, *por corouz qil avoit vers mons' Johan Inge.*
51) *Cartae*, 1101, 1104.
52) *CCR 1323–7*, 27, 141; *CCW*, 544; *CPR 1321–4*, 343.

Chapter 11

1) Phillips, *Edward*, 82, 102, 428-9; F. D. Blackley, 'Adam, the Bastard Son of Edward II', *BIHR*, 37 (1964), 76-7.
2) *Gesta*, 79.
3) *Anon*, 89.
4) K. Warner, *Isabella of France: The Rebel Queen* (2016), 155-8.
5) *CPR 1321–4*, 214.
6) *CPR 1317–21*, 38; *CFR 1307–19*, 363.
7) Davies, *Opposition*, 583; Fryde, *Tyranny*, 67.
8) *Vita*, 136; and see *PROME*, May 1322.
9) J. C. Davies, 'The First Journal of Edward II's Chamber', *EHR*, 30 (1915), 676.
10) *CCR 1318–23*, 541; *CPR 1321–4*, 153.
11) *CCR 1318–23*, 617-8; *CFR 1319–27*, 143, 179.
12) E 101/379/7, fo. 3.
13) *CCR 1318–23*, 577-8, 609; *CPR 1321–4*, 184; E 101/379/4.
14) Davies, 'First Journal', 677; SAL MS 122, 43.
15) *CPR 1321–4*, 221.
16) Davies, 'First Journal', 678.
17) *Flores Historiarum*, 212; *CPR 1321–4*, 232; *Vita*, 128.
18) *CChR 1300–26*, 469.

19) Davies, 'First Journal', 678.
20) *CPR 1321–4*, 227, 229.
21) E 101/379/7, fo. 3.
22) *CCR 1318–23*, 624.
23) SC 1/37/4 and 45.
24) E 101/379/7, fo. 8.
25) *Calendar of Memoranda Rolls (Exchequer): Michaelmas 1326 – Michaelmas 1327* (1968), 296-7.
26) A document is cited, E 403/201, which belongs to September 1322 so cannot possibly refer to the removal of the queen's children two years later, and the membranes cited, 14-15, do not even exist (it has eight membranes); K. Warner, *Edward II: The Unconventional King* (2014), 185-6; ead., *Isabella*, 169-72.
27) *Alianore*: E 101/379/7, fo. 7, E 101/380/4, fo. 32v, SAL MS 122, 4. *Despenser*: E 101/380/4, fo. 19r (which says that it was 'bought for the use of the king by Sir Hugh Despenser the son'), SAL MS 122, 7, 16, *CPR 1324–7*, 172, 278, 325. *Isabele*: *CPR 1307–13*, 97, 402, *CPR 1313–7*, 5, etc. Phillips, *Edward*, 363-4 note 222, for Edward and Eleanor.
28) SAL MS 122, 25, 28, 29, 36, 40, etc.
29) E 101/380/4, fo. 18v; SAL MS 122, 41.
30) *CDS*, 150; *CPR 1321–4*, 277-9.
31) *CPR 1321–4*, 349.
32) E 101/379/17, mem. 2, *son gesine*. Rudham was also said to be Edward's clerk, a typical example of how their households merged: *CPR 1324–7*, 194; SAL MS 122, 66.
33) *CCR 1327–30*, 47-8.
34) *CIM*, 218; *Knights*, vol. 2, 245; *CPR 1321–4*, 256; *CPR 1324–7*, 144, etc.
35) Davies, *Opposition*, 97.
36) *CPL 1305-41*, 231.
37) E 101/380/4, fo. 16r.
38) T. Wright, ed., *A Contemporary Narrative of the Proceedings against Dame Alice Kyteler* (1843), xxiii-xxix. John of Nottingham's arrest was ordered on 11 November 1324, *CPR 1324–7*, 44.
39) *CPL 1305-41*, 461 (1 September 1324).
40) Deposits, 349; *CCR 1323–7*, 198-9, 647; *CPL 1305-41*, 452, 457.
41) Deposits, 351, 360; *CCR 1327–30*, 336; SC 8/311/15528.
42) SC 8/173/8609.
43) *CPL 1305-41*, 42-3, 456-62.
44) J. P. Toomey, *Records of Hanley Castle, Worcestershire, c. 1147–1547* (2001), xx.

45) SC 8/138/6896; SC 8/346/E1399.
46) *CPR 1321–4*, 168-9, 372, 378; *CCR 1323–7*, 87, 101, 120, 126.
47) *CCR 1323–7*, 361 (Pedwardyn); *CCR 1333–7*, 547, 648.
48) *CIPM 1317–27*, 314-40.
49) For what follows, *CIM*, 254-5 (gives Kennington); *CCR 1330–3*, 455-6; *CPR 1334–8*, 234-5 (gives Hertingfordbury); *CPR 1348–50*, 122 (Kennington); SC 8/163/8132; SC 8/310/15484; SC 8/160/7956. For Kennington, *CChR 1300–26*, 442 (it had previously belonged to Roger Damory). Hugh the Younger gave 10 pounds to Nicholas Sudington on 26 October 1324; Deposits, 360-1.
50) *CPR 1324–7*, 116; *CCR 1323–7*, 357; *Sir Christopher Hatton's Book of Seals. To Which is Appended a Select List of the Works of Frank Merry Stenton*, eds. L. C. Lloyd and D. M. Stenton (1950), 125.
51) E 40/4962: SC 8/160/7956; *CChR 1300–26*, 478.
52) *CPR 1324–7*, 188, 206; *CCR 1323–7*, 222, 233, 492, 532.
53) SAL MS 122, 75.
54) Deposits, 362.
55) *CCR 1323–7*, 309.
56) *CPR 1324–7*, 95, 153; *CCR 1318–23*, 288, 395; *CIPM 1317–27*, 393.
57) SC 8/164/8173, SC 8/51/2507 and 8.
58) Pugh, 'Marcher Lords', 172.
59) Fryde, *Tyranny*, 107, 232.
60) *CPR 1334–8*, 343; Deposits, 348, 361.
61) *CCW*, 552-3.
62) SC 8/66/3280.
63) Deposits, 360-1.
64) SC 8/55/2749.
65) *CCR 1323–7*, 383.
66) *CCW*, 553.
67) C. D. Liddy, 'Bristol and the Crown 1326–31: Local and National Politics Early in Edward III's Reign', in W. M. Ormrod (ed.), *FCE III* (2004), 47-8.
68) SC 8/14/671.
69) SC 8/135/6747; SC 8/13/631.
70) SC 8/107/5344; SC 8/171/8534; SC 8/90/4483; *CFR 1319–27*, 423; *CFR 1327–37*, 53. John Botetourt's death: *CIPM 1317–27*, 367-8 (his heir was his seven-year-old grandson). Hugh's letters: SC 1/37/5 (to John), SC 1/36/125 (about Maud). The younger John's pardon: *CPR 1321–4*, 241.
71) *CChR 1300–26*, 448-51; *CCR 1323–7*, 519.
72) *CCR 1323–7*, 335.
73) SC 8/43/2017; *CCR 1323–7*, 125.

74) SC 8/42/2054; SC 8/50/2492.
75) *Early Mayor's Court Rolls*, 24-5.
76) *CFR 1319–27*, 121; Davies, 'First Journal', 674.
77) SC 8/259/12930; *CIM*, 253-4; *CPR 1327–30*, 243-4; *CFR 1327–37*, 95; *CCR 1330–3*, 60-61.
78) *CPR 1340–3*, 39-40.
79) *CPR 1307–13*, 11; *CPR 1307–13*, 478, 494; *CCR 1313–8*, 330-1; *CCR 1318–23*, 422.
80) *CPR 1330–4*, 370.
81) *CPR 1321–4*, 423.
82) SC 8/17/841; see N. Saul, 'The Despensers and the Downfall of Edward II', *EHR*, 99 (1984), 23.
83) *CCR 1323–7*, 217.
84) *CIM*, 239-40, 248-9; *CCR 1327–30*, 63-5; *CCR 1333–7*, 142; *CPR 1338–40*, 521; SC 8/168/8384; SC 8/207/10301; SC 8/310/15476; SC 8/311/15502.
85) *The War of Saint-Sardos (1323–1325): Gascon Correspondence and Diplomatic Documents*, ed. P. Chaplais (1954), 120, 138, 173, 235-6.
86) *CCR 1327–30*, 63-4; Hugh was at Westminster in March 1324.
87) *CCR 1323–7*, 510; SAL MS 122, 28.
88) *CCR 1323–7*, 354; *CCR 1333–7*, 507, 645-6; *CPR 1338–40*, 519.

Chapter 12

1) *WSS*, 173; all translations of Hugh's letters, and letters to him, are mine.
2) *WSS*, 144.
3) *WSS*, 52.
4) *WSS*, 3.
5) *WSS*, 76-7, 145.
6) *WSS*, 123.
7) *WSS*, 1-2, 92, 127, 149-51, 209, 224; SC 1/59/93; SC 1/58/42.
8) *WSS*, 58-9.
9) *WSS*, 107.
10) *WSS*, 209; see also C 61/38, no. 140.
11) *WSS*, 149.
12) *WSS*, 79-80.
13) *WSS*, 119, 139, 143, 145-6.
14) *WSS*, 167-8, 171-2, 218-9, 224-5.
15) M. Prestwich, *Plantagenet England 1225–1360* (2005), 209-10; Phillips, *Edward*, 421 note 83.

16) *WSS*, 64-5.

17) Nicholas Hugate had informed Hugh of this a week earlier: *WSS*, 59-61.

18) *WSS*, 69-71, 74, 119.

19) *WSS*, 119-20.

20) *WSS*, 74.

21) *WSS*, 49, 58, 59, 82, 88, 92, 93, etc.

22) *WSS*, 217, for Surrey's letter; he and Hugh were both descended from Maud Marshal, countess of Norfolk and Surrey (d. 1248). *WSS*, 120, 126, 142-3, 217-9, 236-7 for Kent's letters to Hugh, and 64, 237-8, for Hugh's to Kent. SC 1/37/108 is Hugh's letter to the king which begins *Honurs e reuerencez treshonurable seignur.*

23) *WSS*, 107, 120-1, 124, 224-6, 227, 232, 234-5.

24) *WSS*, 143, 145, 171.

25) *WSS*, 78.

26) *CPR 1307–13*, 476-7. Hugh called him *trescher cousin.*

27) *CCR 1327–30*, 119, 143-4, 147-8; *CIM*, 245, 246-7, 250; SC 8/293/14641; SC 8/169/8553; SC 8/209/10408; SC 8/169/8437. Hugh was replaced as constable of Portchester Castle on 17 July 1324: *CFR 1319–27*, 290.

28) *CFR 1319–27*, 300-2, 308; *CCR 1323–7*, 223, 260.

29) L. Benz St John, 'In the Best Interest of the Queen: Edward II, Isabella of France and the Image of a Functional Relationship', in J. S. Hamilton (ed.), *FCE VIII* (2014), 39.

30) *CCR 1323–7*, 216.

31) *WSS*, 65, 70, 78.

32) Benz St John, 'Best Interest', 37; Warner, *Edward II*, 195-6; *Isabella*, 162-3, 173-7.

33) E 101/380/4, fo. 22r.

34) *Vita*, 143; *CCR 1323–7*, 580.

35) *Vita*, 135.

36) Deposits, 361; *CCR 1323–7*, 49, 258.

37) E 101/380/4, fo. 29v; half a mark was six shillings and eight pence.

38) E 101/380/4, fos. 24v, 30v.

39) *CPR 1324–7*, 130; *CFR 1319–27*, 348.

40) SAL MS 122, 5; *CChR 1300–26*, 441, 451-2, 477.

41) *WSS*, 238.

42) *WSS*, 142-3.

43) *WSS*, 64.

44) *WSS*, 83.

45) *WSS*, 107.

46) *WSS*, 82; SC 1/58/27.

47) *WSS*, 107-8.
48) *WSS*, 143-4.
49) P. Chaplais, *English Diplomatic Practice in the Middle Ages* (2003), 210, 226.
50) *Vita*, 136-8, 140.
51) SAL MS 122, 11, 15, 21; *CCR 1318–23*, 542.
52) SAL MS 122, 20, 21.
53) *CFR 1319–27*, 353-4, 356.
54) SC 8/238/11895; *CFR 1327–37*, 103.
55) *CFR 1319–27*, 356.
56) *Vita*, 142.
57) *Vita*, 140.
58) *Murimuth*, 44.
59) *Vita*, 138.
60) *Vita*, 138-9.
61) SAL MS 122, 22.
62) SAL MS 122, 24.
63) Warner, *Edward II*, 193-6.
64) *Anon*, 120; also *Croniques de London*, ed. G. J. Aungier (1844), 48.
65) *CPR 1324–7*, 161-2, 166-71, 173-5; *CCR 1323-7*, 399.
66) *WSS*, 64, 65, 73-5, 76-7, 77, 94, 101, 156, 167, 172, etc; SC 1/48/149, SC 1/49/147, SC 1/50/3, SC 1/50/82.
67) *WSS*, 75-6.
68) *WSS*, 143.
69) C 61/38, mem. 7d.
70) Benz St John, 'Best Interest', 39.
71) SAL MS 122, 28.
72) SC 1/49/146 and 146A; SAL MS 122, 7, 28, 29.
73) SAL MS 122, 32.
74) SAL MS 122, 34, 37-8.

Chapter 13

1) *Vita*, 142-3.
2) *Vita*, 144-5.
3) SAL MS 122, 38: *Jak Pyk counta au Roi qe le dit mons' Hugh fust tue.*
4) Foedera 1307–27, 615, in French; *CCR 1323–7*, 579-81, in English (my translation differs).
5) SAL MS 122, 40.
6) SAL MS 122, 40-41.
7) SC 1/49/147, 148; Deposits, 361-2.

8)   Deposits, 361; E 101/380/4, fo. 31r.

9)   SAL MS 122, 41; E 101/380/4, fos. 23v, 31r.

10) *CCR 1323–7*, 528; *CCR 1333–7*, 74.

11) SAL MS 122, 41-3, 73; E 101/380/4, fo. 22v.

12) E 101/380/4, fo. 10v; *l'res de secree seal a counte de Cestre et Huchoun le Despens'*.

13) *Vita*, 143-4.

14) Phillips, *Edward*, 487.

15) *CCR 1323–7*, 537-8.

16) *CPR 1321–4*, 15-16.

17) *CCR 1323–7*, 442.

18) *CCR 1323–7*, 543-4.

19) *CCR 1313–8*, 443; *CPR 1321–4*, 368-9.

20) *CPR 1321–4*, 15, 179; *CFR 1319–27*, 167.

21) J. Ward, *Elizabeth de Burgh, Lady of Clare* (2014), 1-3; Underhill, *Good Estate*, 39.

22) *CIM*, 246; *CCR 1327–30*, 83.

23) SAL MS 122, 45-6.

24) SAL MS 122, 46.

25) *CPR 1324–7*, 145-6.

26) *CIPM 1317–27*, 316; *CCR 1323–7*, 288; *CCR 1327–30*, 12, 39; *CPR 1327–30*, 268; *CIPM 1365–9*, 123.

27) SC 1/49/60.

28) SC 8/270/13479; *CCR 1327–30*, 12, 39; *CPR 1327–30*, 25.

29) *WSS*, 199-200, for Isabella's other letter.

30) *Historiae Anglicanae Scriptores Decem*, ed. Roger Twysden (1652), column 2767-8.

31) Blackley, 'Bishop of Exeter', 230-1.

32) *CCR 1323–7*, 543.

33) *CPR 1321–4*, 349.

34) *CPR 1324–7*, 215.

35) SAL MS 122, 50, 69.

36) SAL MS 122, 51-2, 73.

37) SC 1/36/124: E 40/1469; Deposits, 362; *CIM*, 362-3; *CPR 1340–3*, 39-40.

38) *CPR 1334–8*, 314; *CPR 1338–40*, 99.

39) SAL MS 122, 52.

40) SAL MS 122, 53.

41) SAL MS 122, 52-3.

Chapter 14

1) *Foedera 1307–27*, 622-3; *CCR 1323–7*, 577-8.
2) SAL MS 122, 91.
3) SAL MS 122, 66.
4) SAL MS 122, 57-8; Deposits, 362.
5) *CPL 1305–41*, 475.
6) *CPL 1305–41*, 476-9.
7) *WSS*, 136, also 219.
8) *CPR 1324–7*, 4; Deposits, 351, 362.
9) *CPR 1324–7*, 267 (marriage); *CFR 1319–27*, 388; *CIPM 1317–27*, 435 (Braose).
10) *CCR 1323–7*, 222, 291.
11) *CCR 1327–30*, 38; SC 8/165/8212.
12) S. Harris, 'Taking Your Chances: Petitioning in the Last Years of Edward II and the First Years of Edward III', in W. M. Ormrod, G. Dodd and A. Musson (eds), *Medieval Petitions: Grace and Grievance* (2009), 186-7.
13) *CPR 1321–4*, 68; *CFR 1319–27*, 242.
14) SC 8/294/14695; *CPR 1324–7*, 65, 135; *CPR 1327–30*, 117.
15) *CCR 1330–3*, 11-12; *CPR 1334–8*, 204-5.
16) SC 8/95/4739A to H.
17) Deposits, 351, 361; *CPR 1334–8*, 384.
18) Deposits, 360-1; *CCR 1323–7*, 319; *CCR 1337–9*, 534-5; *CCR 1339–41*, 235.
19) *CCR 1323–7*, 572; Deposits, 362; *WSS*, 157. Margaret was already the widow of William Martin, who died shortly before 4 April 1326 only a few weeks before she married Wateville: *CIPM 1317–27*, 446-53.
20) *WSS*, 112, 157, 174-5, 218, 222-3.
21) *WSS*, 157.
22) E 101/380/4, fo. 16r.
23) *CPR 1327–30*, 268.
24) See Appendix 1.
25) SAL MS 122, 65.
26) R. M. Haines, *Archbishop John Stratford* (1986), 167-8; Haines, 'Historia Roffensis', 605; *PROME*, November 1330.
27) *WSS*, 72, 76.
28) *WSS*, 3.
29) SAL MS 122, 65.
30) Deposits, 362.
31) SAL MS 122, 64-5.

32) SAL MS 122, 66 (milk); R. M. Haines, 'Bishops and Politics in the Reign of Edward II: Hamo de Hethe, Henry Wharton, and the Historia Roffensis', *Journal of Ecclesiastical History*, 44 (1993), 605 (quote).
33) 'Roffensis', 605-6, for the preceding.
34) SAL MS 122, 66-7.
35) *CCR 1323–7*, 576-7.
36) SAL MS 122, 70; *CPR 1324–7*, 281.
37) SAL MS 122, 68-9, 75.
38) *AP*, 312-3; *Croniques de London*, 50.
39) SAL MS 122, 78.
40) SAL MS 122, 92.
41) Deposits, 362.
42) SAL MS 122, 75 (*q' sewent mons' Hugh toutes foitz queu p't qil aille*); the eight were the Palington brothers, Roger atte Watre, Robert the Irishman, Richard Wygenhale, John Grey and Nichol Usseton.
43) SAL MS 122, 78-9.
44) *Le Livere de Reis de Britanie e le Livere de Reis de Engletere*, ed. J. Glover (1865), 354-5; *CCR 1323–7*, 593; *CFR 1319–27*, 417-8.
45) *CCR 1323–7*, 175; *CCR 1330–3*, 269, 271; SC 8/238/11876.
46) 'Roffensis', 605.
47) *WSS*, 72.
48) *CPR 1327–30*, 10; *CCR 1323–7*, 608-13.
49) SAL MS 122, 82.
50) *CFR 1319–27*, 421.
51) *CPR 1338–40*, 50.
52) Deposits, 348, 354.
53) W. Rees, *Caerphilly Castle: A History and Description* (1937), 86, 109; M. Burtscher, *The Fitzalans, Earls of Arundel and Surrey* (2008), 23.
54) *CPR 1338–40*, 50; *CPR 1343–5*, 131.

Chapter 15

1) *Croniques de London*, 51.
2) *Anon*, 128; *AP*, 315-6.
3) *CCR 1327–30*, 189, 249.
4) *CPR 1327–30*, 268.
5) *AP*, 314-5.
6) *CCR 1323–7*, 650-1.
7) *Anon*, 124-7.
8) *Anon*, 129-30.

9) SAL MS 122, 90.

10) *CFR 1319–27*, 421.

11) *Murimuth*, 48-9.

12) *CFR 1319–27*, 422.

13) *CCR 1323–7*, 655.

14) SAL MS 122, 90: *qil ne lesseit iames la compaignie mons' Hugh tantcome la vie lui durast.*

15) *Anon*, 92–3.

16) *CPR 1324–7*, 334.

17) *Anon*, 130.

18) SAL MS 122, 90.

19) *CPR 1324–7*, 332; *CCR 1327–30*, 9.

20) Phillips, *Edward*, 514.

21) *CFR 1319–27*, 430. Probably the Gospels found in Edward's chamber when Caerphilly surrendered: Rees, *Caerphilly Castle*, 110.

22) *WSS*, 133.

23) *CCR 1323–7*, 622; *CCR 1327–30*, 445 (Neath).

24) Phillips, *Edward*, 515.

25) *AP*, 318; *Anon*, 130-1.

26) *CCR 1323–7*, 620; *CCR 1327–30*, 16.

27) *AP*, 319, says that Edward was given into Lancaster's custody and taken to Kenilworth, and also that Lancaster was present at Hugh's execution. It names all the men taken with Edward and Hugh correctly, therefore seems reliable. Monmouth to Hereford is under 20 miles.

28) *Extraits d'une Chronique Anonyme intitulée Ancienne Chroniques de Flandre* in *Recueil des Historiens des Gaules et de France*, vol. 22, ed. N. de Wailly (1860), 425 note 4.

29) *Flores Historiarum*, 235.

30) *Brut*, 240.

31) Hamilton, *Gaveston*, 142 note 50; *CPR 1307–13*, 300; *CPR 1321–4*, 187.

32) C 53/112, nos. 3, 5, 6.

33) *Brut*, 239-40.

34) *AP*, 317.

35) Holmes, 'Judgement', 264-7, in French; my translation.

36) *AP*, 319-20. Where exactly Hugh was executed is unclear; possibly his trial took place in the marketplace and his execution at the castle, or perhaps vice versa. See http://www.ladydespensersscribery.com/2008/06/25/execution-day-november-24th-1326/, accessed 22 July 2017.

37) *CPR 1321–4*, 275.

38) *Anon*, 131.

39) *CCR 1323–7*, 621; *CPR 1324–7*, 339-40.

40) *CPR 1324–7*, 339.

41) *CCR 1323–7*, 624.

42) Phillips, *Edward*, 505 note 312.

43) M. Prestwich, 'The Court of Edward II', *RENP*, 71.

44) *CCR 1327–30*, 261, 275.

45) *WSS*, 79, 111, 115, 173-4; *CFR 1319–27*, 430.

46) *CFR 1319–27*, 430; *CFR 1327–37*, 12-13, 14; *CPR 1327–30*, 10, 12, 13, 18, 20.

47) Rees, *Caerphilly Castle*, 83; *CPR 1327–30*, 13, 37.

48) *CPR 1327–30*, 37-9; the hobelars were the Palington brothers, Roger atte Watre and John Grey. Hugh sent Hurley and other carpenters to Caerphilly on 4 March 1326: Deposits, 362.

49) *CCR 1327–30*, 352.

50) *CCR 1330–3*, 175.

51) Harris, 'Taking Your Chances', 186.

Appendix 1

1) *Anon*, 132.

2) *CCR 1330–3*, 325-6; *CPR 1330–4*, 246; SC 8/42/2091 and 2092; *PROME*, September 1331.

3) *CIPM 1336–46*, 78-9; SAL MS 122, 41, 73.

4) *CPL 1305–41*, 553. Elizabeth was the granddaughter of William Montacute (d. 1319), one of Edward's court favourites in the 1310s.

5) Huchon's IPM: *CIPM 1347–52*, 328-42; Alina's: *CIPM 1361–5*, 371-3.

6) *CFR 1327–37*, 421.

7) Devon, *Issues*, 124.

8) *CIPM 1336–46*, 265-6. His fourth son Henry Despenser was 19 in February 1361; see *Petitions to the Pope 1342-1419*, ed. W. H. Bliss (1896), 364.

9) *CChR 1300–26*, 448-51, 466.

10) *CFR 1377–83*, 303, 321, 364; *CCR 1381–5*, 167-8.

11) *CCR 1343–6*, 483; *CCR 1349–54*, 89. The earl of Arundel annulled his marriage to Gilbert's sister Isabella that month in order to marry his second wife, so perhaps Gilbert had demonstrated his displeasure at the earl's shabby treatment of his sister and nephew.

12) *CPR 1377–81*, 404.

13) John Despenser was 30 weeks old on 6 December 1361: *CIPM 1361–5*, no. 47. See also *CFR 1356–68*, 211-2; *CFR 1369–77*, 326.

14) *CIPM 1377–84*, no. 587; *CFR 1377–83*, 303, 321, 363-4.

15) E 101/380/4, fo. 20v: *Jeodi le xxij iour de Nov' a Aleyn Frysebek seler le Roi de Loundr' p' vne sele achate de li p' Johan le Despens' fuitz mons' Hugh le Despens' le fuiz oue le croper e cengles xiijs iiijd* ('Thursday 22 November, to Alan Frysebek, king's saddler of London, for a saddle bought from him for John Despenser son of Sir Hugh Despenser the son, with the harness and saddle-girths, 13 shillings and four pence').

16) *CCR 1349–54*, 322; *CFR 1356–68*, 109; *CPR 1361–4*, 411.

17) *Chronica Johannis de Reading et Anonymi Cantuariensis, 1346–1367*, ed. J. Tait (1914), 175-6. I owe this reference to Brad Verity.

18) *CFR 1356–68*, 344.

19) Stapleton, 'Brief Summary', 340.

20) *CPL 1342–62*, 164.

21) *CPL 1342–62*, 254; *Petitions to the Pope 1342–1419*, 75, 81.

22) *CPL 1342–62*, 164; *CPR 1343–5*, 487-8; *CPR 1345–8*, 18.

23) *CPL 1342–62*, 248, 251.

24) R. C. Palmer, *English Law in the Age of the Black Death* (1993), 397 (I owe this reference to www.soc.genealogy.medieval); *CPR 1367–70*, 321.

25) *CPL 1305–41*, 231.

26) *CIPM 1377–84*, no. 589; *CPR 1343–5*, 138; *CCR 1381–5*, 167-8; *CFR 1383–91*, 86-7, 262-3, 287.

27) *CCR 1349–54*, 285.

28) E 101/380/4, fo. 16r.

29) *CCR 1323–7*, 624, *CMR*, 63 (veiling); *CPR 1324–7*, 153, *CCR 1337–9*, 28 (betrothal).

30) *CCR 1349–54*, 285; *CPR 1334–8*, 464; *CCR 1337–9*, 501.

31) *CCR 1323–7*, 624.

32) *CCR 1327–30*, 47-8.

33) Underhill, *Good Estate*, 90.

34) SAL MS 122, 43: *p' p'er a n're dame p' la dame la Despens' q' dieu la donast hastiue deliu'aunce de son enfaunt xxxs* ('to pay to Our Lady for the Lady Despenser that God granted her a prompt delivery of her child, 30 shillings').

35) *CIPM 1384–92*, 306-7.

36) *Somerset Medieval Wills 1383–1500*, ed. Frederic William Weaver (1903), 289.

Bibliography

Primary Sources

A Descriptive Catalogue of Ancient Deeds, ed. H. C. Maxwell, 6 vols. (1890–1915).

Adae Murimuth Continuatio Chronicarum, ed. E. M. Thompson (1889).

Annales Londonienses 1195–1330, in ed. W. Stubbs, *Chronicles of the Reigns of Edward I and Edward II*, vol. 1 (1882).

Annales Paulini 1307–1340, in Stubbs, *Chronicles*, vol. 1.

The Anonimalle Chronicle 1307 to 1334, eds. W. R. Childs and J. Taylor (1991).

The Brut or the Chronicles of England, part 1, ed. F. W. D. Brie (1906).

Calendar of Ancient Correspondence Concerning Wales, ed. J. Goronwy Edwards (1935).

Calendar of Ancient Petitions Relating to Wales, ed. W. Rees (1975).

Calendar of Chancery Warrants, vol. 1, 1244–1326 (1927).

Calendar of the Charter Rolls, 1257–1326, 2 vols. (1906–8).

Calendar of the Close Rolls, 1272–1333, 11 vols. (1898–1906).

Calendar of Documents Relating to Scotland, vol. 3, 1307–1357 (1887).

Calendar of Early Mayor's Court Rolls, 1298–1307, ed. A. H. Thomas (1924).

Calendar of Entries in the Papal Registers Relating to Great Britain and Ireland: Papal Letters, 1198–1362, ed. W. H. Bliss, 3 vols. (1893–7).

Calendar of Entries in the Papal Registers Relating to Great Britain and Ireland: Petitions to the Pope 1342–1419, vol. 1, ed. W. H. Bliss (1896).

Calendar of the Fine Rolls, 1272–1337, 4 vols. (1911–13).

Calendar of Inquisitions Miscellaneous (Chancery), vol. 2, 1308–48 (1916).

Calendar of Inquisitions Post Mortem, 1272–1369, 11 vols. (1906–38).

Calendar of Memoranda Rolls (Exchequer): Michaelmas 1326–Michaelmas 1327 (1968).

Calendar of the Patent Rolls, 1272–1334, 11 vols. (1891–1903).

Cartae et Alia Munimenta quae ad Domimium de Glamorgancia Pertinent, vol. 3 (1910).

Chronica Johannis de Reading et Anonymi Cantuariensis, 1346–1367, ed. J. Tait (1914).

The Chronicle of Pierre de Langtoft, vol. 2, ed. T. Wright (1868).

Chronicon Galfridi de Baker de Swynebroke, ed. E. M. Thompson (1889).

Collectanea Topographica et Genealogica, vol. 4, eds. F. Madden, B. Bandinel and J. G. Nichols (1837).

Croniques de London, ed. G. J. Aungier (1844).

Flores Historiarum, vol. 3, ed. H. R. Luard (1890).

Foedera, Conventiones, Literae, vol. 2.1, 1307–1327, ed. T. Rymer (1818).

Gesta Edwardi de Carnarvon Auctore Canonico Bridlingtoniensi, in ed. W. Stubbs, *Chronicles of the Reigns of Edward I and Edward II*, vol. 2 (1883).

Historiae Anglicanae Scriptores Decem, ed. Roger Twysden (1652).

The Household Book of Queen Isabella of England, eds. F. D. Blackley and G. Hermansen (1971).

Inquisitions and Assessments relating to Feudal Aids 1284–1431, vol. 1 (1899).

Issues of the Exchequer, ed. F. Devon (1837).

The Chronicle of Lanercost 1272–1346, ed. H. Maxwell (1913).

Le Livere de Reis de Britanie e le Livere de Reis de Engletere, ed. J. Glover (1865).

National Archives records, especially SC 1 (Ancient Correspondence), SC 8 (Ancient Petitions), C 53 (Charter Rolls), E 101 (Accounts Various).

The Parliament Rolls of Medieval England, ed. C. Given-Wilson et al (2005).

Recueil de Lettres Anglo-Françaises 1265–1399, ed. F.J. Tanqueray (1916).

The Roll of Arms of the Princes, Barons and Knights Who Attended King Edward I to the Siege of Caerlaverock, ed. T. Wright (1864).

Royal Charter Witness Lists for the Reign of Edward II 1307–1326, ed. J. S. Hamilton (2001). (I am very grateful to Professor Hamilton for making a copy of this available to me.)

Scalacronica: The Reigns of Edward I, Edward II and Edward III, ed. H. Maxwell (Glasgow, 1907).

Society of Antiquaries of London Manuscript 122 (Edward's chamber account of 1325–6).

Somerset Medieval Wills 1383–1500, ed. Frederic William Weaver (1903).

Statutes of the Realm, vol. 1: 1100–1377 (1810).

Testamenta Vetusta: Being Illustrations from Wills, ed. N. Harris Nicolas, vol. 1 (1826).

Vita Edwardi Secundi Monachi Cuiusdam Malmesberiensis, ed. N. Denholm-Young (1957).

The War of Saint-Sardos (1323–1325): Gascon Correspondence and Diplomatic Documents, ed. P. Chaplais (1954).

Secondary Sources

De Behault de Dornon, A., *Le Tournoi de Mons de 1310* (1909).

Benz St John, L., 'In the Best Interest of the Queen: Edward II, Isabella of France and the Image of a Functional Relationship', in ed. J. S. Hamilton, *FCE VIII* (2014), 21-42.

Blackley, F.D., 'Adam, the Bastard Son of Edward II', *BIHR*, 37 (1964), 76-7.

Blackley, F. D., 'Isabella and the Bishop of Exeter', in eds. T. A. Sandqvist and M. R. Powicke, *Studies in Medieval History Presented to Bertie Wilkinson* (1969).

Bullock-Davies, C., *Menestrellorum Multitudo: Minstrels at a Royal Feast* (1978).

Burtscher, M., *The Fitzalans, Earls of Arundel and Surrey* (2008).

Chaplais, P., *English Diplomatic Practice in the Middle Ages* (2003).

Chaplais, P., *Piers Gaveston: Edward II's Adoptive Brother* (1994).

Davies, J. C., *The Baronial Opposition to Edward II: Its Character and Policy* (1918).

Davies, J. C., 'The Despenser War in Glamorgan', *Transactions of the Royal Historical Society*, 9 (1915), 21-64.

Davies, J. C., 'The First Journal of Edward II's Chamber', *EHR*, 30 (1915), 662-80.

Dodd, G. and A. Musson eds., *The Reign of Edward II: New Perspectives* (2006).

Dryburgh, P., 'The Career of Roger Mortimer, First Earl of March' (Univ. of Bristol PhD thesis, 2002).

Fryde, E. B., 'The Deposits of Hugh Despenser the Younger with Italian Bankers', *Economic History Review*, 2nd series, 3 (1951), 344-62.

Fryde, N., *The Tyranny and Fall of Edward II 1321–1326* (1979).

Gibbs, V., and H. A Doubleday, *The Complete Peerage of England, Scotland, Ireland, Great Britain and the United Kingdom*, 14 vols. (1910–40).

Given-Wilson, C. and A. Curteis, *The Royal Bastards of Medieval England* (1984).

Haines, R. M., 'Bishops and Politics in the Reign of Edward II: Hamo de Hethe, Henry Wharton, and the Historia Roffensis', *Journal of Ecclesiastical History*, 44 (1993), 586-609.

Haines, R. M., *Archbishop John Stratford* (1986).

Haines, R. M., *Edward II: His Life, His Reign, and Its Aftermath, 1384–1330* (2003).

Hallam, E. M., *The Itinerary of Edward II and his Household, 1307–1327* (1984).

Hamilton, J. S., 'Charter Witness Lists for the Reign of Edward II', in ed. N. Saul, *FCE I* (2000), 1-20.

Hamilton, J. S. *Piers Gaveston, Earl of Cornwall 1307–1312* (1988).

Hamilton, J. S. 'Some Notes on 'Royal' Medicine in the Reign of Edward II', in ed. C. Given-Wilson, *FCE II* (2002), 33-43.

Hamilton, J. S., 'The Character of Edward II: The Letters of Edward of Caernarfon Reconsidered', *RENP*, 5-21.

Harris, S. J., 'Taking Your Chances: Petitioning in the Last Years of Edward II and the First Years of Edward III', in eds. W. M. Ormrod, G. Dodd and A. Musson, *Medieval Petitions: Grace and Grievance* (2009), 173-92.

Heebøll-Holm, T. K., *Ports, Piracy and Maritime War* (2013).

Holmes, G. A., 'The Judgement on the Younger Despenser, 1326', *EHR*, 70 (1955), 261-7.

Holmes, G. A., 'A Protest Against the Despensers, 1326', *Speculum*, 30 (1955), 207-12.

Johnstone, H., *Edward of Carnarvon 1284–1307* (1946).

Johnstone, H. *Letters of Edward, Prince of Wales 1304–1305* (1931).

Keen, M., *Nobles, Knights and Men-at-Arms in the Middle Ages* (1996).

Keen, M., *The Laws of War in the Middle Ages* (2015).

Lawrence, M., 'Power, Ambition and Political Rehabilitation: The Despensers, *c.* 1281–1400' (Univ. of York DPhil thesis, 2005).

Lawrence, M., 'Rise of a Royal Favourite: The Early Career of Hugh Despenser the Elder', *RENP*, 205-19.

Liddy, C.D., 'Bristol and the Crown 1326–31: Local and National Politics Early in Edward III's Reign', in ed. W. M. Ormrod, *FCE III* (2004), 47-66.

Lloyd, L. C. and D. M. Stenton, *Sir Christopher Hatton's Book of Seals. To Which is Appended a Select List of the Works of Frank Merry Stenton* (1950).

Maddicott, J. R., *Thomas of Lancaster 1307–1322: A Study in the Reign of Edward II* (1970).

McKisack, M., *The Fourteenth Century 1307–1399* (1959).

Moor, C., *The Knights of Edward I*, 5 vols. (1929–32).

Morris, M., *The Bigod Earls of Norfolk* (2005).

Mortimer, I., *The Greatest Traitor: The Life of Sir Roger Mortimer* (2003).

Oxford Dictionary of National Biography, available at http://www.oxforddnb.com/.

Palmer, R. C., *English Law in the Age of the Black Death* (1993).

Phillips, J. R. S., *Aymer de Valence, Earl of Pembroke 1307–1324: Baronial Politics in the Reign of Edward II* (1972).

Phillips, S., *Edward II* (2010).

Prestwich, M. *Documents Illustrating the Crisis of 1297–98 in England* (1980).

Prestwich, M., *Edward I* (1988).

Prestwich, M., *Plantagenet England 1225–1360* (2005).

Pugh, T. B., 'The Marcher Lords of Glamorgan and Morgannwg, 1317–1485', in ed. T. B. Pugh, *Glamorgan County History, III: The Middle Ages* (1971), 167-86.

Rees, W., *Caerphilly Castle: A History and Description* (1937).

Saul, N., 'The Despensers and the Downfall of Edward II', *EHR*, 99 (1984), 1-33.

Sponsler, C., 'The King's Boyfriend: Froissart's Political Theater of 1326', in eds. G. Burger and S. F. Kruger, *Queering the Middle Ages* (2001), 143-67.

Stapleton, T., 'A Brief Summary of the Wardrobe Accounts of the Tenth, Eleventh and Fourteenth Years of King Edward the Second', *Archaeologia*, 26 (1836), 318-45.

Stevenson, W. H., 'A Letter of the Younger Despenser on the Eve of the Barons' Rebellion, 21 March 1321', *EHR*, 12 (1897), 755-61.

Tomkinson, A., 'Retinues at the Tournament of Dunstable, 1309', *EHR*, 74 (1959), 70-87.

Toomey, J. P., *Records of Hanley Castle, Worcestershire, c. 1147–1547* (2001).

Tout, T. F., *The Place of the Reign of Edward II in English History* (2nd edn., 1936).

Underhill, F., *For Her Good Estate: The Life of Elizabeth de Burgh* (1999).

Vale, M., *The Princely Court* (2001).

Ward, J., *Elizabeth de Burgh, Lady of Clare* (2014).

Warner, K., *Edward II: The Unconventional King* (2014).

Warner, K., *Isabella of France: The Rebel Queen* (2016).

Waugh, S., 'For King, Country and Patron: The Despensers and Local Administration 1321–1322', *Journal of British Studies*, 22 (1983), 23-58.

Waugh, S., 'The Profits of Violence: The Minor Gentry in the Rebellion of 1322 in Gloucestershire and Herefordshire', *Speculum*, 52 (1977), 843-69.

Wells-Furby, B., 'The Gower Prelude to the Marcher Rising of 1321: A Question of Evidence', *Welsh History Review*, 27 (2014), 4-27.

Wilkinson, B., 'The Sherburn Indenture and the Attack on the Despensers', *EHR*, 63 (1948), 1-28.

Wright, T., ed., *A Contemporary Narrative of the Proceedings against Dame Alice Kyteler* (1843).

Online Sources
My blog http://edwardthesecond.blogspot.com/
Jules Frusher's site http://www.ladydespensersscribery.com/
http://news.bbc.co.uk/2/hi/uk/4561624.stm
https://groups.google.com/forum/#!forum/soc.genealogy.medieval

Index